Research on Educational Innovations

Fourth Edition

Arthur K. Ellis

EYE ON EDUCATION
6 DEPOT WAY WEST, SUITE 106
LARCHMONT, NY 10538
(914) 833–0551
(914) 833–0761 fax
www.eyeoneducation.com

Library of Congress Cataloging-in-Publication Data

Ellis, Arthur K.
  Research on educational innovations / Arthur K. Ellis.—4th ed.
    p. cm.
  ISBN 1-930556-96-9
        1. Education—United States—Experimental methods. 2. Educational inno-
  vations—United States. 3. Education—Research—United States. I.
Title.

  LB1027.3.E45 2005
  370'.7'2073—dc22

                                                                    2004028879

10 9 8 7 6 5 4 3

Editorial and production services provided by
Freelance Editorial Services
52 Oakwood Blvd., Poughkeepsie, NY 12603-4112
(845-471-3566)

Also Available from EYE ON EDUCATION

What Great Principals Do *Differently*:
15 Things That Matter Most
Todd Whitaker

Great Quotes for Great Educators
Todd Whitaker and Dale Lumpa

What Great Teachers Do *Differently*:
14 Things That Matter Most
Todd Whitaker

BRAVO Principal!
Sandra Harris

Stepping Outside Your Comfort Zone:
Lessons for School Leaders
Nelson Beaudoin

Dealing with Difficult Teachers, Second Edition
Todd Whitaker

Journey Into Community:
Looking Inside the Community Learning Center
Steve R. Parson

The Principal as Instructional Leader:
A Handbook for Supervisors
Sally J. Zepeda

Instructional Leadership for School Improvement
Sally J. Zepeda

The ISLLC Standards in Action:
A Principal's Handbook
Carol Engler

Data Analysis for Continuous School Improvement
Victoria L. Bernhardt

About the Author

Arthur K. Ellis is Professor of Education and Director of the International Center for Curriculum Studies at Seattle Pacific University. Previously, he taught in public schools in Oregon and Washington and at the University of Minnesota. He is the author or coauthor of 18 published books and numerous journal articles, book chapters, and scholarly papers. He consults to numerous government and private agencies and foundations and to various school systems in the United States and abroad.

Table of Contents

1

What Research
Is of Most Worth?

*By turning away from science, educational researchers would
be freed from the annoying requirement to base their arguments on evidence.*

Richard E. Mayer

*No Child Left Behind is indelibly launched. A culture of ac-
countability is gripping the American educational landscape.*

Rod Paige (former U.S.
Secretary of Education)

*During the last 50 years at least, scholars and researchers in
all disciplines have acknowledged that there are different
ways of knowing the world, and thereby investigating it and
that the particular kind of science...called "sci-
ence-as-usual"...is only one of them.*

Elizabeth Adams St. Pierre

*We hope the field will move beyond quantitative versus qual-
itative research arguments because, as recognized by mixed
methods research, both quantitative and qualitative research
are important and useful.*

R. Burke Johnson and
Anthony J. Onwuegbuzie

Writing in the *Educational Researcher*, American Educational Research
Association President Marilyn Cochran-Smith (2005) noted that "Today,
in part because of the federal government's enlarged role in education as a
whole and in education research in particular, the research community is

once again (or, more accurately-still) struggling with questions about the nature of educational scholarship: What kinds of research 'count'? Do some 'count' more than others? Who gets to do the counting? For what purposes and what contexts? Should certain kinds of research be elevated (and funded) over others? As Ellen Condliffe Lagemann and others remind us, these are enduring questions in the century-long history of educational inquiry, involving debates about science and scientism, the development and institutionalization of fields of study, and the emergence of knowledge hierarchies that hardened (though, at certain times, they became more fluid and permeable) during the 20th century. These are the same enduring questions that are concurrent with the development of many fields of scholarship" (p. 20).

Cochran-Smith goes on to cite a more than quarter-century-old commentary in which the celebrated educational researcher Robert Grinder (1982) quoted a then quarter-century-old letter to the Educational Researcher. The author of that letter was another educational researcher of some note, Percival Symonds, who wrote in 1958 that educational research should be limited to "that which is scientific, empirical, pragmatic, experimental" (quoted in Cochran-Smith, 2005, p. 20). The debate is hardly a new one as we shall see.

In 1859 the English philosopher and scientist Herbert Spencer published what proved to be a rather influential essay "What Knowledge Is of Most Worth?" The title alone focused attention on one of the most important issues in the annals of education. The question, of course, comes more easily than the answer. Given the realities of the knowledge explosion, Spencer's question is even more relevant today than it was when he first asked it. For his part, Spencer concluded that knowledge of science is of the most worth because it holds the key to our survival as a species. Whether his answer was right or not, it proved to be highly influential. It was only a matter of years after its publication that Spencer's idea took hold in schools and universities. The sciences achieved parity with the humanities in America's universities and high schools. The curriculum would never be the same. Latin and Greek gave way to modern languages. Rhetoric and declamation gave way to chemistry and physics. And today when questions about the origins of life or the cosmos arise, answers are sought from science.

Yes indeed, science. Although not everyone agrees that science offers the most profound solutions to our many problems, it is fair to say that science has gained the upper hand as explainer. The philosopher Jurgen Habermas (1971) has noted on more than one occasion that the rise of science as explainer has led to as many problems as it has solved. For example, he cites the "expert culture" syndrome as having invaded our lives to the point that ordinary adults have become infantilized, cowed by expert advice givers. That aside, with regard to educational innovations and the funding of educational research projects, the National Research Council has made it clear that the scientific study of education is the key to educational improvement. In other words, answers to questions of improved academic achievement are to be found in scientific inquiry.

But what exactly is science? The legendary anthropologist Margaret Mead published the book, *Coming of Age in Samoa* in 1928, which was based on ethnographic studies Mead had conducted among teenage girls in that island country. Mead had done graduate work at Columbia University where she obtained her PhD, studying under such luminaries in the field of anthropology as Franz Boas and Ruth Benedict. At the time, anthropology was finding its place in the scheme of things as one of the emerging "social" sciences. Employing anthropological or ethnographic methods, Mead relied on field notes, interviews, and observations rather than statistical data to make inferences and reach conclusions about the customs, folkways, and mores of her subjects. In other words, she did *qualitative* research. *Coming of Age in Samoa* was highly praised by critics for its content and for its methodology; and to be fair, it has been criticized as well regarding both the accuracy of Mead's observations and the soundness of her conclusions. But similar praise and criticism has been leveled at much of the natural science research of nearly 100 years ago. Mead's credentials as a scientist were confirmed by the American Association for the Advancement of Science (AAAS) in 1973 when she was elected to the presidency of that prestigious organization.

At roughly the same time Margaret Mead was completing her graduate work and beginning her career as an ethnographer, Ronald Fisher published his celebrated text, *Statistical Methods for Research Workers* (1925). The book, which became a standard in the annals of quantitative research, was based on the idea that one could infer knowledge gained from carefully selected representative samples to entire populations. In essence, Fisher's ideas on the use of statistical methods were seminal to our knowledge of the study of populations, variation, and reduction of data. Applications of statistical methods could readily be made by researchers in such diverse fields as agriculture, medicine, genetics, and of course, education. At the heart of the research process, as Fisher and others described it, is the experiment with its accompanying ideas of simple random selection of subjects combined with appropriate research designs and accompanying statistical measures. Among other things, he developed the statistical procedure known as analysis of variance or ANOVA with its familiar F (for Fisher) ratio.

Evidence-Based Education

Now, in this first decade of the twenty-first century we are informed that only "scientifically based" educational research involving randomized field trials has the capacity to advance knowledge in the profession (National Research Council [NRC], 2002). We learn further of the NRC's "depiction of a community of investigators with a strong scientific culture as the key to a healthy research enterprise" (Feuer, Towne, & Shavelson, 2002, p. 8). This would seem to eliminate the arts, but beyond that whimsical thought one quickly encounters lexical problems. What exactly is meant by a "scientific culture," and how inclusive is the "community of investigators"? These questions are far more easily posed than answered.

The term "evidence-based education" derives from the older term "evidence-based medicine," a term made popular in Britain and that signifies empirically based findings, particularly empirically based findings resulting from random assignment of subjects to treatment groups. Empirical evidence, the cornerstone, according to the No Child Left Behind Act (NCLB) "means research that involves the application of rigorous, systematic and objective procedures to obtain reliable and valid knowledge relevant to educational activities and programs" (No Child Left Behind Act of 2001).

Even though "from a research perspective, education poses challenges absent in fields such as medicine, welfare, and workplace safety" (MDRC, 2004), the U.S. Department of Education is officially on record as favoring randomized trials or true experimental methods as the most definitive means of determining the value of teaching and learning procedures. Below that, in order of descending respectability according to evidence-based advocates, are quasi-experimental comparison group studies, followed by pre-post comparisons, correlational studies, case studies, and anecdotal evidence. Advocates of evidence-based education research are convinced that theirs is the only way to restore respectability to research findings in education, whereas their critics decry the lack of "real-world" authenticity to be found in such outcomes.

In a well-reasoned article appearing in the Educational Researcher (2004), Johnson and Onwuegbuzie argue for mixed-methods research, as a "third paradigm." They define mixed methods research as "the class of research where the researcher mixes or combines quantitative and qualitative research techniques, methods, approaches, concepts or language into a single study" (p. 17). Basically, it seems that their premise is one of bringing to bear the reliability found in quantitative approaches (that is, the statistical findings that confirm similar outcomes in hypothetical repeated trials) and the validity found in qualitative approaches with their careful, thick descriptions of conditions found in a particular setting. They list among the strengths and weaknesses of quantitative and qualitative research those noted in Figures 1.1 and 1.2 (p. 6).

Figure 1.1 Strengths and Weaknesses
of Quantitative Research

Strengths

1. Testing and validating already constructed theories about how phenomena occur.
2. Testing hypotheses that are constructed before the data are collected.
3. Can generalize research findings from data based on random samples.
4. Can generalize findings replicated on different populations.
5. Useful for obtaining data that allow quantitative predictions.
6. Can eliminate confounding variables, allowing cause and effect assessments.
7. Provides precise, quantitative, numerical data.
8. Data analysis is relatively less time consuming using statistical software.
9. Results are relatively independent of the researcher (e.g., effect size, statistical significance).
10. May have greater credibility with people in power (e.g., administrators, politicians, funding agencies).
11. Useful for studying large numbers of subjects.

Weaknesses

1. Categories and theories used by researcher may not reflect local constituents' understandings.
2. Researcher may overlook certain phenomena not accounted for by focus on predetermined theory or hypotheses being tested.
3. Knowledge produced may be too abstract and general for direct application to specific local situations, contexts, and individuals.

Adapted from Johnson, R., & Onwuegbuzie, A. (2004). Mixed methods research: A research paradigm whose time has come. *Educational Researcher, 33*(7), 14–26.

Figure 1.2 Strengths and Weaknesses
of Qualitative Research

Strengths

1. Data are based on participants' own categories of meaning.
2. Useful for studying a limited number of cases in depth.
3. Useful for describing complex phenomena.
4. Provides individual case information.
5. Can conduct cross-case comparisons and analysis.
6. Provides understanding and description of peoples' personal experiences of phenomena.
7. Can describe, in rich detail, phenomena as they are situated and embedded in local contexts.
8. The researcher identifies contextual and setting factors as they relate to the phenomenon of interest.
9. The researcher can study dynamic processes.
10. The researcher can use "grounded theory" to generate inductively a tentative but explanatory theory about a phenomenon.
11. Can determine how participants interpret "constructs" (e.g., self-esteem, IQ).
12. Data typically collected in naturalistic settings.
13. Responsive to local situations, conditions, and stakeholders' needs.
14. Researcher can respond to changes that occur during conduct of a study and may shift focus as a result.
15. Qualitative data in the words and categories of participants lend themselves to exploring how and why phenomena occur.
16. Determine idiographic causation (i.e., determination of causes of a particular event).

Weaknesses

1. Knowledge produced may not generalize to other people or settings.
2. Findings may be unique to those researched.
3. It is more difficult to make quantitative predictions.
4. It is more difficult to test hypotheses and theories.
5. Result may have lower credibility with administrators, etc.
6. It is generally more time consuming to collect data.
7. Results are more easily influenced by the researcher's personal biases and idiosyncrasies.

Adapted from Johnson, R., & Onwuegbuzie, A. (2004). Mixed methods research: A research paradigm whose time has come. *Educational Researcher, 33*(7), 14–26.

The Current Scene

Title 1 of the Elementary and Secondary Education Act of 1965 was reauthorized by the Congress of the United States in 2002 in the form of PL 107–110, the so-called NCLB Act. What might seem a routine matter, that is, reauthorizing a document now more than 40 years old, has in fact resulted in a considerable amount of controversy, both academic and political. For starters, NCLB incorporates the Comprehensive School Reform Program. Although Title 1 specifically targeted low income, low performing schools, (NCLB) expands the agenda to call for "evidence based research" that links the standards movement, with its explicit concerns for accountability, to school reform in general. Comprehensive School Reform is defined by the U.S. Department of Education as a wide-ranging, 11-part list of requirements with as its bottom line "scientifically based" support for improved achievement (Borman, Hewes, Overman, & Brown, 2003) (see Figure 1.3, p. 8).

Whether this is yet one more example of political intrusion into scientific work is arguable but probable. If this is the case, however, it won't mark the first time. Basically, the Congress has enacted legislation implying that much educational research has been of questionable scientific worth and that federal funds supporting research in the future will be granted only to those individuals, groups, and agencies that conduct rigorous, replicable, cause-and-effect studies.

There are many fascinating aspects of the school reform movement, but for the purposes of this book, the issue of what constitutes valid educational research stands out. The National Research Council (2002) has made clear its own stance that the scientific study of education involves principles of inquiry shared by science in general. To be exact, all scientific endeavors

- pose significant questions that can be investigated empirically;
- link research to relevant theory;
- use methods that permit direct investigation of the questions;
- provide a coherent and explicit chain of reasoning;
- yield findings that replicate and generalize across studies;
- disclose research data and methods to enable and encourage professional scrutiny and critique.

Figure 1.3 U.S. Department of Education
Components of Comprehensive School Reform

To qualify for CSR funding, the following program components must be met:

- Employs proven methods for student learning, teaching, and school management that are founded on scientifically based research and effective practices and have been replicated successfully in schools;

- Integrates instruction, assessment, classroom management, professional development, parental involvement, and school management;

- Provides high-quality and continuous teacher and staff professional development and training;

- Includes measurable goals for student academic achievement and establishes benchmarks for meeting those goals;

- Is supported by teachers, principals, administrators, and other school staff by creating shared leadership and a broad base of responsibility for reform efforts;

- Provides for the meaningful involvement of parents and the local community in planning, implementing, and evaluating school improvement activities;

- Uses high-quality external technical support and assistance from an entity that has experience and expertise in schoolwide reform and improvement, which may include an institution of higher education;

- Includes a plan for the annual evaluation of the implementation of the school reforms and the student results achieved;

- Identifies the available federal, state, local, and private financial and other resources that schools can use to coordinate services that support and sustain the school reform effort; and

- Meets one of the following requirements: Either the program has been found, through scientifically based research, to significantly improve the academic achievement of participating students; or strong evidence has shown that the program will significantly improve the academic achievement of participating children.

Source: Borman, G., Hewes, G., Overman, L., & Brown, S. (2003). Comprehensive school reform and achievement: A meta-analysis. *Review of Educational Research, 73*(2), 127.

A careful reading of this list and its wider implications has led a number of educational researchers (Berliner, 2002; St. Pierre, 2002; Erickson& Gutierrez, 2002) to question the NRC's focus on positivist principles of educational research in an increasingly postmodern world. Roughly speaking, this translates into the *quantitative* versus *qualitative* debate in educational research. This debate has its antecedent conditions. The terminology is certainly current, but the essence has been manifest for a long time. Consider the essentialist/progressive divide, the phonics/whole language controversy, and the direct instruction/discovery learning argument, to mention just a few. They differ, but the clash of world views is more similar than different in each case. All are highly susceptible to the *either/or* mentality so inviting to the sophist. Much time and energy are devoted to chronicling the shortcomings of the other, to the point that less than helpful definitions begin to emerge based on what we are not.

Certainly, there are voices of reason, people who call for the strategic use of a variety of carefully crafted research methods the better to inform us all. A cursory examination of the types of educational research considered to be legitimate indicates that both quantitative and qualitative methods now find support. For example, the *American Educational Research Journal* published 13 quantitative and no qualitative research studies in its spring 1984 edition. In its spring 1994 edition, three qualitative and four quantitative studies were to be found. And in its spring 2004 edition, there were three of each.

Given the NRC's obvious preference for quantitative research, the question of censorship inevitably arises. Does NCLB mean the end of qualitative inquiry and other forms of investigation in education? Not necessarily any more than decisions by federal agencies not to fund certain kinds of artistic creativity mean that artists are no longer free to express themselves as they wish. It simply means they may have to work without federal funds. In the United States there are many foundations that are open to funding other types of educational research, and many journals are dedicated to a wider point of view regarding what constitutes legitimate educational inquiry.

Political decisions influence the conduct of research in any given field. This is so in physics, medicine, agriculture, and other fields. It always has been the case. And the present situation calls for funding scientifically based educational research that fits the guidelines found in Figure 1.3 (p. 8). For now, the essentialists and positivists appear to have the upper hand. But the most reasonable thinking seems to be that the *either/or* argument is specious, that judicious combinations of both types will in fact yield the best results if progress is to be made. Stay tuned.

2

Nature of Educational Innovation

One doesn't discover new lands without consenting to lose sight of the shore for a very long time.

André Gide

Each generation must answer anew a set of age-old questions. Those questions go to the heart of our existence. They are questions of purpose, being, destiny. They are questions of justice, relationships, goodness. The fact that previous generations have grappled with the same questions is helpful but not sufficient. The questions are so basic that we must address them; we ignore them at our peril. Others cannot answer them for us, although they can give us insights, and we can benefit from their experience. We must seek our own answers, however different or similar to those arrived at by our predecessors. This is so because the search is as important as the outcome and because situations change over time. It is the process of arriving at answers, however tentative or even deficient, that makes us human.

Just as we seek answers to life's larger questions, we seek answers within the frames of our professional existence, in this case teaching and learning. As teachers and administrators, we seek answers to questions about the nature of knowledge, learning, and teaching. We ask ourselves if there are better ways to organize teaching, present ideas to young people, and assess learning. We grapple with such dualisms as control versus freedom, cooperation versus independence, time-on-task versus creativity.

As practical people working in school settings with all the complexities one finds in such socially contrived environments as playgrounds and lunchrooms, and such academically contrived environments as high school physics laboratories and primary reading classes, we wonder what to teach, how best to teach it, and even if what we teach has lasting value. These questions tend to deplete our energy, especially when we are continually reminded by the popular press that American schools are poorly preparing the nation's young for an increasingly complex future.

At the same time, the educational literature is filled with ideas and strategies for innovation: mastery learning, whole language learning, interdisciplinary curriculum, learning styles, developmentally appropriate practice, cooperative learning, effective teaching, school restructuring, site-based management, and the list goes on. Each of these innovations is touted by its proponents as the key to an improved school experience for teachers and students. Administrators read about a given innovation and wonder whether it could be the answer for their school. A teacher attends a workshop where the presenter makes a compelling case for some new paradigm. Like wandering nomads in search of the next oasis, we move from fad to fad in search of the next wellspring with the vague hope that we might find a permanent place to settle. Of course, we never do.

Still, the waves of innovation are received with mixed reactions. What is the source of our ambivalence toward innovation in education? On the one hand, we seem ready, as educational historian Herbert Kliebard has pointed out, to grasp at anything so long as it is *new*. There is a feeling, almost a fear, that our school could be left behind. On the other hand, seasoned teachers and administrators have seen so many so-called innovations come and go that a certain degree of cynicism sets in when they are told at fall meetings, "We are going to adopt a site-based management approach," or whatever.

In this book I have attempted to provide teachers, administrators, counselors, and other school personnel with insights to a carefully selected set of innovations. The innovations chosen to appear in these pages have nationwide (if not international) impact. They have application across a range of grade and subject levels. And they have considerable staying power. As you read about them, you should gain knowledge not only of certain specific innovations but insights into the nature of innovation itself and how and to what extent a particular innovation, perhaps one that is yet to appear, is not merely new, but worthwhile.

At this point a cautionary note must be sounded. No new idea, no matter how well researched, is worthwhile outside a context of purpose. For example, if we were asked, "Is an interdisciplinary curriculum a good idea for my school?" we would be forced to respond by asking, "What is the purpose of your school?" No one can answer that question meaningfully except the people who have a genuine interest in your school. Now this can seem rather simplistic and even obvious to everyone. But the history of failure and disappointment in educational innovation starts with confusion of purpose. It inevitably leads to cynicism and the "we tried that" syndrome.

So somewhere in the matrix of your individual and school goal structures, you must measure any new educational idea's worth. The more meaningful question is not, "Is it the latest trend?" but "Is it good for us?"

Each educator, school faculty, and school community must face the same basic questions:

+ What does our school stand for?
+ What should students learn?
+ What are the best conditions for learning?
+ What experiences enhance learning?
+ How should classes and schools be organized?
+ How can we know if we are attaining our goals?

...and so on. The questions are endless because

+ Teaching is as much an art as a science.
+ Learning is a poorly understood process.
+ Students are diverse and they respond differentially.
+ Societal needs and demands change.
+ Local and site-specific needs differ considerably.

What Is an Innovation?

Innovation and *novelty* come from the same Latin root. They both imply that something is new. The idea that something is new is dear to our hearts. We have been conditioned by advertisers and promoters to associate "new" with "improved," whether the product is a detergent or a curriculum. The *Oxford English Dictionary* (1971) defines innovation as "the introduction of novelties." Innovation is a noun related to the verb "to innovate," first found in print in 1561 in T. Norton's *Calvin's Instructions,* in which the sentence appears, "A desire to innovate all things moveth troublesome men." So, the term appears to have reached through to the emotions, negative and positive, from that time to this day.

In the school-based world of teaching and learning, innovation seems to be all-important. Schools often express a desire to be on the cutting edge of things, and know the latest trends, to avoid being old-fashioned or out of date. The teacher workshop and inservice training business, which employs educational innovations as its stock-in-trade, is a multimillion-dollar industry in the United States and Canada.

Where Are They Now?

A generation ago, a series of innovations entered the world of education. Depending on your age or your powers of recollection, you may recognize some of them. They included team teaching, career education, values clarification, multicultural education, human relations training, open schools, competency-based education, peace education, back to the basics, bilingual education, and a few others. Where are they now? The answers vary. Some disappeared without a trace. Some are the forerunners of present-day reform efforts. Some are still around in one form or another. This will always be the case. Today's trend is often tomorrow's forgotten dream. Some of the innovations that sweep through the school scene are nothing more than fads. Some have greater staying power. Let's look at why this might be so.

Research Based?

A common claim of most educational innovations is that they are research based. The intent, apparently, is to give school personnel cause to think that a particular program is valid and reasonable for them to use because it will yield improved results. The term *research based* lends almost mystical qualities to the innovation, making it difficult, if not impossible, for the average teacher, administrator, or school board member to challenge the claims made on behalf of the innovation. Who among us, after all, is going to challenge *research*? The fact is that many school personnel simply do not understand the arcane procedures of educational research with its language of statistical analysis, control groups, experimental designs, and so on. As a result, they are left to the mercy of persuasive arguments by so-called experts who tell them what the research says and what they should therefore do. I will demystify the process.

It is useful to consider examples of research from the field of natural science because science has served as the paradigm for most social science research, of which educational research is a subset. I'll begin with the idea of theory. Theories are *tentative* ways of explaining and predicting phenomena. A theory represents a carefully considered set of ideas about something. The development of a theoretical model is the quest of persons doing pure or basic (as opposed to applied) research. While working in the field of physics, Albert Einstein developed his theory of relativity, a theory that stated that all motion must be defined relative to a frame of reference. In other words, space and time are relative, not absolute, concepts. They take on meaning in relation to their context. Einstein proposed his ideas as a theoretical model to be tested, not as a fact. Other physicists conducted research on the theory, finding much supportive evidence for it. Today the theory of relativity serves as a useful model for the explanation and prediction of the behavior of matter and energy. As a theory, however, it is subject to new interpretation, and in time it may well be modified considerably in the light of new knowledge.

Most often, scientific theory emerges as the result of some preliminary research in a particular field. When Charles Darwin sailed aboard HMS *Beagle* to the Galapagos Islands and to the South Pacific in the nineteenth century, he made careful, systematic observations of certain animals and their unique characteristics. From his data collecting, he advanced the hypothesis that changes in the physical characteristics of animals were the result of a continuous evolutionary process. More than a century later, his theory of evolution remains the object of scientific study, although it has itself evolved considerably over time. Many questions have been answered, but far more questions remain. And research on the topic continues.

Our first two examples are about the behavior of matter and energy and adaptive change in the physical characteristics of animals. As complex as those issues are, they seem pure and uncomplicated when compared to theories advanced within the frame of the social sciences. The theories of Sigmund Freud and Karl Marx, for example, were social theories. Freud developed a theory of personality based on research with patients who were mainly institutionalized, sexually abused women. In time, he built a huge amount of scaffolding around his observations, and his ideas became so pervasive that whole terminologies entered the vocabulary of the middle class (e.g., Freudian slip, ego) as a result of his work. To many his ideas seemed more like solid findings than theories, and they found their way into literature, film, and everyday life, not to mention introductory psychology classes. Today his ideas seem rather quaint, and unlike those of Darwin or Einstein, they are not really the basis for advancements in the field of psychological research.

The theories of Karl Marx were tried out on about half the world's population under the name of Communism, and they still prevail in one form or another in certain countries. Marx theorized a leadership of the working class and a utopian society unfettered by religion, private ownership, competition, and other traditional forms of thought and practice. One might argue whether Marx's pure theory was in fact what was institutionalized in the former USSR, its satellites, and so forth. As bizarre and ugly as the socialist *experiment* called Marxism was, it does serve to make a point to consumers of educational research: Theories of human behavior have real, lasting consequences when we try them out on human beings, so we had better be careful when we consider applying them to our classrooms and schools. The leap from theory to practice is often quite a jump, and one fraught with imminent peril.

How Educational Theories Develop

Basic or pure research findings from psychology and other fields are often used to develop theoretical models of teaching and learning. Those theoretical models are then used to derive implications for education. A specific school program emerges when certain educational implications are in turn developed into a coherent set of teaching strategies, materials, learner activities, and classroom or school structural changes. Therefore, the developer exhorts us, change what you are doing at present and adopt this innovation. Why? Because it is better, and the so-called research shows that to be true or we would not ask you to do it.

Three steps are involved along the way to your classroom or school: (1) pure research, (2) educational implications, and (3) suggested classroom or school practice. Let's examine the steps one at a time using a specific example, _cooperative learning_.

Level I

In the 1940s and 1950s, social psychologist Morton Deutsch (1949) used his research findings to develop a theory of social interdependence. Like most good scientific researchers, Deutsch was familiar with prior research, especially, in this case, the work of Kurt Lewin in the 1930s. Lewin had developed an idea called field theory, which said in essence that a group is actually a _dynamic whole_ rather than a mere collection of individuals. Lewin meant that the behaviors of members in a group are interactive, thereby creating the potential for greater outcomes than one might get merely by adding the sum of the parts of a group. "Deutsch theorized that social interdependence exists only when the goals of individuals in a group are affected, for better or worse, by the others." It was "better" that intrigued him. Building on Lewin's insights to motivation, inclusion, and democratic processes, Deutsch theorized that when people with common goals worked with each other in cooperative fashion, something better happened than when they either worked alone or competed with each other. Deutsch went on to theorize that the process is enhanced when individuals perceive that they can reach their goals only if other members of their group can also reach their goals. In repeated experiments, Deutsch found that his theory seemed to hold up. He published his results, thus allowing others to support, extend, or challenge his findings in the free marketplace of intellectual endeavor. Others, of course, contributed to the theoretical construct. One can, for example, readily trace its origins to Gestalt theory, which emerged in nineteenth-century Austria and became noted for its pioneering studies in perception. Gestalt theory took issue with reductionist, atomistic processes popular at the time. The Gestalt theorem that "the whole of anything is greater than the sum of its parts" is fundamental to cooperative learning.

Level II

In time educational researchers began to show interest in the theory of social interdependence. They reasoned that what worked in small groups and workplace settings where the theory had originally been field tested might also work in classrooms. School classrooms seemed like a logical place to apply the theory of social interdependence because a typical room has about 30 kids who traditionally each work alone, or who, even when placed in groups, may not have the skills to identify and achieve a common goal. Also, because of tradition among other things, most students (and often their parents) probably do not *perceive* that they can better attain their academic goals if other students improve as well. It almost seems contrary to common sense. The research studies in classrooms, of which there have been many, were driven by questions of increased achievement, increased motivation to learn, and attitude toward school and fellow students, as well as by other outcomes. Among the leading Level II researchers are Robert Slavin of Johns Hopkins University, and David and Roger Johnson of the University of Minnesota, who, in collaboration with their associates, have conducted many empirical studies of the effects of cooperative learning in school settings. As the efficacy of cooperative learning became increasingly clear, especially its beneficial effects in conceptual and problem-solving tasks, the argument for teachers and administrators to use it in classrooms became compelling.

Level III

Efficacious outcomes for cooperative learning were increasingly reported at professional meetings and in research in education journals throughout the 1970s, 1980s, and 1990s. Many of the reported studies had been conducted in school classrooms across a range of grade and subject matter levels. The word began to spread. It was at this point that schools of education began to incorporate cooperative learning methods into teacher education courses; and workshops, sometimes conducted by the researchers themselves, sprang up around the country. Any teacher or administrator interested in applying cooperative learning in the classroom or school had little trouble finding workshops, institutes, retreats, classes, or professed practical articles in such magazines as *Instructor* and *Learning*. In short, cooperative learning was sweeping through the educational community like wildfire. The workshops, institutes, retreats, classes, and articles were mainly focused on practical applications of the theory and were available in both initial and advanced forms. Teachers and parents wanted answers to such questions as, "How do I know the slower students won't just copy the ideas of better students?" "How do I measure individual achievement?" "What do I do if a kid won't cooperate with other members of the group?" "How is this different from just assigning kids to committees?" "Won't this slow down higher achievers?" Out of these excellent, practical questions came new educational research studies, journal articles, and books such as David and Roger Johnson's *Leading the Cooperative School* (1989a).

Thus more than 50 years after the theory of social interdependence began to crystallize, and more than a century since the origins of Gestalt psychology, the refinement of school and classroom applications of cooperative learning continues. At this point, more than 300 research studies conducted in classroom settings and school districts are available. Thousands of policy articles can be found on the topic. And all of this is completely necessary simply because it's a long leap from a theory of social interdependence formulated by social psychologists in the 1930s to a third-grade science class near the turn of the twenty-first century.

A final note is in order. A theory exists in relatively pure form. Its empirical test comes when researchers try it out under controlled conditions. These tests make it possible to accept, modify, or reject the theory in specific settings. However, the fact that a theory tests well under controlled conditions does not guarantee that it will survive the inevitable distortions that come with real-world applications by individuals and groups who choose it or are told to use it. These insights have been enriched through the rise of the qualitative research movement where life in classrooms is chronicled on the basis of careful observations, interviews, and so forth. In summary, Level I is theory building, pure research, or both; Level II is empirical research, either quantitative, qualitative, or a combination thereof; and Level III is program evaluation where it becomes possible to learn the extent to which a program or curriculum is successful when its implementation becomes widespread in schools or entire districts.

I selected cooperative learning as a case study in the nature of educational innovation because it strikes me as a positive example of the gradual unfolding of the process of how a theory germinates and how it ultimately finds its way to classroom practice. If the theory has real promise, it will interact with classroom practice in such a way as to cause further refinement of the theory. Thus, the process is cyclical rather than linear. If it were linear, we would simply impose the finished product on a classroom. This has been done with disastrous consequences. The exciting aspect of the teacher's or administrator's role is that they can be a basic part of the process. This is so because they are key figures in the refinement of an idea, not because they say whether an idea is good or not. The practical application of ideas by teachers and students in real-world educational settings represents the best test of an idea's staying power.

Conclusion

Each of the educational innovations examined in this book began as a theory far removed from classroom life. Each has found its way into the classrooms and schools of America. I propose to examine how that happened. Our analysis of each raises a basic set of questions:

- How good was the original theory on which the idea is based?
- How appropriate is the research that advocates the use of this theory in school settings?
- What does this theory purport to do that will improve life in schools and classrooms?
- What claims are made on behalf of the theory as a necessary part of the school curriculum?
- What are the requisite conditions of the theory for school success?
- Why would someone want to use the ideas that flow from this theory in school settings?

Classroom life unfolds within a complex set of conditions. The list of human and material variables is endless. No two individuals and no two classrooms are the same, just as no two schools or communities are the same. The presence or absence of one student in a classroom changes the circumstances. Each teacher's personal, practical sense of teaching and learning is different. The leadership is variable from one school to the next, ranging from dynamic to nil. The public's perception and support of schools in each community has much to do with a school's success or failure. And of course, what happens in families matters even more than what happens at school.

As teachers and administrators, we are always trying to improve ourselves. We want our efforts to help young people to learn to be productive. Therefore, we seek the help of others who also care and who can help us. And that is what this book is about.

3

The Structure of Educational Innovation

Out of every ten innovations attempted, all very splendid, nine will end up in silliness.

Antonio Machado

It can be argued that there is little that is new in education. It can also be argued, and has been, that there is nothing new under the sun. Most things have been tried before in one form or another, but our experiences are different from those of the previous generation because they are our experiences. As we consider the many problems of teaching and learning, new perspectives emerge and compete for our attention. In these times of sustained criticism of the educational system, new ideas, terminology, and reform programs are abundant simply because people sincerely want to improve things. It is as simple as supply and demand. In fact, the proliferation of new programs, which run the gamut from well to poorly researched, has reached a level of staggering proportions.

At this point it will serve us well to return to some of the ideas presented in Chapter 2. Figure 3.1 (p. 22) illustrates how innovative programs emerge and are developed. Initially someone identifies an idea or research that suggests the possibility of a theory about human behavior. The theory might emerge from insight into human behavior, thinking processes, or perceptions of reality, for example. Regardless, the theory can have implications for how teachers teach and under what conditions students learn best. Jean Piaget's (1970) theory of the development of the intellect, for example, clearly identified age-related stages through which one progresses. Furthermore, the theory stated that persons in a particular stage of development are capable of certain intellectual activities and incapable of others that must happen later. This theory intrigued a number of educational researchers who wished to apply Piaget's ideas to school settings, something Piaget had never done. Some researchers hypothesized that intellectual development could be accelerated with enriched programs. But to the best of our knowledge, this idea does not have anything close to sufficient empirical support. This line of thinking amused Piaget; he called it the "American question" (Piaget, 1970).

Figure 3.1 Development of Innovative Programs

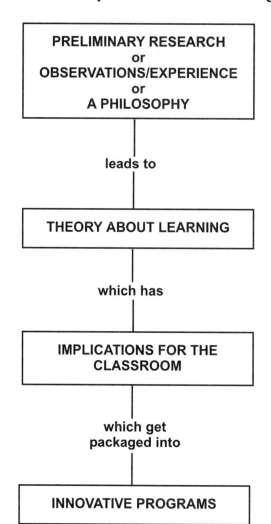

At some point someone in the education field thinks through the implications of a given theory and develops the ideas into a program or curriculum suitable for use in educational research. The program might be designed to change teacher behaviors, student behaviors, or classroom environments to conform to the ideal set of conditions on which the theory is predicated.

Reaping the Whirlwind

What is the role of educational research in all of this? How is educational research different from systematic program evaluation? The claims are that many of these innovative programs are research based. I must point out that there is a difference between saying that a program is research based and when research has shown a program to be effective under certain conditions. Unfortunately, many educators do not make this crucial distinction. *In fact, the best that many developers can claim is that the theory and resulting programs are developed from basic research, often in psychology, into programs for teaching and learning. Often, however, innovative programs are questionably based on theoretical models, with scant evidence to support or justify exactly how the program is truly a practical application of the theory.* This is the initial realm of question posing that educators should enter with those who tout a particular program.

Ideally, before expenditures of time and money are spent on the widespread implementation of educational innovations, those programs should be subjected to careful, unbiased investigation through the evaluation of pilot programs. Unfortunately, as educational researcher Robert Slavin has pointed out, this generally tends to happen toward the end of the cycle of the innovation, after the rush has died down, and educators have cynically moved on to some other new activity or program. Thus, we reap the whirlwind.

How did our profession get caught up in this succession of fad-driven spirals of innovation based on newness rather than goodness? Slavin (1989), one of the most careful researchers in the educational community, has observed and examined this phenomenon over the years. His insights into the process are rather revealing:

> Generational progress does occur in education, but it is usually a product of changes in society, rather than changes in educational techniques themselves. For example, the clearly beneficial trend toward desegregation and more equal treatment of minorities represents true generational progress, but it arose from social and legal changes, not from educational innovation. More often, education resembles such fields as fashion and design, in which change mirrors shifts in taste and social climate, and is not usually thought of as true progress. (p. 752)

Slavin states further that

> one of the most important reasons for the continuing existence of the educational pendulum is that educators rarely wait for or demand hard evidence before adopting new practices on a wide scale. Of course, every innovator claims research support

for his or her methods; at a minimum, there is usually a "gee whiz" story or two about a school or district that was "turned around" by the innovation. Alternatively, a developer may claim that, while the program itself has not been formally evaluated, the principles on which it is based are supported by research. (p. 753)

The Hunter Model: "One More Such Victory and We Are Undone"

Pyrrhus, King of ancient Epirus, left us the term Pyrrhic victory, an allusion to his battle field triumphs accompanied by horrendous causalities among his own troops. There are many such so-called victories in the annals of education, but here is a recent example. Slavin examines the Madeline Hunter model in detail. He calls Hunter "perhaps the most popular educational trainer of our time" (p. 754). I have not included a chapter on Hunter's program because the movement itself appears to have faded. But it can serve as an excellent example of what happens in the name of educational innovation.

Because it is almost inconceivable that educators today have not heard of the Hunter program or model, I will give it only the briefest overview here. The model is sometimes called Instructional Theory Into Practice (ITIP) or Program for Effective Teaching (PET). It emerged in the early 1970s with a series of books and workshops by Madeline Hunter. Throughout the 1970s and well into the 1980s, schools—and oftentimes entire districts and states—provided inservice Hunter model training. Entire staff development programs and faculty evaluation procedures were based on it. District personnel officers would routinely quiz prospective teachers on their knowledge of the Hunter model. Courses for preservice and inservice teachers, where people actually got college credit for studying ITIP, were offered throughout the land. Student teachers were expected to develop lesson plans and units that used the ITIP steps to effective teaching as a template. Teachers themselves were often divided over the program. Many became advocates and some were themselves trained as ITIP trainers, creating a multiplying effect. Some teachers shrugged it off as one more fad they had to endure. A few brave souls openly questioned the validity of the entire thing, but that took courage in light of its overwhelming popularity and near-complete dominance. The amazing thing is that as it disappears, there are no apologies; seemingly no regrets. But the lesson to be learned by those who wish to profit from it is enormous. It draws out the danger present in what the philosopher Francis Bacon called The Idol of the Tribe. When the Idol of the Tribe is worshipped, few dare question events—after all, everyone is doing it. It's the in thing to do. Basically, a mentality is created where criticism is not welcome, to say the least.

The ITIP or PET program itself is a method for analyzing the key elements of a lesson with suggested procedures for lesson development. It was purportedly based on educational and psychological theory and research. It focused on four elements: (1) teaching to an objective (generally a behavioral objective), (2) teaching at the correct level of (cognitive) difficulty, (3) monitoring and adjusting instruction (i.e., formative evaluation and reteaching, mastery learning), and (4) using established principles of learning (e.g., reinforcement, motivation, transfer, etc.).

The ITIP movement followed the pendulum swing described by Slavin. It serves as a classic example. The program was proposed in the early 1970s and implemented in a few school districts. Anecdotal claims of great success were made. The word spread rapidly that here at last was a research-based program that worked in real-world school settings. ITIP became de rigueur among staff developers. Schools of education incorporated it into their teacher training programs. By the late 1970s and early 1980s, the movement was sweeping the country, even though there were no quality studies that showed the program was at all effective in increasing student learning. Complaints by researchers and other critics were either ignored or deemed sour grapes. Anecdotal stories proliferated to verify the program's success.

The program's originator, Madeline Hunter, appeared at conventions, wrote books and articles, and consulted with school districts directly. Where she was unavailable, surrogates took her place. Thousands of teachers and administrators attended workshops at beginning and advanced levels. It became generally expected that anyone who was current knew the ITIP protocols. At its peak, the Hunter program was being used, and in many cases enforced by district officers, in all 50 states. Its popularity exceeded any phenomenon in modern school practice history.

By the mid-to-late 1980s, interest in the program began to wane as staff developers moved on to other topics such as learning styles and outcome-based education. They did this not because the latter were proven to be any better but because they had become the latest fad. At about this time, evaluation results of ITIP programs showed that the program had impact that was no more positive on student learning than random efforts by teachers. The research results mattered little because by the time they weighed in ITIP had pretty much run its course. New fads had taken its place.

In Retrospect

What was touted as an educational program based on purported research was actually a classic example of the process of implementation I described previously. Many of the elements of ITIP were based on psychological research and learning theory. But the implementation of the program itself had not been evaluated with quality research to determine its effectiveness in increasing student learning. For example, reinforcement was identified as one of the key parts of ITIP. Psychological research has, in fact, clearly shown that positive reinforcement of learning predictably results in increased learning. Similarly, psychological research has also shown that the immediacy of feedback, another ITIP protocol, can serve as a motivating factor in learning. Both of these are elements of ITIP that have a substantiated research base. Other elements of ITIP, such as the correct level of difficulty, were based on theoretical models. In this instance, ITIP used Benjamin Bloom's taxonomy of educational objectives in the cognitive domain, a model the very vocabulary of which raises basic questions.

In this manner, ITIP was presented as a research-based model of teaching and learning; and in one sense it was. Certain individual elements were based on psychological research in the area of learning. In other words, specific elements of the program may have been sound in and of themselves under given conditions. But when the entire package was put together as a unified model—that is, when individual research findings and theories were combined to form one unified construct (usually in the form of lesson plans) called ITIP—it was no longer actually correct to say that ITIP was research based. The act of conceptualizing ITIP resulted in a new construct consisting of many divergent research findings and theories. It was, therefore, a new entity that as such had not been researched at all. And in retrospect, that may be giving ITIP too much credit. Actually, the German educator Johann Herbart had conceptualized an almost identical scheme in the nineteenth century, one that identified five points in effective teaching. It, too, swept across our landscape like a prairie fire! Today, only a handful of educators have even heard of it or of Herbart. As the poet and philosopher George Santayana noted, "Those who cannot remember the past are condemned to repeat it."

Perhaps an analogy will serve us well to explain the complex issue of validating an educational innovation, even one allegedly based on sound theories. We know from the laws of physics that a billiard ball struck at a certain angle by another billiard ball will behave in a predictable fashion, at least on a flat, well-made, felt-covered, billiard table where there are no competing, interfering variables such as an imperfectly shaped ball, a gale-force wind, a table with uneven legs, molasses poured on the surface, and so forth. But what happens to our billiard ball, even under optimum conditions, if the table is littered with a dozen other balls? The laws of physics still work, but the situation is complex because of the probable interactions of the other balls with the initial ball. Now we have balls going in all directions. Actually, a billiard table littered with billiard balls is a fairly simple situation compared to a classroom filled with 30 students. Thus, a theory about motivation developed under controlled conditions during psychological experiments has only limited predictive validity in the seemingly random, infinitely complex world of classroom life. The theory itself may indeed be valid, but now the theory no longer stands in the splendid isolation of controlled laboratory conditions. It interacts with and becomes a mere part of an infinitely more complex situation. Our point is not to disparage educational or psychological research. On the contrary, we find it helpful when it is done well. It is the misapplication and overreaching of research findings that bother us. It is the misapplication and over-reaching of research findings that should bother you. What I wish to say is that the claims made by someone who talk about what "the research shows" must be carefully considered before we enter into wholesale policy or curriculum change.

The business of teaching and learning in school settings is a serious trust. All of us involved in the work of schools must do our best to honor that trust. We know that all is not well in the world of teaching and learning in America. As educators, we are vulnerable to new nostrums and fixes that will make things right at last. Change is a necessary condition of progress, and it behooves us to make the most meaningful changes possible. The hope is that as you examine the various attempts at innovation found in this book, you will learn to ask the right questions and that you will find useful answers.

4

"The Research Says…"

There aren't any embarrassing questions—
just embarrassing answers.

Carl Rowan

Have you ever found yourself at a meeting or conference listening to a speaker who pauses dramatically and states in august tones, "Well, the research says…?" Everyone, including you, quickly puts pen to paper in anticipation of some significant pronouncement that will change school life forevermore. If we only had a nickel for each time an education hustler has used such a phrase! If only it were as significant a statement as it appears to be to the uninitiated. The only appropriate response that comes to mind in the midst of such confusion is, "What research?"

In fact, the claim of most innovators or purveyors of innovation is that research has in some strategic way played an important part in the evolution and development of their ideas, programs, or materials. And in some sense, the claim is generally true but often misleading. For example, if someone claims a program for elementary children is based in part on learning transfer, we may be impressed. After all, the concept of transfer of learning is well documented in the annals of psychological research. But the leap from research in a laboratory setting to classroom application is long and difficult.

What "Kind" of Research?

I will show you a classification system that should prove helpful as you attempt to sort out different kinds of research. With this knowledge you will be able to determine for yourself what is behind the statement, "the research says…"

The term *research* has become so generic that it can and does refer to a wide range of activities. For example, you can research the cost of an airline ticket by checking on prices from five different airlines. To a freshman, a research paper is often little more than a collection of what other people have said about a topic. There is the old story of the student who searched the library for ideas before reaching the insight that, to make his term paper truly meaningful, he needed to research the topic. To an

29

advanced engineering student, research can mean mainly controlled experimental studies. We have the teacher-as-researcher model, often referred to as action research, which is typically a narrative of classroom events. This approach has led to collaborative research between teachers and university scholars. Now, there is the perennial debate over the relative value of two research paradigms—quantitative and qualitative. The origins of the debate are profoundly philosophical, and the nature of the debate is at times heated, with each side claiming to do research that is more valid. Others, searching perhaps for the golden mean, cite the necessity of doing both.

In spite of these problems of definition, it is helpful to conceptualize educational research in the following manner. I propose a model of research with three levels, each of which has different but related implications for educational innovation. The first is basic or pure research done theoretically and in so-called laboratory settings; the second is applied research done under controlled conditions in school settings; and the third is evaluation research applied to school programs once they have been implemented. Each is different from the others, and each yields its own unusual types of conclusions (see Figure 4.1).

Level I Research

Level I research is basic or pure research on learning and behavior. It is most commonly conducted in experimental or laboratory settings by psychologists, learning theorists, linguists, and others. Its purpose is to establish a theoretical construct or idea as having some validity. For example, Jean Piaget constructed a theory of stages of intellectual development through which children pass on their way to adult thought (Piaget, 1960). Jerome Bruner (1960) constructed a theory of the structure of knowledge that included alternative ways by which knowledge of some reality could be represented to learners (Bruner, 1966, 1996). And Howard Gardner has constructed a theory of multiple intelligences which essentially broadens the definition of the term *intelligence* (Gardner, 1983).

The research from which a theory emerges can come from controlled studies employing traditional empirical methods, or from qualitative, subjective observations, or from both. Invariably, it also takes into account prior contributions to the topic, modifying or possibly even rejecting them. This type of theory development is referred to as *grounded theory*. It is a process of deriving constructs and theories directly from immediate data that the researcher has collected. However, the usefulness of the constructs and theories grounded in the specific data must be validated with further research.

Figure 4.1 The Three Levels of Educational Research

LEVELS OF RESEARCH

PRELIMINARY RESEARCH or OBSERVATIONS/EXPERIENCE or A PHILOSOPHY

Level I: **Basic research on learning.**

leads to

THEORY ABOUT LEARNING

Level II: **Experimental research on educational outcomes.**

which has

IMPLICATIONS FOR THE CLASSROOM

which get
packaged into

INNOVATIVE PROGRAMS

Level III: **Program evaluation research on large-scale implementation.**

It is important to note that not all educational theories are derived from such research. It is possible for a learning theory to emerge out of a philosophical or religious belief, which may or may not have empirical support. For example, if a person is convinced of the inherent goodness of human beings, that person can readily propose that children's learning and their accompanying desire to learn would increase in a supportive, nonrestrictive, open environment. For the theory to be taken seriously, of course, it would need to have a well-established rationale. Such examples of theory building based on philosophical positions probably account for as many or more theories than do theories grounded in empirical data. More often, a well-grounded theory contains elements of both.

[Although Level I research can serve as a foundation for curriculum development, it is not designed to answer applied educational questions directly.] Piaget claimed on the basis of his research that most 8-year-olds are in a stage of concrete operations, leading many builders of innovative curriculum packages to put together mathematics and science activities that involved manipulative materials. And right or wrong, they did so on the assumption that the message from pure research could be applied to groups of 25 or 30 children learning together in a classroom setting. The extent to which it is reasonable to do this becomes a function of Level II research.

Level II Research

Level II research involves studies whose purpose is to determine the efficacy of particular programs or instructional methods in *educational* settings. Educational researchers who are interested in applying theories and procedures developed at the pure or basic level generally conduct such studies. For example, an educational researcher might attempt to set up controlled conditions in several classrooms for the purpose of comparing, say, cooperative learning in social studies with independent student learning. The experimental conditions might call for randomly assigning students and teachers to different treatment modes or conditions where the same material is studied. Pretests and posttests can be administered to all participants and comparisons made to determine whether a statistically significant difference occurred between or among treatments.

Level II research is applied research because (1) it is conducted in the same or similar settings that are actually found in schools, and (2) it makes no attempt to develop a theory but attempts to make instructional or curricular applications of a given theory. At its best, Level II research provides practical insights that cannot be derived directly from pure research. Thus, even though we can agree that reinforcement has been shown to be a powerful psychological concept by pure researchers, it remains for the Level II researcher to demonstrate how it might be advantageous to apply reinforcement in teaching in classroom settings.

Level II research is crucial to the process of validation of programs or methods of instruction. But time and time again, this step is simply ignored or poorly crafted as program developers or purveyors urge teachers and administrators to adopt a particular product. To return to the ITIP or PET theory-into-practice model for a moment, in retrospect we can see that it claimed its validity on the basis of such pure or basic research constructs as reinforcement, transfer, retention, and so forth, which are real enough. But it was almost totally lacking in any proof of what happens when one takes those constructs and *packages* them as a template for use by teachers in classroom settings. The same thing can be said for a number of other programs that have swept the country such as Assertive Discipline, TESA, and higher-level thinking strategies.

One of the best sources for school personnel to search at Level II is the journal, *Review of Educational Research*, published by the American Educational Research Association (AERA). This journal carries reviews and meta-analyses of various programs, projects, and packages. Doing so will give you insight into the quantity and nature of applied research that has been conducted in a given area.

A final point about Level II research is that each study, even if it represents good research, is severely limited in its generalizability. For example, if a study were conducted of teaching methods of reading and literature with fourth-grade, inner-city children, then whatever the results it would be unwise to generalize them to, for instance, rural eighth-grade students. This is why large numbers of good investigations about a given program should be carried out before school districts jump on this or that bandwagon. Cooperative learning, to cite an example where this has been done, has been and continues to be investigated in such a wide variety of school-based settings that its Level II foundation is secure, especially compared to most other innovations. Level II research in education is invariably improved by carefully crafted replication studies, something that is all too rare in our field.

Level III Research

Level III research is evaluation research designed to determine the efficacy of programs at the level of school or district implementation. It is by far the least likely of the three types to be carried out in any systematic way, and because of this, programs (good, bad, or indifferent) usually go through phases from initial enthusiasm to gradual abandonment, replaced by the next fad.

Examples of Level III research include evaluation studies that examine the overall effects on teachers and students of a particular district- or schoolwide innovation. If a district changes, for instance, from basal reading instruction to whole language learning, it is the job of evaluation researchers to determine exactly what changes were brought about and what the results of those changes were. This might involve interviews with teachers, students, and parents; the application of classroom environmental scales and observations to determine student perceptions of whole language learning; assessments of the amount and nature of support for the innovation; and analyses of achievement data over time.

It is important to note that an educational theory can have sound research support at Levels I and II and yet still may not be successful when implemented on a larger scale. This could happen for a number of reasons. For example, Level II research may have been conducted with highly trained teachers or with teachers who were supportive of the new program and volunteered for the Level II research. When the program was implemented on a districtwide scale, however, many teachers may have been skeptical of it, were reluctant to participate, were poorly trained, or decided on their own to make certain adaptations to the program. The availability of strategic and tactical support in the form of administrative and inservice leadership, as well as parental reaction, also represents factors that become known only over time. These and other variables make it crucial that Level III research or program evaluation be conducted.

A generation ago when the New Math swept the country, it had a pretty firm foundation at Levels I and II, but what little evidence we did gain at Level III revealed that many teachers were actually subverting the New Math, preferring to teach traditional arithmetic whenever they could. Mixed to negative parental reaction was seriously underestimated to say the least. And even the more farsighted of developers probably underestimated the drumbeat of criticism that arose in the popular press. So even if you are convinced that the theory behind some new program is sound, and even if you have seen published evidence of controlled studies in classroom settings that are supportive of the theory's application, you're still not home free. You must have seen the results of evaluation studies that indicate that this program really works in large numbers of regular classrooms.

Now you may be thinking that this represents quite a few gates for a new program to have to open before it proves its worth. And that is exactly the point! If we are to become less susceptible to fads, then it will be because we have become more deliberate and cautious along the way to adopting new programs.

Figure 4.1 (p. 31) illustrates the process that ideally unfolds in the cycle of educational innovation. The process begins with theories derived from pure or basic research. The theory is then tested under experimental or quasiexperimental conditions in school settings. Finally there is the program evaluation stage where assessment is made based on data from real classrooms that operate under typical day-to-day conditions.

It is true that these levels are somewhat arbitrary. There is not necessarily a linear flow from pure to applied to evaluation research. Sometimes there is, but often the situation is more chaotic than that. In some cases, the theoretical construct is less the source of energy than is the simple fact that something is available for educational use that was not available previously. Computers and calculators are obvious examples of this.

Summary

Comparison to medicines

In the world of prescription medications, the Food and Drug Administration (FDA) subjects new medicines to a long and exhaustive review before allowing them to be prescribed by doctors and dispensed by pharmacists. And even this process is a far cry from releasing a product to over-the-counter sales. Some critics of this system have pointed out that in many cases it takes years from the time we read about an experimental drug in the newspapers and its availability to the public. The role of the FDA is to play gatekeeper as tests are conducted, effects examined, potential drug interactions investigated, and so on. As a result, some drugs never make it to the marketplace and some do eventually.

With respect to educational innovations, however, we have no counterpart to the FDA. Therefore, programs can be rushed into the schools with little or no testing at any stage of the game. This may please those who are in a hurry to jump on the latest bandwagon, but it disadvantages those who would prefer to be consumers of thoughtfully tested and refined programs. Too often whole districts have adopted particular curriculums and teaching procedures that had basically no research foundation. This renders our profession vulnerable to criticisms that are difficult to refute.

In this chapter, it has been suggested that research be conducted at three distinctly different levels along the way to validating or invalidating educational innovations. Those three levels are (1) basic or pure research, (2) applied research in school settings, and (3) evaluation research where the effects of the large-scale implementation of an innovation are studied. *Time* All of this takes time, and rightly so. The only way to improve educational practice is to approach educational innovation with such a deliberate, measured sense of its worth.

Of course, schools adopt new ideas on the basis of something more than educational research. Economic, political, and cultural considerations will always play a role in this process. Welcome to the real world. But where we can be more thoughtful about change on the basis of a thorough examination of the merits of a given change, we ought to proceed cautiously.

Years ago there was a radio show called "It Pays to Be Ignorant." The theory behind the show was that people could win cash prizes and major household appliances by proving to the world, or at least to the huge nationwide radio audience, that they really were ignorant when it came to answering questions put to them by the genial host of the show. It was a great concept and a successful program. But I wish to say as clearly as possible that it doesn't pay to be ignorant when it comes to spending the public's tax dollars on educational innovations that really haven't proven themselves.

The Following Chapters

The chapters that follow contain overviews and analyses of current innovations in education. The process of selecting these topics involved a careful look at a wide variety of state and school district inservice offerings, college and university courses, and staff development institutes. During this process it became obvious that many of the offerings were simply variations of a more limited number of basic ideas or concepts. It is these basic concepts, or golden threads, that are the focus of the following chapters. Of course, the manifestation of the concepts can differ somewhat from one region of the country to another, or from one packager to another. The focus, however, is only on programs that have truly nationwide impact, whatever their regional calling cards happen to be.

Each of the following chapters contains a reasonably common format for the presentation of the topic under review. Each chapter begins with an overview of the concept to clarify exactly what is being talked about. I have depended heavily on primary sources for these sections. At times, this has required synthesizing the writing and ideas of many authors because for many of these topics there is no single developer who speaks for or represents the entire area. For example, the *brain research* movement in education is not dependent on the work of one person; it represents a compilation of ideas from many investigators and promoters. Even in the instances where one individual is clearly identified with a topic, such as Madeline Hunter for the Hunter Model, I have expanded the discussion past that individual to include descriptions of the programs as they are being implemented and expanded by others. The "main players" in each particular field of endeavor are identified; that is, those most closely associated with the topic and related programs. Although reference is made to various individuals and their programs as examples, the interpretations and descriptions of the concepts and programs are mine.

I have also provided specific examples of the structural effects these programs have, or would have if implemented, in the schools. For example, a teacher who adopts a whole language approach for the classroom will organize (1) the classroom, (2) the curriculum, and (3) instruction differently from a teacher following, say, a basal-reader approach. Similarly, a school following a direct instruction model will have a different focus and decision-making process from that found in a goal-free approach to schooling. Each of these chapters illustrates in specific terms what changes might occur if you implement a given program. In other words, ideas have consequences when they become reality, and I wish to be clear about that with you.

Included in each chapter is a critique of the given topic. It is fair to say that the work of the proponents of these ideas and programs is not above criticism, and I am not at all reluctant to do just that. Some programs have been carefully developed and come complete with a sound research foundation. Others are faddish and lacking both a theoretical and research base. In some cases, certain programs are antithetical to one another and the attempt to adopt both or to blend them will lead only to a confusion of purpose. Cautionary notes will be sounded about the implications that should be considered before wholesale changes in an educational system are undertaken. Who knows? What you are presently doing may be better than what will happen if you implement a certain highly touted program.

Proponents' claims about the degree to which the programs are supposedly research based are presented for your consideration. But do bear in mind that the term *research-based* can be a little like the term *low fat* found on product labels. It can be rather misleading. At the very least, one must know how to interpret the claims.

5

Setting Standards

The high stakes recently attached to standardized tests have given teachers incentives to revise the priorities of their instruction, especially for lower-class children, so that they devote greater time to drill on basic skills and less time to other, equally important (but untested) learning areas in which achievement gaps also appear.

Richard Rothstein

This standards-based movement seems to be hanging around a bit longer than we imagined it would.

Kenneth Sirotnik and Kathy Kimball

The standards movement holds the promise of revolutionizing teaching and learning in our schools.

Mary Diez

[F]ar too many news stories this year began with sentences like these: "To give her third-graders an extra 50 minutes of reading daily, the principal has eliminated music, art, and gym."

Gerald Bracey

Recently, when asked whose economy would be the strongest in 75 years, most of a group of Nobel-prize winning economists selected China. Not many of the economists thought the United States would be a contender for that title in 75 years because both China and the European Union will have larger populations and better educated workers. These thoughts were noted by Christine Culver, a federal education official in remarks she made to a gathering of citizens in Lawrence, Kansas. She also mentioned that for every engineer who graduates from a U.S. college, 40 graduate in China (Fox, 2004).

The much-touted No Child Left Behind Act of 2001 (NCLB) set a target date of 2014 for all students to be proficient in mathematics and reading.

This is somewhat more modestly stated than the Goals 2000 Act, which called for American students to be foremost in the world. But whether it is any more realistic is another question, although one could quibble over the meaning of the word *proficient*. In any event, as implied at the beginning this chapter, economic competitiveness remains at the forefront of reasons given for our desire to improve academic achievement by American students.

What Standards?

The answer to increased academic achievement, notably in reading and mathematics, is thought by many in the setting of high standards with mandatory testing to determine to what extent those standards are being met. But before I go any further, let us look at some different things people mean when they use the term *standards*. For starters, there are academic standards, content standards, and performance standards (Phelan, 2004).

Academic standards are designed to illustrate what students should know and be able to do in academic subjects at each grade level. *Content* standards describe what experts concur constitutes the essential knowledge that students should know in each academic subject area or discipline. *Performance* standards indicate the specific level of competent performance qualifies students to be described as advanced, proficient, below competence, and so on.

The current standards movement was officially inaugurated with the publishing of *Curriculum and Evaluation Standards for School Mathematics* (1989) by the National Council of Teachers of Mathematics (NCTM). Previously, several influential mid-eighties publications were instrumental in setting the process in motion. Among those were *A Nation at Risk* (1983), Diane Ravitch's book, *The Schools We Deserve* (1985), E. D. Hirsch Jr.'s *Cultural Literacy* (1987), and Allan Bloom's *The Closing of the American Mind* (1987). Each of these in its own way made the same case: American schools were failing to make the grade academically, largely because we have no cohesive, rigorous core curriculum.

By 1989 President George H. W. Bush had convened the National Governors' Association at an Education Summit in Virginia to set national educational goals to be achieved by the year 2000. Bush's successor, President Bill Clinton, continued the effort that included six goals, among them the curious goal: "By the year 2000, U.S. students will be first in the world in science and mathematics achievement." Perhaps our elected leaders attended too many high school basketball games where the cheer, "We're number one!" has become so common over the years. This goal was set without any apparent reference to historical evidence that we ever had been number one in these areas of the school curriculum.

It Was Better in the Old Days, or Was It?

In fact, Columbia University Professor William Bagley's address to the National Education Association Annual Convention of 1938 emphasized the following points:

- American elementary and secondary students fail to meet standards of achievement by students in other countries.
- An increasing number of high school students are basically illiterate.
- Notable deficiencies exist in mathematics and grammar throughout the grade levels.
- More money is being spent on education than ever before, but such problems as the crime rate continue to increase.

Plus ça Change, Plus C'est la Meme Chose

"The more things change the more they remain the same." Needless to say, the goal of being first in the world in mathematics and science achievement was not in evidence in 1938, nor was it in 2000, and it has yet to be achieved. The other goals—there are six altogether—are less disputable, at least on the grounds that they do not represent measurable outcomes. Therefore, whether "all children will start school ready to learn," to note another goal, has been achieved as a goal is dubious but debatable.

The Movement Gathers Steam

During the 1990s other major professional education organizations followed the NCTM lead of setting standards, each in its own respective subject matter area. At this point, standards have been published by the professional organizations representing the five core areas of the school curriculum: mathematics, reading, writing, science, and social studies, as well as in such areas as health, the arts, and life skills. The idea in each case is to identify the salient characteristics of school subjects to give teachers and students a clear sense of what those subjects are actually about (see Figure 5.1, p. 42). Why is this necessary? The answers to that question appear to range from concerns over lagging achievement—especially as noted in international comparisons—to a felt need for order, common content coverage, and overwhelming pressure from business and universities. Business and universities are key players simply because these are mainly the two places where students go after high school.

Figure 5.1 Standards Defined

The term *standards* has come to refer to two different but related ideas: content and performance. Content standards identify what students should know and be able to do, and performance standards identify *how* students will demonstrate their proficiency.

Academic Content Standards describe what every student should know and be able to do in the core academic areas (e.g., reading, mathematics, science, history, etc.). Content standards should apply equally to students of all races and ethnicities, from all linguistic and cultural backgrounds, both with and without special learning needs.

Performance Standards answer the question: "How good is good enough?" They define how student demonstrate their proficiency in the skills and knowledge framed by states' content standards.

An example from the Washington State Commission on Student Learning, Essential Academic Learning Requirements in Mathematics:

The content standard in mathematics requires students to: *understand and apply concepts and procedures from probability and statistics.*

The corresponding *performance standard* (4th-grade level, probability benchmark) requires students to demonstrate their mastery of the standard by showing that they

◆ understand the difference between certain and uncertain events.

◆ know how to list all possible outcomes of simple experiments.

◆ understand and use experiments to investigate uncertain events.

Adapted from *Standards: What Are They? Improving America's Schools*, Spring, 1996. U.S. Department of Education, and from the *Essential Academic Learning Requirements Tech Manual*, 1998, Olympia, WA: Washington State Department of Education.

The Role of the States

The American school curriculum is in many ways a curious artifact of our educational history. Not only is there no national curriculum, but the fact of the matter is that beyond the state, district, and building levels, classroom teachers are basically given free rein to emphasize whatever they want in the subjects they teach. There is no controlling legal authority with the power to say to a classroom teacher, "This is what and how you must teach." Thus two educators teaching U.S. history in adjoining rooms of the same school can cover widely divergent topics. This is less so in areas such as algebra or biology, but even a cursory examination of textbooks makes the point that the curriculum is not completely agreed on in any subject. There is no common core. In the same building, one primary teacher can take a whole language approach to the teaching of reading while that teacher's next door neighbor takes a phonics-based approach. Of course, state and district guides do prescribe certain coverage, but just as in the case of the doctor's prescription, the patient does not have to swallow it.

Further evidence of the unusual (when compared to most other countries) nature of our curriculum is found in the obvious discontinuities among textbooks, standardized tests of achievement, and content emphasis by classroom teachers. It is not at all unusual for teachers to note that skills and knowledge sought on standardized achievement tests were not even taught by them. The linkage between standardized tests and textbooks is tenuous at best, given the fact that any two textbooks that are said to cover the same subject will actually cover some topics in common as well as other topics not held in common. In other words, the curriculum is not standardized.

The standards movement is just that: an attempt to standardize the curriculum through the publishing of content standards by the influential professional associations representing the various subject matter disciplines. The thinking is that a standardized curriculum is a more tightly coupled curriculum. For the first time textbook publishers and test authors have a clear frame of reference for what material should be taken into account. So too, do classroom teachers. Of course we have no national curriculum, so the standards suggested by the professional organizations are exemplary at best. Now, 49 states have or are in the process of adopting standards for the various subjects of the school curriculum. Thus it appears more possible now than ever before to get everyone on the same page, so to speak.

As each state sets about the business of articulating standards, we might ask why. Why not one national set of standards? The answer is found in the Ninth Amendment to the U.S. Constitution, which makes it clear that all matters not specifically relegated to the federal government fall within the jurisdiction of the individual states. Education is not mentioned in the Constitution; therefore, by inference it is a state matter. However, the professional organizations such as the National Council of Teachers of Mathematics, The International Reading Association, the National Council of Teachers of English, the National Science Teachers Association, the National Council for the Social Studies, and others do have national prominence to say the least, and their setting of standards for the various disciplines of the core curriculum has indeed proven to be highly influential at the state level. Still, one of the emerging critical problems is the disagreement on what standards are. Recently, I was at a meeting of middle school experts, one of whom, having examined the mathematics standards proposed by one particular state, said, "These aren't standards, they're activities." Problems of definition and articulation will no doubt continue to plague the process.

Another curiosity is that although we have witnessed the development of discipline-based standards in nearly every state, we have yet to see much evidence of standards held in common across the curriculum, except by inference. This is so in spite of the fact that all the national (professional organization documents) and state standards reports stress the need for subject matter integration, project-based learning, and so on. In Canada, for example, the Ontario Ministry of Education and Training has published *The Common Curriculum: Policies and Outcomes Grades 1–9*. This thoughtful document sets forth a curriculum framework on the basis of four program areas as opposed to the traditional discipline-based approach. Each of the program areas addresses various elements of content integration and application (Hargreaves and Moore, 2000).

Accountability and Standards

It is one thing to publish standards to better inform all those involved in the education of our children. It is yet another thing to expect that teachers, once informed, will follow suit. State and district guides, for example, have been around for years as a means of informing educators of the essential knowledge and skills they should teach. However, as often as not, such guides are paid little notice. It is not at all uncommon for teachers, having been given the district guide at the beginning of the school year, to say they unable even to find it when asked, something that they would have little trouble doing if they took the district guide as seriously as, say, their car keys.

Given such a history, one could reason that some teachers will take the standards seriously and many will not, relegating them to the same dust-gathering status as other documents. But this time around, besides seeking greater standardization of curriculum content and offering the hope of linking curriculum content with textbook coverage and achievement test coverage, the standards movement is also accompanied by articles of assessment. Several states, most notably Washington, Vermont, and Maryland, have focused on the development of *high-quality* performance assessments designed to measure the extent to which standards-based curriculum and teaching result in improved student abilities to solve complex problems. An example of such a performance assessment is shown in Figure 5.2.

The development of assessment instruments tied to the standards can or cannot have been the original intent of the professional associations. The fact is, however, that this is what has happened and is continuing to happen. Standards-referenced test instruments, typically in the form of what are called *performance assessment* tests, are cropping up in nearly every state. Thus what began as a curriculum movement, in which content

Figure 5.2 Example of Performance Assessment

Mathematics Sample Short-Answer
Mathematical Concepts and Procedures Item

Component: The student understands and applies the concepts and procedures of mathematics: algebraic sense.

Benchmark: The students recognizes, creates, and extends patterns and sequence.

The ancient Greeks discovered that certain numbers, when arranged in dot patters, form definite shapes. **Triangular numbers,** for example, have dot patterns that can be arranged into triangles. A sequence of triangular numbers is shown below.

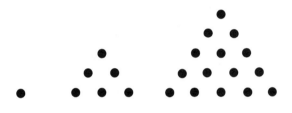

What is the next triangular number in this sequence? Clearly explain or show the reason for your answer.

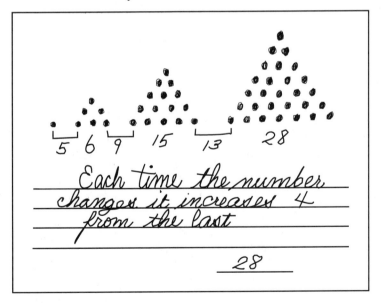

Source: Washington State Office of the Superintendent of Public Instruction. (1999).

standards were articulated, has become as well an outcomes or assessment movement in which *performance* standards are increasingly prescribed.

Another way to think of the evolution of the standards movement is offered in an insightful article by Marzano and Kendall (2000). They suggest that it is crucial to consider the difference between content standards, which describe what students should know and be able to do, and curriculum standards, which describe what should take place in the classroom, or in other words, the desired methods of instruction. They give as an example of a content standard from NCTM: "Use estimation to check the reasonableness of results." Note how generally applicable such a skill would be. On the other hand, they give as an example of a curriculum standard, also from NCTM: "describe, model, draw and classify shapes." Marzano and Kendall's clear preference is for the setting of clear content standards because content standards represent achievement goals without being prescriptive as to how teachers might go about teaching. Thus if a state or district wished to suggest methods of instruction designed to reach the goals, that is another matter.

Points of Origin: Level 1

The origins of the standards movement can be traced in part to its essentialist philosophical roots. In fact, standards are often known as *essential* learnings. Essentialist philosophy, which generally disdains but sometimes cooperates with progressive educational philosophy as we shall see, can be described as follows:

> Essentialism is rooted in the belief that there is a core of essential knowledge and skills that must be transmitted to students. This essential core is represented by the various subject matter disciplines that represent the essence of school learning. Essentialism represents a search for objective truth that can be known, and this results in emphasis on discipline-based science, mathematics, language, arts, history, physical education, and other essential school subjects.

Of course, things are never that simple. The standards movement also has roots in the social efficiency tradition, a phenomenon that has been with us since the early days of the twentieth century. Social efficiency asks the question: "How can we make teaching and learning more efficient and productive in order to best serve society?" The efficiency movement, which began in industry and which was clearly articulated in Frederick Winslow Taylor's book, *The Principles of Scientific Management* (1911), soon jumped the rails from industry to education, and the search was on for ways to make schools more effective—which meant then and means now, more efficient.

Efficiency as an educational concept represents what is known as the technical interest. The technical interest, as described by the philosopher Jurgen Habermas (1971), is a means–end approach. That is, the technical interest seeks means to control situations toward certain predetermined ends: "If we do this, we will get that." Put another way, prediction equals control. This should be familiar territory to those acquainted with such standards-movement precursors as behavioral objectives, time-on-task analysis, competency-based education, and outcomes-based education.

According to Habermas, the more the technical interest encroaches into the world of such interests as the practical and the reflective, the more our lives become diminished. One can be assured that teachers and students, who live in the practical world of classroom life, have not been in the forefront of the standards movement. Speaking from an anecdotal perspective, I can say that more and more teachers are telling me that they no longer involve their students in project learning and other related activity-centered experiences. They are simply "too busy" getting their students ready to do well on the standardized tests and performance assessments.

Essentialist Goals, Progressive Means

Although the standards movement clearly represents an essentialist goal structure, the means suggested for achieving the goals are just as clearly progressive. For example, a recommendation that comes from nearly all the major professional groups is that there be *less* whole-class, teacher-led direct instruction, and that there be *more* experiential, hands-on learning. This seems at first glance to give rise to some measure of discontinuity. Consider, for example, the oft-noted observation that Japanese mathematics teachers, who apparently are more academically successful than their U.S. counterparts, and who do indeed use a whole-class, teacher-directed approach, do indeed teach fewer topics in greater depth.

This point takes us back to Marzano and Kendall's cogent observation that content standards and curriculum standards are basically two different things. Thus a content standard can demand a certain skill, knowledge, or ability, whereas a curriculum standard can suggest the purported best means for instructing students toward such achievement. However, this matter does raise serious concern over the wisdom of linking the achievement of certain content goals with certain methods of instruction in the absence of clear and convincing evidence that those methods are the best route to those goals.

In their book *Best Practice: New Standards for Teaching and Learning in America's Schools* (1998), Zemelman, Daniels, and Hyde wrote:

A more general, progressive paradigm is emerging across content boundaries and grade levels. This coherent philosophy and spirit is reaching across the curriculum and up through the grades. Whether it is called Best Practice, or Whole Language, or integrated learning, or interdisciplinary studies, by some other name, or by no name at all, this movement is broad and deep and enduring. It is strongly backed by educational research, draws on sound learning theory, and, under other names, has been tested and refined over the years. (p. 7)

Zemelman and colleagues (2000) identify "thirteen interlocking principles, assumptions, or theories that characterize this model of education" (p. 7). Whether everyone would agree with the extent to which these clearly progressive principles of teaching and learning, if used by teachers and students, will bring about higher levels of achievement remains another matter. What we can see, however, is that the standards movement is an amalgam. The legendary frontiersman Davy Crockett, at least in his Disney incarnation, used to describe himself as half alligator, half bear, with a touch of snapping turtle—bad mathematics, perhaps, but a colorful description. Perhaps the theoretical construct of the standards movement is somewhat Crockettesque in that it seems to be half essentialist, half progressive, with a touch of social efficiency.

Research at Levels II and III

Given that the standards movement is reasonably recent, one might expect not to find much research connected with it. This is increasingly less the case as investigators make their inquiries. The research that looks at the effects of setting standards on achievement is not easily classified. Typically, it looks more like Level III research than it does Level II; what could be called program effects are at stake.

Mayer (1998) investigated the extent to which the NCTM teaching standards in mathematics were a factor in raising achievement among eighth- and ninth-grade algebra students. Specifically, he asked the question: "Do students taught in NCTM-like classrooms perform differently on standardized assessments than students taught in traditional classrooms?" (p. 54) Mayer identified classrooms in 41 schools in a large school district where algebra was taught using either a primarily traditional emphasis or using primarily NCTM-prescribed instructional procedures such as student-led discussion, group investigation, writing about problems, different means of solving problems, multiple solutions, and so on. He found that the measured knowledge of algebra of both lower- and higher-GPA students "grows faster" in the NCTM-like classrooms among students at the eighth-grade level. At the ninth-grade level, which was dominated by students who were not selected to take algebra in their

Figure 5.3 Principles of Best Learning Practices

- **Student-centered:** The best starting point for schooling is young people's real interests; all across the curriculum, investigating students' own questions should always take precedence over studying arbitrarily and distantly selected content.

- **Experiential:** Active, hands-on, concrete experience is the most powerful and natural form of learning. Students should be immersed in the most direct possible experience of the content of every subject.

- **Holistic:** Children learn best when they encounter whole ideas, events, and materials in purposeful contexts, not by studying subparts isolated from actual use.

- **Authentic:** Real, rich, complex ideas and materials are at the heart of the curriculum. Lessons or textbooks that water-down, control, or oversimplify content ultimately disempower students.

- **Expressive:** To fully engage ideas, construct meaning, and remember information, students must regularly employ the whole range of communicative media—speech, writing, drawing, poetry, dance, drama, music, movement, and visual arts.

- **Reflective:** Balancing the immersion in experience and expression must be opportunities for learners to reflect, debrief, abstract from their experiences what they have felt and thought and learned.

- **Social:** Learning is always socially constructed and often interactional; teachers need to create classroom interactions that "scaffold" learning.

- **Collaborative:** Cooperative learning activities tap the social power of learning better than competitive and individualistic approaches.

- **Democratic:** The classroom is a model community; students learn what they live as citizens of the school.

- **Cognitive:** The most powerful learning comes when children develop true understanding of concepts through higher-order thinking associated with various fields of inquiry and through self-monitoring of their thinking.

- **Developmental:** Children grow through a series of definable but not rigid stages, and schooling should fit its activities to the developmental level of students.

- **Constructivist:** Children do not just receive content; in a very real sense, they re-create and reinvent every cognitive system they encounter, including language, literacy, and mathematics.

- **Challenging:** Students learn best when faced with genuine challenges, choices, and responsibility in their own learning.

Source: S. Zemelman, H. Daniels, and A. Hyde. (1998). *Best Practice: New Standards for Teaching and Learning in American Schools,* 2nd ed. Portsmouth, NH: Heinnenman.

eighth-grade year and who were therefore typically lower-skilled students, there seemed to be little achievement difference between students in traditional classrooms and those in NCTM-like classrooms.

Mayer's findings should be considered highly tentative because his study did not attempt to control a range of factors affecting external and internal validity. Nonetheless, his work does represent real-world-of-school research and a set of findings that offer qualified endorsement to the use of the NCTM principles for students who qualify for and take eighth-grade algebra.

There is no shortage of reporting from states and school districts about how the implementation of standards-based reforms has resulted in increased student achievement. Whether the standards movement is to be given all or part of the credit, the fact is that National Assessment of Educational Progress (NAEP) mathematics and reading scores have risen in recent years in a number of states that have taken reform seriously. The problem with attempting to unravel cause and effect relationships—or even more realistically trying to figure out meaningful associations—is that *any* findings are fraught with uncontrolled variables such as changed or differentially defined drop-out rates, greater or lesser retention of students, inclusion or exclusion of special-needs students, inclusion or exclusion of limited-proficiency English students, and other factors which could severely restrict meaningful comparisons.

In spite of these issues, we find the Seattle Public Schools, where emphasis on high academic standards has been coupled with site-based management, reporting 1999 reading and mathematics test scores at both third- and eighth-grade levels well above statewide averages, a rare outcome for this large urban district. In Milwaukee and Philadelphia, similar success stories have been reported in the wake of adopting higher academic standards (2000). Again, problems surface when one considers the confounding effects arising in each of these situations because a number of reforms have been implemented simultaneously of which a focus on higher academic standards is only one.

On the seven National Assessment of Educational Progress (NAEP) tests given to fourth and eighth graders from 1990–1996, Texas and North Carolina, two states that have placed great emphasis on the standards-based reform and accountability, made the greatest average gains in the nation (National Alliance of Business, 2000). Although these outcomes initially appear to be a positive thing, on further examination one encounters so many rival hypotheses for why this might be so as to make it difficult to attribute these gains to the implementation of standards. In other words, broad policy decisions typically contain so many uncontrolled educational variables as to make cause and effect conclusions nearly impossible.

The Council for Basic Education (CBE) assessed the "rigor" of mathematics and language arts standards on the basis of a review of standards documents from 43 states (Joftus & Berman, 1998). The Council's review yielded a number of significant findings, notably that state mathematics standards tend to be more rigorous than language arts standards. Most states' mathematics standards "contain few major gaps in the concepts and skills included," and even states with less rigorous standards tend to address the most essential skills and concepts. On the other hand, CBE investigators noted that although most states' standards address basic skills they often do not address "literature study, research, or even language study such as word origins and differences between standard usage and slang" (p. 1).

So the evidence is clear that standards, although subscribed to by nearly every state, mean different things to different people. CBE's conclusion is that there is considerable range to be found with some states setting "very rigorous" standards, others setting "rigorous" standards, and still others setting standards with low levels of rigor. The CBE findings comport with assessments by a number of other researchers who noted similar discrepancies in the quality of standards set by various states.

The eminent researcher Robert Linn (2000) notes four reasons why, in spite of quality issues, the standards movement has sustained itself. He notes that testing and test results are and probably will remain an integral part of the movement. Those reasons include the fact that tests are relatively (compared to other curricular and instructional changes) inexpensive, testing changes can be implemented quickly; test results are highly visible and draw media attention; and testing can bring about other changes that would be difficult to legislate. He writes that in spite of the problems posed by standards-based assessment, there are some cues that policy makers and other educators should take to heart.

The Critics' Corner

Obviously not everyone is enamored of the standards movement. Alfie Kohn has called the standards movement a "horrible idea." Kohn notes that the standards movement is "fatally flawed" in five separate ways. Kohn argues that the standards movement gets the following things wrong: motivation, pedagogy, evaluation, school reform, and improvement. He discusses these issues at length in a number of sources (2004). Kohn points out that the movement oversimplifies why children might want to learn, how they are best taught, and how improvement might best be brought to a complex system. The idea of demanding higher test scores, Kohn notes, will accomplish little more than studying for tests, emphasizing rote learning, and tightening control over classrooms by people who do not spend their time in classrooms.

Figure 5.4 Ten Suggestions for Policymakers

♦ Set standards that are high, but attainable.

♦ Develop standards, *then* assessments.

♦ Include all students in testing programs but provide accommodations for

  • those with the most severe disabilities, and

  • students who have not yet transitioned into English language programs.

♦ Develop new high-quality assessments each year that are comparable to those of previous years or results will be distorted.

♦ Important decisions about students and schools must not be based on one single test.

♦ Compare change from year to year rather than from school to school.

♦ Set both long- and short-term school goals for all schools.

♦ Uncertainty should be reported in all test results.

♦ Unintended negative effects must be considered as well as intended positive effects when evaluating testing systems.

♦ Testing alone will not improve the educational system as a whole; the way to narrow the achievement gap is to provide all children with the teachers and resources needed to reach our high expectations.

Source: Linn, R. (2000). *Standards-based accountability: Ten suggestions.* Retrieved August 1, 2000, CRESST Policy Brief: www.cse.ucla.edu.

Gerald Bracey (2004), editor of a research column in *Phi Delta Kappan,* has been particularly critical. He has spoken out against the No Child Left Behind Act as well as against the standards movement, particularly the standardized testing that has come to be part and parcel of the movement. He writes,

> Many of us saw No Child Left Behind (NCLB) as a piece of Orwellian doublespeak from the beginning. My first anti-NCLB essay appeared January 2001 in *Newsday.* That's right, 2001, a year before the plan was signed into law. For most observers, though, the arc of accelerating animosity required time. (p. 160)

Bracey notes further, observing the high price paid in terms of what might be called by some nonstrategic subjects:

> In what might be considered its swan song, the Council for Basic Education conducted a survey and found NCLB producing "academic atrophy" in social studies, history, geography, civ-

ics, languages, and the arts. A little more of this, and we can declare, "No Education Left." (p. 166)

Marzano, Kendall, and Cicchinelli (2000), who are not particularly critical of the movement, note an apparently overlooked problem with addressing the standards. Their calculations show that, given the demands of the standards and accompanying benchmarks from the various subject matter areas, it would take more than 15,000 hours to adequately address the necessary content. This would mean some drastic alteration of the amount of time spent in school because K–12 education has only a little more than 9,000 hours now. Those readers of this book who possess some mastery of fractions will note that this would call for 15/9 of the time we presently spend. Put another way, Marzano, Kendall, and Cicchinelli say the implication for coverage would be to extend school from K–12 to K–21. They conclude that one possible solution would be to extend the amount of time given to instruction, and another would be to decrease the number of standards.

Maehr and Maehr (1996) offered rather pointed criticisms of the standards movement when they wrote:

> The recommendation to establish and apply "standards" emerges as a prime example of looking to past evidence of known flaws, and being unmindful of a changed and changing world into which these standards are now supposed to work....It sounds good on its face perhaps, but it is a simplistic solution at best and a demonic one at worst. Implied is a school that doesn't exist, a commitment that cannot work, a course of action that will prove debilitating to many students and the schools they attend. (p. 21)

Maehr and Maehr go on to list four "major concerns" they have about the call for standards. They point out that although it is easy to point to failing schools, in fact it is society that has failed. They note that schools already have standards and that adding on new ones in the absence of clear mission is folly. They question the extent to which standards and their accompanying assessment protocols are in fact motivators toward excellence. And they predict an erosion of school culture in which true learning and growth and development are sacrificed in the attempt to meet external standards.

Asa Hilliard (1998) takes the standards movement to task in no uncertain terms. He notes that many of the people advocating tougher standards "have no idea of the importance of quality teaching and leadership." Hilliard argues that without a national curriculum, the result of allowing each state to set its own standards will inevitably lead to validity problems in any meaningful kind of national assessment.

In an article not meant to be directly critical of standards, James Popham (1999) makes a useful distinction between types of standardized tests and their accompanying results, which of course, are pointed to by standards advocates as proof of declining achievement as well as the ultimate measures of how well standards might it. Popham distinguishes between *aptitude* tests, which predict how well students are likely to perform in some subsequent educational setting, and *achievement* tests, which measure what students know. The most familiar aptitude tests are the SAT (Scholastic Assessment Test) and the ACT Assessment. Both of them are used as predictors of college or university academic performance.

Achievement tests, he notes, typically cover four subject areas (mathematics, language arts, social studies, and science), and are designed to provide information to be used for comparisons between and among groups regarding student knowledge and skills. Popham lists the five most used achievement tests as the *California Achievement Test, Comprehensive Test of Basic Skills, Iowa Test of Basic Skills, Metropolitan Achievement Test,* and *Standard Achievement Test.*

Popham cites three reasons why schools should not be judged on the basis of standardized test scores. The first reason he notes is that of the mismatch between what is taught and what is tested. Of course, the response of standards advocates is that by setting clear standards, it becomes far more possible to close the gap between curriculum and assessment. This is so because textbook companies will have a clearer idea of what to include, and teachers will have a clearer idea of what is essential.

Popham's second reason is that standardized tests do not measure the most important things that teachers teach. And by definition, they cannot do so. Here is his reasoning: Standardized tests need to produce a large spread of scores. This means that the most effective test items are those that are answered correctly by only about 50 percent of the test takers. He writes that test items that are answered correctly "by large proportions of students, for instance, 80 percent or more, are usually not put in standardized tests in the first place..." (p. 2). The problem is that these are the significant items that teachers typically teach. So, a kind of reverse Darwinian procedure emerges in which success is weeded out.

The third problem noted by Popham is that over time teachers become familiar with the content of standardized tests, and that leads to an inflation of test results because teachers, knowingly or not, end up teaching to the test. Does this really mean higher achievement? Probably not. It means that teachers are taking their cues about what to teach from the tests.

Where Does This Leave Us?

The standards movement would appear to be one that will not go quietly into that dark night. It may well have a certain staying power, a certain elemental appeal. Who could really argue that the setting of standards in the subject matter disciplines is a wrong-headed idea? As we have seen, the movement does have its detractors, but their objections seem to be mainly over the assessment issues. To convene a body of experts in the field, subject matter, and pedagogical authorities, and to ask them to decide on the salient characteristics of, say, geometry, is hardly an affront to a geometry teacher's dignity or professional academic freedom. Even the most creative teachers, who have developed their own courses of study, would surely want to know what the experts say is significant, if for no other reason than that this could be a point of departure, a model from which to deviate.

Further, although the content standards themselves do represent a disciplinary approach to curriculum, there is no reason to think that a team of teachers from different disciplines would be restricted in their attempts to integrate studies. In fact, one could argue that standards are helpful in such a situation because they define the essence of the various aspects of content to be merged by a team. One of the arguments against interdisciplinary teaching has always been that subjects such as mathematics tend to get short shrift. A team that starts with a set of standards representing each subject is armed with a means of preventing that from happening.

It should also be noted that the professional organizations that have taken the lead in the development of standards have in every case encouraged team teaching, higher order thinking, interdisciplinary learning, inquiry, constructivist approaches, experiential learning, and even less use of and reliance on standardized tests. Therefore, it is incumbent on educators to think through the difference between advocating standards and simply assuming that standardized tests are the main or only way we can know whether standards are meaningful guides to teaching and learning. There may be all the difference in the world in these two points of view.

6

Innovations From Brain Research

The disciplines of brain science and education haven't had a lot to say to each other—mostly because they live in isolation. I think this estrangement is puzzling, because the two are naturally aligned. A simple but crude experiment can prove the point of intersection. Cut off someone's head, and try to teach what's left.

John Medina

Over the past 20 years or more, neuroscientists have amassed a wealth of knowledge on the brain and its development from birth to adulthood. And they are beginning to draw some solid conclusions about how the human brain grows and how babies acquire language, sight and musical talents, and other abilities. The question now is: How much of these data can educators use? The answer is uncertain.

Debra Viadero

There are more possible brain states than there are particles in the universe.

Vilayanur Ramachandran

Dr. Read Montague, a neuroscientist at Baylor University's College of Medicine, recently conducted a study of soft drink preference involving Coca Cola and Pepsi Cola (Ha, 2004). He and his colleagues found that when subjects were given the two drinks to compare without knowing which was which, the ventral putamen of the brain became highly active. When the subjects had knowledge of which cola they were drinking beforehand, however, the medial prefrontal cortex of the brain became activated. In the blind tests, Pepsi was preferred, but in the case of tests where subjects were informed of the brand name, Coke was the winner. This study has obvious implications for the world of advertising, and no doubt more resourceful persons will see connections to teaching and learning.

Brain researcher John Medina (2003) of the Talaris Institute has noted that "if brain scientists and educators were allowed to work together, they would probably turn both disciplines upside down." He cites among other problems the lack of a common vocabulary. Educators and brain researchers simply tend to live in different worlds.

Medina, lamenting what could be construed as a "no-contact order" between the two disciplines, has identified a number of potential collaborative research topics that could definitely lead to new insights in brain-based teaching and learning. Figure 6.1 lists those topics.

Figure 6.1 Topics for Collaborative Research Involving Brain Specialists and Educators

The following brain rules have been identified by researchers in brain function. These rules could serve as focal points for much needed research into the implications of brain function for teaching and learning.

+ Repetition is critical for memory
+ Sleep is important to the learning process.
+ Every brain is different from every other brain.
+ We process meaning before details.
+ People are natural explorers.
+ We are visual learners.
+ Exercise aids learning.
+ Focused attentional states facilitate learning.
+ Stressed brains do not learn the same way as nonstressed brains.

Source: John Medina (2003). *Response.* Autumn, 2003.

What Medina has identified is a potentially powerful research agenda. The promise is there, to paraphrase that most quotable English writer Alexander Pope, to furnish us with a map rather than a maze, as the list of terms in the next paragraph might suggest to most teachers. If Medina's agenda is taken seriously by teams of educational and brain science researchers, we should know a great deal more in the not-too-distant future about how people learn and how they might be taught more effectively.

Meanwhile, take a moment to consider the following: structural and transportational cellular systems, glial cells, neurons, dendrites, amino acids, neurotransmitters, peptides, corpus callosum, and anterior commissure. These terms, which are a focus of brain research, have little meaning to most teachers and administrators. Yet the research in this area may well have implications for how we should teach and how schools should be organized. Robert Sylwester, a leading figure in the field of brain research and school learning, points out that educators have stressed the environmental aspects of learning potential, largely without an understanding of how the brain actually works. However, medical research advances have made possible the startling recognition that the human brain is on the verge of understanding itself! In the light of this development, Sylwester concluded that

> Our profession has tended to think of the nurture side as dominant, but these new theories argue that nature plays a far more important role than previously believed—or that the dichotomy itself is not an irrelevant issue. They also suggest that many current beliefs about instruction, learning, and memory are wrong. (1995, pp. 14–15)

The current love affair on the part of education with brain research flows from the belief that if we can figure out how the brain functions—how information is received, stored, retrieved, and otherwise processed—we can then design educational programs based on that knowledge. Brain research represents for many the ultimate pedagogical frontier. Once this new territory is explored and mapped, the promise of maximizing the learning potential of each student will be realized. Sylwester's bold statement indicates that we may need to make essential changes in the ways we go about the business of school learning and teaching.

The basic research in this area began with Paul Broca's celebrated nineteenth-century theory of hemispheric dominance. Research into this and other areas of brain function has continued apace in the twentieth century, and in 1981, Roger Sperry received the Nobel Prize for his split-brain research. In more recent years, medical research into brain function has expanded into a variety of areas to include brain development in childhood, short- and long-term memory, attention, emotions, gender differences, effects of aging, consciousness, creativity, sensory input, intelligence, sexuality, and others. It is all technical and overwhelming for those outside the world of scientific investigation even to consider.

The Pendulum Is Well Into Its Swing

It was not long after certain findings from brain research became publicized that educators jumped into the breach with ideas about how the findings should alter educational practices (Reiff, 1992; Carnine, 1990;

Caine & Caine, 1990; Springer & Deutsch, 1989; Wittrock, 1981). A wide range of supposed educational theories has emerged on the heels of medical investigations. More than 25 years ago, Robert Sylwester wrote, "The brain is the most magnificent three pounds of matter in the universe. What we now know about the human brain and what we'll discover in the years ahead may well transform formal education" (Sylwester, 1981). Whether what we think we know about the brain will prove useful or not, educators have jumped on the bandwagon with article after article about the educational implications of medical research. Sylwester went on to say, "but can we afford to wait until all problems are solved before we begin to study the education issues implicit in this research? When mass media begin to report discoveries, parents will expect us to respond" (Sylwester, 1981, p. 8).

In at least a comparative sense, Sylwester was cautious, believing that it was too early to implement curricular and instructional changes based on the medical research. He was no doubt well aware of the tendency of some educators to make wild claims and advocate unproven methodologies based on theories alone, and he remains cautious to this day. As he later wrote, "We've already demonstrated our vulnerability with the educational spillover of the split-brain research: the right brain/left brain books, workshops, and curricular programs whose recommendations often went far beyond the research findings" (1995, p. 6).

Other educators have been less restrained in their enthusiasm. It is fair to say that they have responded to the medical findings by developing activities and strategies designed to influence life in classrooms. The topic has become a common offering at conventions, workshops, and inservice meetings. Those who wish confirmation of this claim need only review the list of presentations found in the catalogues of major education conferences.

An example of learning implications derived from medical research is reflected in the work of Caine and Caine (1990, 1994, 2004). They have developed, they write,

> brain principles as a general theoretical foundation for brain-based learning. These principles are simple and neurologically sound. Applied to education, however, they help us to reconceptualize teaching by taking us out of traditional frames of reference and guiding us in defining and selecting appropriate programs and methodologies. (1990, p. 66)

They go on to say that

> [i]f these principles are as sound as we believe they are, then they provide us with a framework for learning and teaching that moves us irrevocably away from the methods and models

that have dominated education for more than a century." (1994, p. 87)

Pretty heady stuff.

Figure 6.2 summarizes Caine and Caine's brain-based learning theory. Each of the 12 learning principles has direct implications for teaching and learning. For example, the second principle states that "brain-based teaching must fully incorporate stress management, nutrition, exercise, drug education, and other facets of health into the learning process" (p. 66). The sixth principle states that "vocabulary and grammar are best understood and mastered when they are incorporated in genuine, whole-language experiences. Similarly, equations and scientific principles are best dealt with in the context of living science" (p. 67). These are interesting conclusions in any educational context, but to state that they are based on brain research gives them, one supposes, heightened credibility. At any rate, these assertions sailed past the editorial gatekeepers of *Educational Leadership*, a policy journal in the field of education.

Figure 6.2 Caine and Caine's
Brain-Based Learning Principles

1. The brain is a parallel processor.
2. Learning engages the entire physiology.
3. The search for meaning is innate.
4. The search for meaning occurs through "patterning."
5. Emotions are critical to patterning.
6. Every brain simultaneously perceives and creates parts and wholes.
7. Learning involves both focused attention and peripheral perception.
8. Learning always involves conscious and unconscious processes.
9. We have two types of memory:
   a. a spatial memory system, and
   b. a set of systems for rote learning.
10. The brain understands and remembers best when facts and skills are embedded in natural spatial memory.
11. Learning is enhanced by challenge and inhibited by threat.
12. Each brain is unique.

Source: Adapted from Caine, R.N., & Caine, G. (1994, 2004). *Making connections: teaching and the human brain.* Menlo Park, CA: Addison-Wesley.

The application of basic brain research to education has also resulted in an emphasis on learning styles, particularly among proponents of hemisphericity (right and left brain preference) in learning. It is worth noting that both learning-styles advocates and brain-research educators support a *whole-brain* approach to teaching. That is, they both claim that it is necessary to teach to both sides of the brain, providing a wide and complementary range of strategies and activities to stimulate learners. This results in a model that is best understood in comparison to *traditional* models, as shown in Figure 6.3.

Figure 6.3 Caine and Caine's Brain-Based Learning Teaching Model Compared to Traditional Methods

	Traditional	Brain-Based
Source of Information	Simple. Two-way, from teacher to book, worksheet, or film to student	Complex. Social interactions, group discovery, individual search and reflection, role-playing integrated subject matter.
Classroom Organization	Linear. Individual work or teacher-directed.	Complex. Thematic, integrative, cooperative, workstations, individualized projects.
Classroom Management	Hierarchical. Teacher-controlled.	Complex. Designated status and responsibilities delegated to students and monitored by teacher.
Outcomes	Specified and convergent. Emphasis on memorized concepts, vocabulary, and skills.	Complex. Emphasis on reorganization of information in unique ways, with both predictable outcomes, divergent and convergent, increase in natural knowledge demonstrated through ability to use learned skills in variable contexts.

Source: Adapted from Caine, R. N., & Caine, G. (1994). *Making connections: Teaching and the human brain.* Menlo Park, CA: Addison-Wesley.

Other educational implications cited by brain-based teaching advocates include:

- balanced teaching to engage both hemispheres;
- growth spurts and their implications for individualization, pacing, year-round schooling, acceleration, and failure policies;
- matching structure and content of curricula, environments, activities, and interactions to cognitive abilities;
- curriculum integration to provide meaningful contexts and connections among and between subjects; and
- schema theory, to furnish a learning environment that provides stability and familiarity as well as challenge and discovery.

Wider ranges of contextual and sensory cues in learning to increase the number of links made with each new concept, thus leading to improved long-term memory and transfer.

Bernice McCarthy's 4MAT System (1987) is an example of a hybrid program that incorporates brain research and learning styles. McCarthy developed a comprehensive instructional approach to meeting individual needs by combining research on brain hemispheres with David Kolb's Learning Cycle (1985). The 4MAT System identifies the learning needs of four types of learners and accompanying strategies for the integration of both right and left brain processing skills. It, along with other learning styles inventories, is promoted to preservice teachers for the noble goal of reducing stereotypes (Beck, 2001), but rarely is the premise of "bilateral hemispheric engagement" challenged nor are there any conclusive studies connecting their use to student achievement. Ironically, their use can result in merely replacing one set of stereotypes with another if the novice teachers assume the *modes* or preferences are stable.

Research on Education and the Brain

The research at Level I is classic basic research into brain function. The researchers themselves admit that the research base is just developing, and it has barely scratched the surface. Sylwester (1995) identifies two approaches taken by scientists who study the brain: from the bottom up, and from the top down. The bottom up-approach characterizes the work of neuroscientists who focus on the working of small units—individual cells or small systems of cells. The top-down approach focuses on complex cognitive mechanisms or functions, such as movement, language, and abstract analysis. These studies include the normal and abnormal functioning of single neurons, networks of neurons, and the factors that affect neuron activity. All of this (and much more) is accomplished through the use of CAT scans, EEGs, PETs, MRIs, and other tests. Some of this research is conducted on animals, as well as on people with brain damage or mental illness. Other studies are done in laboratory experiments with normal primates and humans, using brain imaging technology to determine chemical composition, electrical transmission, and blood flow patterns that occur normally and during the conduct of certain tasks. All of this sounds technical, and it is.

A variety of theories and ideas have emerged from the basic research into brain function. Two of the earliest theories still prevalent in education circles coalesce around two major concepts: hemisphericity and growth spurts.

Sperry's research supports the idea that the two hemispheres of the brain serve differing but complementary functions. A person uses both hemispheres when learning or functioning, but one can dominate the other and determine a person's style or preferred way of learning. Each hemisphere is thought to contribute specialized functions to tasks. The left hemisphere of the brain is associated with verbal, sequential, analytical abilities. The right hemisphere is associated with global, holistic, visual-spatial abilities. Two related ideas are full *lateralization* and *parallel processing*. In lateralization, the left hemisphere dominates in language expression, whereas the right hemisphere dominates in nonverbal processing. In parallel processing, research indicates that the brain hemispheres perform many tasks simultaneously.

The concept of different functions for the two hemispheres of the brain seems now to be widely accepted, with the left brain controlling linear activity and the right brain controlling global activity. Programs have emerged to teach to both sides of the brain or to compensate for a weaker hemisphere. However, this conclusion is questioned by a number of researchers and psychologists. For example, Zalewski, Sink, and Yachimowicz (1992) concluded that "there is little empirical support for educational programs that supposedly train students to compensate for hemisphericity through teaching integrative process techniques," and that "the notion of cerebral dominance has limited theoretical or practical value for educators..." (pp. 55–56).

Herman Epstein's medical research, done in the 1970s, seems to indicate that the brain grows in spurts rather than in a continual, uninterrupted process. This finding is often used to support the Piagetian model of cognitive development. Growth spurts in school age children often occur between the ages of 6–8, 10–12, and 14–16 years. And they often occur in summer when school is not in session. Myelination has to do with the process of nerve fiber maturation, which occurs in stages that seem to parallel Piagetian stages of cognitive growth and development. Connecting nerve systems are the last to myelinate in childhood, indicating that a child could be said to have a "functionally split brain."

A number of other topics are now the focus of investigation. Nobel Prize winner Gerald Edelman (1992) proposed a biological brain theory model based on evolutionary theory emergent from a type of jungle environment. He stresses the biological nature of learning and consciousness, which can have implications for the classroom; but it is not certain at this point what they might be. Another Nobel Prize winner, Francis Crick, has undertaken a biological search for the soul (or consciousness) within neural networks. His book, *The Astonishing Hypothesis: The Scientific Search for the Soul* (1994), has generated considerable interest. The implications of Crick's book for education are also unclear, but its nearly total focus on materialism puts it at odds with many religious beliefs, a surefire prescription for controversy.

Exploration in the area of gender differences and brain function continues apace. For example, it has been well documented that males and females differ in the way they solve intellectual problems and experience emotions. Males generally perform better on certain spatial tasks and mathematical reasoning, whereas females typically outperform males on tasks of perceptual speed and verbal fluency. The extent to which these differences exist because of environmental factors or combinations of factors is problematic, but it is also theorized that they are because of different hormonal influences during brain development (Kimura, 1992).

Noteworthy are two other avenues of thought emerging from recent findings in brain research. Daniel Goleman (1995) has become famous with his construct of emotional intelligence, about which he cites research on the brain and emotion. His thesis is that individual success can be predicted better by emotional health than by standardized IQ tests. He says, "[i]n a very real sense we have two minds, one that thinks and one that feels." And Peterson (1994) presents an interesting look at brain research and the idea of critical periods; that is, certain periods of development are crucial if not vital to the development of specific cognitive and neurological functions. Each of these has potential implication for how schools go about the business of teaching and learning.

There are a number of other areas of brain research that may well have educational implications, but they remain beyond our pedagogical grasp simply because the medical knowledge itself is still limited. These include endorphin molecules, memory, hyperactivity, attention span, creativity, and others. Just to cite an example, researchers at the UCLA Medical Center have discovered that children below the age of 10 have brain activity that is unusually rich in the secretion of theta waves, thought to be associated with creativity. Whether in the future this knowledge will stop teachers from handing out worksheet after worksheet to these naturally creative little characters remains a matter of speculation. The general opinion of experts is that we have barely scratched the surface in our knowledge of the human brain. Brain research centers recently opened in Cardiff Wales and Singapore (2004) testify to the fact that the frontier remains rich with possibilities.

A review of materials for this chapter turned up scores of purported research findings and implications for education from brain research. The following list is only a sample of what educators and researchers are saying based on brain research. Our purpose is not to endorse these recommendations or even to suggest that ample evidence exist in their support. Some current, possibly valid, but unsubstantiated claims:

◆ Critical periods exist for learning some skills.

◆ Early experience, education, and environment play a primary role in determining who we are.

◆ Emotion drives attention, and attention drives learning and memory.

◆ Music trains the brain for higher forms of thinking.

◆ Knowledge is retained longer if children connect not only aurally but also emotionally and physically to the material.

◆ Complex subjects such as trigonometry or foreign language should not wait for puberty to be introduced.

◆ Teens' biological clocks are set later than those of their fellow human beings and therefore high school should start later in the morning.

◆ Children need to be more physically active in the classroom.

◆ If sensory neural connections are not repeatedly stimulated in the first few months of life when the brain is still in its formative period, they atrophy and die.

◆ Females seem to have stronger connections between the two halves of their brain than do men.

This is quite a list; but remember this is only a fraction of the ideas emerging from the claims that invoke brain research. Some of the claims are far more wide ranging than the few that appear above.

Complicating any attempts at an analysis of the research at Levels II and III is the variety of claims being made in the name of brain research. On many of the specific claims, research at Level II has not been able to catch up with all the various findings and possible implications for education. At this point, however, there are too few objective, well-designed studies identifying specific educational purposes and methodologies based on brain research to provide an acceptable and reliable base in support of such claims. Moreover, the topic becomes confusing because so many innovators are now claiming brain research as a reason to do this or that. For example, learning styles advocates often point to brain research in support of their claims, but the applied research that does exist is often of poor quality. Similarly, brain-based teaching advocates such as Caine and Caine (1994, 2004) call for brain-based educational methodologies that include the integrated curriculum, thematic teaching, and cooperative learning.

The Brain Compatible Approach (Roberts, 2002) is another version of this, linking experiential education to the key principles advocated by brain-based teaching. For example, one recommendation is to balance students' experience with 60 percent ritual-based activity and 40 percent novelty, that is, suspense, surprise, and disorder. This is geared toward the ideal emotional balance purported to understand learning: It is enhanced by challenge and inhibited by threat (see number 11 in Figure 6.1, p. 58). However, it is unashamedly an attempt to articulate progressive *learn-by-doing* ideas to standards-based critics of the experiential approach. Roberts acknowledged that experiential education is considered subversive and outside the mainstream, and thus recommends quantifying the outcomes of the approach. As it stands, it is yet another attempt to apply neurological findings and joins a host of other projects that have not been systematically tested.

So the Level II research in these areas may well point to the efficacy of specific methodologies, but to do so may or may not necessarily be an accurate inference flowing from the brain research findings to date. John Medina's (2003) list of possible topics (see Figure 6.1, p. 58) for collaborative research efforts involving brain specialists and educators seems an reasonable place to begin serious Level II research.

Medical and psychological research will continue and, of course, educators will undoubtedly continue to draw inferences for teaching and learning from it. But we are too close to the frontiers of knowledge in this area to legitimately cite research that promises improved test scores, or much of anything else for that matter. It is not surprising, therefore, that no evidence of Level III program evaluation studies demonstrating that either school or district adoption, or teacher training or workshop participation in brain-based programs result in better school practice, however one might choose to define it. Many of the school restructuring efforts seem to coincide with what certain educators are saying the brain research points to, that is, cooperative learning, smaller groups, search for deeper meaning, and so on, but those ideas have been touted on grounds independent of brain research as well. Possibly, however, future research in brain function will lend support to these efforts.

Conclusion

It is probably useful for educators to be informed of the research in brain function. The problem is, however, that it tends to be highly technical research from another field, that of medical research. The extent to which medical research will trickle down to the point that it yields real educational implications remains to be seen. Much of what is touted by brain-based teaching advocates resembles good sense teaching, so in that way it is harmless at worst and useful at best. We, however, may be a number of years away from any major revelations that are directly applicable to life in classrooms or that provide a coherent set of principles for teaching and learning.

It makes sense for you to attempt to keep informed of developments in this field. The research base at Level I will continue to grow exponentially. Our knowledge right now is primitive, but it won't stay that way. Look for a host of new insights down the road. I recommend caution in investing your time in inservice activities in which methodologies are founded primarily on brain research because they will tend to be faddish and probably premature. The fact that the direct classroom applications are not clearly there should not blind us from the realities that will emerge in the future. This area will in time come to have more to offer to teaching and learning than we can presently imagine.

7

Self-Esteem and Self-Efficacy

There is within this movement an implicit (and increasingly explicit) intuition, an assumption—a faith, if you will—that an essential and operational relationship exists between self-esteem and responsible human behavior, both personal and social.

John Vasconcellos

There is no getting around the fact that most educators who speak earnestly about the need to boost students' self-esteem are unfamiliar with the research that has been conducted on this question....Very few people in the field seem to have any feel for the empirical literature as a whole—what the evidence really says and how meaningful it is.

Alfie Kohn

No clear consensus exists regarding the definitions of self-concept and self-esteem, so discussion of these constructs can be confusing.

J. Lewis and H. Knight

[C]ultural beliefs regarding self-esteem and its influence on individual behavior provide a powerful counterbalance to academic knowledge claims on the topic. This cultural commitment leads to widespread support for self-esteem despite the consistent failure of sympathetic researchers to demonstrate a causal connection between it and various forms of prosocial behavior.

Joseph Kahne

If you search for a more strongly held belief within the American school system than the trust in the importance of self-esteem to school success—and indeed to success in general—you won't find one. It is a deeply embedded cultural belief that permeates nearly every facet of teaching and curriculum.

Indeed, the notion that positive self-esteem promotes achievement is widely accepted as fact. Trying to convince certain teachers that it might not be so is like trying to convince them the sun rises in the west. This causal relationship theory is so prevalent and strong that Barbara Lerner (1996) has suggested, "Many teachers will be hard pressed to think of a contrasting theory. The self-esteem theory of educational development has been the reigning orthodoxy for so long that they were never taught anything else" (p. 10). There are rival theories, as we shall see, but they are given little credence in education circles.

What is Self-Esteem?

The National Association for Self-Esteem (2004) describes self-esteem in terms of experience and being. They define self-esteem as "the experience of being capable of meeting life's challenges and being worthy of happiness." The term *self* seems to have taken on a life of its own in American popular culture. There is even a trendy magazine called *Self*. One book on learning theories (Schunk, 2000) has indexed the following self-related terms: self-actualization, self-concept, self-efficacy, self-evaluation, self-fulfilling prophecy, self-instruction, self-instructional training, self-judgment, self-monitoring, self-reaction, self-regulation, self-reinforcement, self-reports, self-schemas, and self-worth. Psychologists, counselors, and educators use a range of terms to capture the elusive concept of self-esteem. Generally speaking, however, *self-concept, self-esteem, self-regard,* and *self-image* are used interchangeably by educators, and all refer to how we view ourselves, abilities, appearance, self-worth, and so on; in other words, one's perception of oneself. The idea is that, for each of us, our self-measure can vary considerably, both quantitatively and qualitatively. On a continuum, we see ourselves as valued, or not valued, capable or less so, worthwhile or not. The idea that self-esteem is a viable construct and one worth considering from an educational point of view is a fairly recent one, and its case is problematic at best. From the point of view of useful educational research, a problem with self-esteem that occurs from the start is that of definition.

It is instructive to consider some of the instruments that purport to measure self-esteem, because instruments provide us, for better or for worse, with operational definitions. For example, the *Coopersmith Self-Esteem Inventory* (Coopersmith, 1987) defines self-esteem as "the evaluation a person makes and customarily maintains of him- or herself; that is, an expression of approval or disapproval, indicating the extent to which a person believes him- or herself competent, successful, and significant and worthy." The *Culture-Free Self-Esteem Inventories* (Battle, 1992) define self-esteem as "a composite of an individual's feelings, hopes, fears, thoughts, and views of who he is, what she is, what he has been, and what she might become." And the *Piers-Harris Children's Self-Concept Scale* (Piers & Harris, 1984) defines self-concept as a "relatively stable set of self-attitudes reflecting both a description and an evaluation of one's own behavior and attitudes." Although the word choice varies somewhat, you will note that the definitions are more similar than different. This, then, is at least a place to start. However, a distinction must be drawn between a definition written as a sentence or two on the one hand, and an *operational definition*, which is an interpretable score derived from an instrument that purports to measure the construct. A review of the three instruments just listed leads one to the inescapable conclusion that they are not measuring the same thing. This, of course, is a validity issue.

In pursuit of further clarification, three ideas should be noted. First, psychologists have differentiated between global and narrow constructs of self-esteem. For example, one might have an overall high opinion of oneself but could hold oneself in low esteem as an athlete. One might score high on an academic self-esteem inventory, but low on a musical one. This suggests that self-esteem is not a broad construct at all, but that each of us has multiple constructs of self-esteem. Thus, one's self-esteem may be dependent on the area of life in question. A perhaps more useful term, one often associated with more narrowly defined self-abilities is *self-efficacy*, an idea described by the psychologist Albert Bandura (1997) as personal beliefs about one's capabilities to learn or perform actions at designated levels.

Such distinctions are at odds with the view held by those educators who consider self-esteem as a unified, global construct. However, more and more evidence seems to be emerging to support a multidimensional and differentiated rather than a global view of self-esteem (DuBois and Hirsch, 2000).

Second, the construct is also convoluted by the tendency to equate self-esteem with human dignity, rendering it an entitlement of personhood in a civil society. Keep in mind, however, that just because all people are of equal worth, it does not follow that they can perform all tasks with equal skill. The doctrine of equal value as human beings is a broad construct of self-esteem, but it confuses attempts to get at the more narrow constructs of self-esteem in specific areas of endeavor. It is probably useful in this regard to separate the idea of *being* from that of doing. That, however, is much easier to propose than to carry out.

Third, there is the issue of perceptions of reality. The broad construct of self-esteem (equal value as human beings) should not necessarily cause a problem here, but the narrow constructs do because some people's views of themselves are so far removed from reality that it does them a disservice. In fact, they can be better or worse at certain things than they think they are. For example, in a five-nation comparison of mathematical abilities of 10-year-olds made in 1989, American children finished last in mathematics achievement and South Korean children finished first. However, the American children had the highest self-estimate of their mathematical abilities, and the South Korean children had the lowest.

A review of the literature indicates a broad and sustained interest in the topic. Dubois and Hirsch note that they were able to identify 1,463 articles pertaining to self-esteem at the early adolescent level alone (2000). Whether the construct is real or imagined, it is nonetheless a part of American culture, and it continues to be a major focus of attention among educators and educational researchers.

The Claims and the Programs

At the heart of the matter are the claims made by certain educators and psychologists that feeling good about oneself is important for constructive life choices, helps prevent destructive behaviors, and even leads to higher achievement. The idea is that people who view themselves favorably are able to work and learn more effectively. It is claimed that self-esteem and academic achievement are positively associated, that there is a causal relationship between the two (in the esteem–achievement direction), and therefore, to increase achievement we should try to raise students' self-esteem. Consider the following comment in Carl Rogers' classic book, *Freedom to Learn* (1969, 1994). Rogers quotes a teacher with whom he was working at the time as saying, "I cannot explain exactly what happened, but it seems to me, that when their [the students] self-concept changed, when they discovered they can, they did! These 'slow learners' became 'fast learners'; success built upon success" (p. 22).

Consider as well this comment by Madeline Hunter (1994) in an attempt to justify the wide ranging benefits of her teaching model: "Outside evaluation demonstrated substantial increases in student learning and self-esteem…" (p. 34). Yet nowhere does there seem to be published, empirical evidence that self-esteem was carefully measured in connection with the use of Hunter's model under anything approaching controlled conditions. And it is well to keep in mind that even those instrument developers who believe in the global self-esteem construct would say that self-esteem is a deeply imbedded phenomenon not subject to rapid change.

not so ? correction.

A New Vaccine?

The strength of these beliefs runs deep, and as Lerner pointed out, it is so ingrained that teachers cannot even come up with a rival theory. The cause-and-effect theory, however, goes well beyond achievement. In the late 1980s, legislation was passed that created the California Task Force on Self-Esteem. With a $700,000 budget the task force was to place self-esteem at the center of a social science research agenda, with the intent of ameliorating the pressing social issues of welfare dependency, drug and alcohol abuse, school failure, child abuse, and teenage pregnancy. John Vasconcellos, who created the legislation, stated:

> As we approach the twenty-first century, we human beings now—for the first time ever—have it within our power to truly improve our human condition. We can proceed to develop a social vaccine. We can outgrow our past failures—our lives of crime and violence, alcohol and drug abuse, premature pregnancy, child abuse, chronic dependence on welfare, and educational failure. (California Task Force, 1990, p. ix)

What Jonas Salk had achieved in the crusade against polio, the California Task Force would achieve in the crusade against low self-esteem. Roll up your sleeves. Help is on the way!

The California Task Force proposed to "vaccinate" children against a disease that had plagued students for years. Nothing, it seems, is as powerful as an idea whose time has come. As the belief that self-esteem, and therefore achievement and other things, could be boosted by informed teachers became more widespread, two concurrent developments emerged. First, educational practices in general began to change in an attempt to alleviate any ostensible damage being done to students by traditional practices and promote greater self-esteem through the use of different strategies and curriculum. Practices dropped, or at least attacked, included various grading procedures in which students failed: tracking of students by ability, negative reinforcement, the monocultural curriculum, competition, and autocratic procedures in general. These were replaced by positive reinforcement from teachers, grade inflation, self-talk, identifying personal strengths, opportunities to study one's own culture, counseling, creative spelling, Ebonics, among others. Obviously, this coincided with many other developments congruent with progressive educational practices, but the self-esteem movement was evident in most of them.

The second development was the use of prepackaged self-esteem curriculum programs that took root, quickly sprouted, and which continue to flower to this day. It is a big business. Examples include Esteem Builders, Power of Positive Students (POPS), Phoenix Curriculum, and even the DARE program for drug prevention, although it has fallen into a state of rapid decline in the wake of several influential articles noting its failure to produce predicted results. These are merely a few of the better-known programs. All focus, variably, on the activities mentioned in the preceding paragraph.

Consider for a moment the following excerpt from *Bridges: A Self-Esteem Activity Book for Students in Grades 4–6* (McGuire & Heuss, 1994). The activity in question is titled *How to Develop a High Self-Esteem.*

> How does a person who has low self-esteem go about raising it? Well, the best way is to change his thought patterns. It's true— we feel the way we THINK we feel! The more positive you are, the better you'll feel. And the better you feel, the higher your self-esteem will be. GO FOR IT! (p. 59)

This use of teacher and student time away from such real issues as character formation, academic achievement, and hard work, with its focus on feeling good, is presented by the authors as though *raising* one's self-esteem were a simple matter of changing one's thought patterns and doing the many other activities found in the program. In economic theory *opportunity cost* suggests that choosing to do one thing also means giving up certain others. What is the opportunity cost of spending time in these activities? The school day contains only so many hours. The reader is informed on the book's back cover that the authors' mission is to promote positive self-esteem, but nowhere in the activity book is there a shred of theory, research, documented findings, or empirically validated linkages between self-esteem and anything else beyond feeling good about oneself. It is also worth mentioning that some advocates have adopted the causation theory as a useful explanation of why certain minority groups continue to lag academically. Indeed, many multicultural curricula are designed to promote students' self-esteem based on their ethnic identity and the idea that all cultures are worthwhile and have made valuable contributions (e.g., Vann & Kunjufu, 1993). Figure 7.1 illustrates two different self-esteem programs and their claims. See what you think.

Figure 7.1 Descriptions of Two Social Vaccine/Self-Esteem Programs

The Phoenix Curriculum

The goal of the Phoenix Curriculum (Youngs, 1989) is to help teenagers gain an understanding of their potential and an appreciation of themselves. The curriculum consists of a 10-module program for grades 6, 7, and 8, divided into three units focusing on self-esteem, getting along with others, and goal setting and achievement; and a 20-module program for high school divided into five units focusing on self-esteem, personal relationships, responsibility, happiness and success, and goal setting and achievement.

The Phoenix Curriculum provides an organized, well-focused approach to overcome boredom, negativity, and defeatism. The real strength of the program is that, as students learn about goal setting and personal choice, it allows them to take more and more responsibility for themselves and for learning. Students learn to trust themselves and to take pride in who they are. Once they have that self-confidence—the belief that they can achieve whatever they set their minds to—teachers can proceed with the traditional part of their job: providing opportunities for learning.

The Power of Positive Students (POPS)

Mitchell and McCollum (1983) based their plan on the relationship between self-concept and achievement in school:

> Because the school experience is a primary influence on how students perceive themselves, and because students with a positive self-concept are more effective learners, self-esteem must be a major concern of those who plan and implement the school curriculum. The psychological, social, emotional, and moral development of a child is not incidental to education but the foundation on which it is built. Building self-esteem as part of the curriculum is a worthy end in itself.

Their purpose was to modify the total instructional environment to sustain the positive feelings that most children have about themselves when they enter school. Their strategy was to enlist the cooperation of all persons who compose a child's human environment:

> To achieve a positive climate, and a positive self-concept, we repeated in endless variations, morning, noon, and night, the message, *You can succeed if you want to,* and *Everybody is somebody....*We deliberately surrounded children with assurances of their self-worth.

This included slogan contests and the incorporation of positive thinking into curriculum. Most activities, however, focused on recruiting stakeholders to the perspective of optimism and encouragement, such as districtwide programs with nationally known motivational speakers and frequent briefings to community members enlisting their support. Most tellingly, they devoted a great deal of attention to their central administrative staff who needed to be oriented to the theoretical base, aims, and methodology of the plan and kept them current through weekly meetings.

With no formal results reported, I can only surmise that increased communication and cohesiveness could not hurt.

The Critics

In recent years, the critics of these strategies and programs have become more and more vociferous. The attacks have come from a wide range of sources on either side of the political spectrum. They have come largely from the popular press, but also from some conservative essentialist writers in education. Cartoons regularly lampoon the efforts and programs by educators in this area. There have been editorials by nationally syndicated columnists such as Charles Krauthammer, George Will, and John Leo blasting the ludicrousness of it all and generously citing the more bizarre examples to be found. Some see it as simply the latest incarnation of the long-standing emphasis on positive thinking and self-help.

Most of the critics are in basic philosophical disagreement with the causation theory, and they point to the almost total lack of empirical data to support that theory. For example, Thomas Sowell (1993, p. 97), a senior fellow at the Hoover Institution stated, "The very idea that self-esteem is something earned, rather than being a prepackaged handout from the school system, seems not to occur to many educators." Alfie Kohn (1994, p. 277) stated, "the whole enterprise could be said to encourage a self-absorption bordering on narcissism," and that the programs are superficial, consisting of such drivel as "I am special because…," essays "all about me," and chanting hollow phrases like "I think" and "I feel."

It is more difficult to find critics within the educational establishment, but there are a few. For example, Elizabeth McPike (1996), the editor of *American Educator,* the journal of the American Federation of Teachers (AFT), wrote:

> [W]ell-intentioned but misguided notions about self-esteem have become, if anything, even more deeply embedded in the culture of many, many schools. These notions get played out in various ways and constitute one of the most serious threats to the movement to raise academic and disciplinary standards and improve the learning opportunities and life chances of our nation's children. (p. 9)

Roy Baumeister (1996) goes even further, advising educators to "beware the dark side" of teaching self-esteem and advises schools to "forget about self-esteem, and concentrate on self-control." And, as we shall see, a number of researchers are also troubled by the claims of causation, and even relationship, between self-esteem and achievement and prosocial behaviors. But these critics within the profession are rare. Even more rare

are those who challenge the multicultural claims about self-esteem and students' success as have O'Donnell and O'Donnell (1995).

Level I Research

It is best to think of the Level I research in two separate ways: First, let us consider theoretical models, followed by a look at empirical studies examining the relationship between self-esteem and achievement and prosocial behaviors.

Chapter 3 described how educational theories often derive from a variety of sources: philosophy, experience, observations, and basic research (often done in other fields, such as psychology). Consider two scenarios. First, someone can conduct exploratory research—collecting data on a variety of people, analyzing them statistically in search of relationships between variables. Then, on the basis of those relationships, either a theory of causation—that one variable has a directing influence on the other variable—or a theory of relationship—that where one variable is found, the other(s) probably will be also—is developed. For example, an economist can find a positive correlation or relationship between a person's amount of education and income. The data show that as the amount of a person's education increases, his or her income also increases. One might theorize a cause-and-effect relationship between the two variables: Education determines income. This makes a certain amount of sense. Educated people in our society can usually demand a higher salary than those less educated.

However, the nature of correlation is sometimes confusing. In this case, one could just as easily have theorized that income drives education because people with money are more likely to be able to afford to go to college. This theory also seems plausible. But, it is just as plausible that both variables are driven by something else. The German social scientist, Max Weber, advanced a theory in the late nineteenth century of the relationship between Protestantism and success in capitalist ventures. Weber had noted a significant statistical correlation between the two variables. His critics, however, have pointed out that highly developed capitalist enterprises existed before the advent of Protestantism and can also be found in Asian cultures where Protestantism is hardly present. Weber was well aware that other preconditions, material, and psychological, are often present for the development of successful capitalism, and even he admitted that a cause-and-effect relationship is tentative at best.

The second scenario develops somewhat differently. Based on a philosophical perspective or worldview of human nature, one might develop a theory independent of much empirical data. At this point, it is a theory with little or no evidence. It becomes the work of empirical researchers to see if the theory fits reality, that is, whether there is reason to think it is true or workable in certain circumstances. Sometimes evidence is gathered to a degree that the theory is accepted as true or valid. Other times the evidence is lacking and the theory is rejected as insufficient to explain reality. A celebrated example of this is the phenomenon known as *phrenology*. The theory of phrenology, conceptualized by the Austrian doctor Franz-Joseph Gall around the turn of the eighteenth century, posited that the conformation of the skull is indicative of mental faculties and character traits. Phrenology enjoyed popular appeal until well into the twentieth century when it became discredited for lack of scientific evidence. As a field, education is replete with such examples, the most recent of which is the Instructional Theory into Practice (ITIP) model referred to earlier.

Self-esteem theory appears to have developed by way of the latter. Scheirer and Kraut (1979) concluded that many of the self-esteem ideas can be traced back to early humanist psychologists. They state:

> Professional psychologists as early as William James emphasized that a person's beliefs about himself will influence his decisions and actions. The forefathers of American social psychology, C. H. Cooley and George Herbert Mead, described the self as a social entity formed by appraisal reflected from other persons. Following Mead and Cooley, symbolic interactionists hypothesized that a positive self-concept will lead to constructive, socially desirable behavior, and conversely that a distorted self-concept will lead to deviant, socially inadequate behaviors. (p. 131)

Thus a correlation between self-esteem and prized behaviors, not to mention a cause-and-effect relationship, was hypothesized early on. What is noteworthy here is that these things were theorized as ways to explain human failure and "deviant, socially inadequate behaviors." One might just as easily have theorized the opposite: People's socially inadequate behavior leads them to feeling bad about themselves. Or a third hypothesis is that the causative agents sit somewhere outside the correlation.

Earlier I mentioned that Lerner (1996) noted that self-esteem theory has been the reigning orthodoxy for so long that, "Many teachers will be hard pressed to think of a contrasting theory." What many educators have never even thought of is that there are rival theories to this orthodoxy. For example, Lerner contrasts the orthodoxy with the ideas of Alfred Binet (of Stanford-Binet fame), who theorized:

> [A] self-critical stance was at the very core of intelligence, its sine qua non and seminal essence....[H]e saw self-criticism as the essence of intelligence, the master key that unlocked the doors to competence and excellence alike....[H]is view on the

natural inclinations [one of egotism] of children [was] not novel at all,…that egotism was the natural state of childhood. Teachers who took this view saw it as their job to help children overcome their egotism…and [learn] to see themselves and their accomplishments in a realistic perspective in order to take realistic steps toward excellence. (p. 10)

Lerner calls this "earned self-esteem" as opposed to "feel-good–now self-esteem." In this contrasting theory, self-esteem is earned. "It is not a precondition for learning but a product of it" (p. 10). This point of view, as well as those of other rival theories, seems hardly to have been given serious consideration if one were to judge by the curricular artifacts available.

What empirical evidence exists to support the reigning self-esteem theory? Not much that I, or anyone else apparently, have been able to find. In fact, the thousands of studies done on self-esteem in the past four decades have been reviewed many times (e.g., Scheirer & Kraut, 1979; Hansford & Hattie, 1982; Byrne, 1984; California Task Force on Self-Esteem, 1990; Skaalvic & Hagtvet, 1990; Kohn, 1994; Baumeister, Smart, & Boden, 1996), and the conclusions are always the same: The relationship between self-esteem and achievement and other related behaviors is minimal at best, and more likely nonexistent. And most of the researchers consistently point out that even with those factors for which a small relationship is found, it is usually so small as to have no practical significance. Additionally, these small correlations are in no way supportive of any type of cause-and-effect relationship.

Scheirer and Kraut (1979) examined the wealth of research and concluded that, "little direct evidence exists in either psychological or sociological literature that self-concept has an independent influence on behavior" (p. 132). Regarding academic achievement in particular, they stated, "the overwhelmingly negative evidence reviewed here for a causal connection between self-concept and academic achievement should create caution among both educators and theorists who have heretofore assumed that enhancing a person's feelings about himself would lead to academic achievement" (p. 145), and "neither the internal needs model nor the identification with one's ethnic group model has stimulated an educational program with positive results linking self-concept with academic achievement" (p. 144).

Things had not changed much 25 years later when Alfie Kohn came to several conclusions:

[T]he findings that emerge from this [self-esteem] literature are not especially encouraging for those who would like to believe that feeling good about oneself brings about a variety of benefits. (p. 273)

In sum, high self-esteem appears to offer no guarantee of inclin-
ing people toward pro-social behavior—or even of steering
them away from antisocial behavior. (p. 275)

The implication is that the better the research, the less significant the connection it will find between self-esteem and
achievement. (p. 275)

Among the more interesting developments in this intriguing realm
are the actions of the California Task Force on Self-Esteem (1990). The
Task Force was composed almost wholly of strong proponents of the
self-esteem theory. The report of the Task Force stated, however, "We
who served on the task force were determined that our findings would be
grounded in the most current and valid research available" (p. 43). And
what did they conclude?

The associations between self-esteem and its expected consequences are mixed, insignificant, or absent. The nonrelation-
ship holds between self-esteem and teenage pregnancy, self-esteem and child abuse, self-esteem and most cases of alcohol and
drug abuse....If the association between self-esteem and behavior is so often reported to be weak, even less can be said for the
causal relationship between the two. (Smelser, 1989, pp. 15, 17)

This did not stop advocates of the causal theory, however, who forged
ahead with a wealth of new programs. How could this have happened,
given the evidence? Joseph Kahne (1996), who studied this outcome from
the California Task Force for Self-Esteem, noted, "Findings that questioned the likelihood of ameliorating social problems by promoting
self-esteem were ignored. More precisely,...they were overruled" (p. 12).
Such is the strength of cultural beliefs, so much so that evidence itself
seems not to matter and can simply be overruled by those who do not believe it. The task force itself offered this explanation:

Many of us on the task force are convinced that a sizable number of practitioners in functioning [self-esteem] programs are
well ahead of academic researchers in their appreciation of
self-esteem's central role in the social problems that plague our
society. (p. 43)

So much for humility.

Figure 7.2 Exploding the Self-Esteem Myth

The following excerpts are taken from the article "Exploding the Self-Esteem Myth," which appeared in the January 2005 issue of *Scientific American*. The authors of the article make the following points about the relationship of self-esteem to academic achievement:

Item: Boosting people's sense of self-worth has become a national preoccupation. Yet surprisingly, research shows that such efforts are of little value in fostering academic progress or preventing undesirable behavior.

Item: Logic suggests that having a good dollop of self-esteem would enhance striving and persistence in school, while making a student less likely to succumb to paralyzing feelings of incompetence or self-doubt. Early work showed positive correlations between self-esteem and academic performance, lending credence to this notion. Modern efforts have, however, cast doubt on the idea that higher self-esteem actually induces students to do better.

Item: ...[R]esults, which are now available from multiple studies, certainly do not indicate that raising self-esteem offers students much benefit. Some findings even suggest that artificially boosting self-esteem may lower subsequent performance.

Item: Even if raising self-esteem does not foster academic progress, might it serve some purpose later. Say, on the job? Apparently not. Studies of possible links between workers' self-regard and job performance echo what has been found with schoolwork: the simple search for correlations yields some suggestive results, but these do not show whether a good self-image leads to occupational success, or vice versa. In any case, the link is not very strong.

Source: Baumeister, R., Campbell, J., Krueger, J., and Vohs, K. (2005). Exploding the self-esteem myth. *Scientific American, 292*(1), 84-91.

One other matter of note: From the decades of research on self-esteem, an interesting counter-theory has emerged suggesting that self-esteem strategies can have detrimental effects. Wesley Burr (1992) suggested that out of this emphasis on self-esteem have emerged greater selfishness, excessive individualism, and processes that are undermining the health of families. Baumeister and colleagues (1996) have taken this charge a step further. Their examination of the research concluded that there is a lack of empirical evidence to support the idea that low self-esteem leads to anti-social behavior. They write, "The traditional view that low self-esteem is a cause of violence and aggression is not tenable in light of the present evidence" (p. 26). From the research, however, they have theorized that

> one major cause of violent response is threatened egotism, that is, a favorable self-appraisal that encounters an external and unfavorable evaluation....In particular, unrealistically positive or inflated view of self, and favorable self-appraisals that are uncertain, unstable, or heavily dependent on external validation, will be especially vulnerable to encountering such threats. (p. 12)

Finally, they theorize that "[a]n uncritical endorsement of the cultural value of high self-esteem may therefore be counterproductive and even dangerous" (p. 29).

New research even draws into question the cherished notion that higher self-esteem leads to more socially acceptable behaviors. Whether linkages can be established between self-esteem and adjustment by children and adolescents remains problematic in the sense that any such linkages that might exist appear to be highly differentiated and complex. Dubois and Tevendale (1999) note that even directional patterns of influence, that is to say, between cause and effect, are probably recursive. They go on to write that

> there appears to be a potential for high levels of self-esteem to have *negative* [italics added] or unfavorable consequences for the adjustment and well-being of young adolescents, rather than only the health-promoting benefits that have been assumed previously. (p. 8)

Dubois and Hirsch's conceptual model of self-esteem in early adolescence illustrates the many factors imbedded in the construct, including context, developmental status, and types of adjustment. The model emphasizes the bi-directional nature of self-esteem.

In summary, what does the Level I research say? It says that the construct of self-esteem as a global, unified entity is probably not established and most probably does not exist as such, self-esteem is more likely differentially held by individuals depending on context, and it represents a complex, interrelated set of factors. As to its cause and effect properties, the latest theoretical thought is that it is bi-directional, serving as both cause and effect in such matters of adjustment and achievement. Although research findings do support that higher self-esteem is in some sense desirable, it does not account for more than approximately 5 percent of the variance in criterion measures of achievement, a moderate contribution to say the least (Dusek, 2000). Given the latest theory building and research findings, self-efficacy seems a more reasonable school-based pursuit than does self-esteem.

Levels II and III Research

Not surprisingly, the popular educational literature is replete with anecdotal stories that inform the reader of schools and students "turned around" by "innovative" school programs and practices designed to promote self-esteem. But it is difficult to disagree with Alfie Kohn's (1994) conclusion, "Hard data to support the efficacy of such interventions [self-esteem programs] are…virtually nil." Even the sympathetic California Task Force on Self-Esteem reached similar conclusions: "There is no solid evidence that counseling and psychotherapy can increase self-esteem." If that type of intense treatment cannot change self-concepts, it seems improbable that slogans and other such efforts will have little effect on achievement and other prosocial behaviors.

It is one thing to ponder whether teachers can play a significant role in raising the self-esteem of their students, a prospect that seems complex and problematic, in spite of claims made by program developers. However, there is a certain amount of research to indicate that certain elements of self-esteem, especially self-efficacy, do play a role, however limited and however directional, in certain valued school outcomes.

Sterbin and Rakow (1996) investigated the linkages between academic achievement on standardized tests and locus of control and self-esteem. Reviewing some 12,260 student test scores from the National Education Longitudinal Study 1994 database, they did find moderate but positive correlations between locus of control and achievement (r=.29) and self-esteem and achievement (r=.16). They concluded that the findings suggest that the constructs of locus of control and self-esteem need improved, more situation-specific operational definitions. Finally, they stated that "self-esteem is significantly related to socioeconomic status, gender, and locus of control, variables that must be taken into account before the effects of self-esteem on achievement can be assessed" (p. 1).

Pajares and Viliante (1997) studied the influence of writing self-efficacy, writing apprehension, perceived usefulness of writing, and writing aptitude on 218 fifth graders' essays. They noted that "students' beliefs about their abilities directly influenced apprehension, perceived usefulness, and performance, and partially mediated the effects of gender and writing aptitude on apprehension, perceived utility, and performance" (p. 1). Writing aptitude emerged as a clear predictor of writing performance. The significance of this thoughtful study is that the investigators recognized the emergent knowledge of self-efficacy as differentiated, situation specific, and related to perceived importance of task.

A study by Roeser and Eccles (1998) examined the relationships between adolescents' perceptions of their middle school and achievement among other variables. They found that student perceptions of their school's climate, including such matters as school goal structure, provision for autonomy, and positive teacher regard of students were associated with increased academic success. Of course, this is correlational rather than cause and effect research, but it is supportive of clear school goals, student autonomy and choice making, and a positive attitude on the part of teachers toward their students.

A meta-analysis conducted by Multon and colleagues (1991) tested the hypotheses that self-efficacy beliefs are related positively to academic performance and persistence outcomes. The investigators reported a positive and statistically significant relationship between self-efficacy beliefs and academic performance and persistence outcomes across a wide variety of school subjects. It is important to note here that I am talking about self-efficacy and not about global self-esteem.

Related to self-efficacy are problem-solving skills and dispositions such as self-determination and self-advocacy. Poock and colleagues (2002) reported that a program called Learning and Education About Disabilities (LEAD) implemented in one school district used "a number of research-supported practices to successfully promote self-advocacy and other self-determination skills for students with LD [learning disabilities]" (p. 210). These would be defined as "goal-directed, self-regulated, autonomous behavior." The logic of the program is "[a]n understanding of one's strengths and limitations together with a belief in oneself as capable and effective are essential to self-determination."

The report acknowledged other similar programs on which it was modeled, but did not cite any empirical studies that supported the assertion that its practices were "research-supported" nor did the authors quantify the claims of success. This is not surprising considering that the happy results so claimed are rather difficult to define in clearly demonstrated terms:

> Ultimately, LEAD has succeeded in helping students develop not only the critical skills of self-advocacy and self-awareness, but also fostering an altruistic philosophy that, when combined with leadership skills, can be effective in changing society's views of individuals with LD.

Raising student achievement was not an objective and no data was collected. These experiments might provide some basis for a controlled study, but all such programs must be considered anecdotal at most: inspiring but hardly generalizable to other environments.

The Positive Action (PA) program survived a more rigorous study (Flay & Alfred, 2003). PA is grounded in a broad theory of self-concept that includes the belief that making positive and healthy behavioral choices results in feelings of self-worth. The program is designed to "enhance the development and integration of affective and cognitive brain functions" while remaining consistent with many social learning theories. PA and Non-PA schools were compared to assess program effects on elementary student achievement and behavior. The effects on violence, suspensions, and absenteeism were marginally significant, but out-of-school suspensions were far less so. One interesting aspect of the study was the comparison of middle schools based on their feeder system to track those with high, medium, or low proportions of graduates of the PA program in attendance. The difference was significant, with medium-PA and high-PA schools having 31–37 percent fewer problem behaviors, including violence, *dissing* behaviors, and property crimes. This study provides some support for the strength of such a program and for the more general argument that comprehensive programs can have broad and long-lasting effects.

There is one major Level III research study worth noting. The U.S. Office of Education started Project Follow Through, a comprehensive program in the primary grades of 170-plus communities (see Chapter 12, Mastery Learning). The largest and most expensive educational study ever conducted by the Office of Education, it involved research on a wide range of instructional approaches from open classrooms to highly structured, teacher-controlled methodologies. Researchers (Stebbins et al., 1977) concluded that the models of instruction that produced the largest gains in self-esteem were those that assumed that competence enhanced self-esteem (Lerner's *earned self-esteem*) and not the other way around. Those instructional programs concerned with affective outcomes and their causal influence on learning (Lerner's *feel-good-now self-esteem*) produced minimal or even negative affective outcomes, as well as the lowest academic achievement. The sad note, however, is that given their popularity and the time and money spent on self-esteem programs, there is so little school-based evidence to support them.

Conclusion

Finally, it is up to you to decide whether self-esteem programs in school settings are worthwhile. There is limited evidence at Levels I, II, and III to support their pursuit. Caution, therefore, is the watchword if you decide to go ahead. Some time ago I had a conversation with a professor of education who works at another university. She is a staunch advocate of raising self-esteem in the classroom through specific strategies that lead, in her opinion, to higher achievement. To the remark that the evidence is lacking, she simply replied that the work is too important for us to be sitting around waiting for research results that may not be useful anyway.

Even the National Association for Self-Esteem (2004), although clinging to the vaccine metaphor, concludes that difficulties do exist. They write:

> Definitive research on self-esteem has been difficult due to the variety of definitions and the many self-esteem measures being used, and the multiple factors which influence it. Nevertheless, the preponderance of evidence underscores the significance of self-esteem and its relationship to so many of the problems facing youth today. It is also evident that programs to foster self-esteem can serve as a "social vaccine" in reducing the incidence of many such problems.

So, as Abraham Lincoln once observed, "[p]eople who like that kind of thing find that's just the kind of thing they like." And, apparently, many are sold on the idea. The question ultimately is not whether we all want young people to have positive opinions of themselves. Of course we do. Rather, the question is how does that come about? Perhaps the answer is found in the pursuit of old-fashioned virtues such as disciplined effort, helping others, showing courtesy and kindness, and applying ourselves diligently when it comes to hard work on serious matters. But that, too, is just a theory waiting to be tested.

A final note is in order here. It is probably time for teachers to stop thinking of self-esteem as a global construct. Too much evidence exists to indicate that it is situation specific, multidimensional, varies tremendously for a given individual based on perceptions of importance and self-efficacy, and is bidirectional and recursive in relation to significant school and life outcomes.

8

Teaching for Intelligence

Intelligence, in a word, reflects a micro-culture of praxis: the reference books one uses, the notes one habitually takes, the computer programs and databases one relies upon, and perhaps most important of all, the network of friends, colleagues, or mentors on whom one leans for feedback, help, advice, even just for company.

Jerome Bruner

Although we cannot turn mentally retarded individuals into intellectual geniuses, we can achieve meaningful increases in intellectual abilities. Any conclusions to the contrary can result only from failing to cite or take seriously the full range of the relevant data.

Robert Sternberg

One of the functions of intelligence is to take account of the dangers that come from trusting solely to the intelligence.

Lewis Mumford

This chapter and the one that follows examine the research base for two closely related topics, teaching for intelligence and thinking skills. Any decision to separate them into two parts is to some extent rather arbitrary. There is overlap, to be sure. However, the topic of teaching thinking skills seems to have taken on tactical forms that are manifest in specific, often commercial, concrete programs, whereas teaching for intelligence represents a more strategic, generic set of ideas about teaching and learning. This chapter contains several views of the broad construct of intelligence and methods that have been used to bring these ideas to the classroom. Chapter 9 presents specific efforts that are being made to teach those elusive mental processes called thinking skills.

What is Intelligence?

The term *intelligence* is not easily defined, as Stephen Wolfram (2002) reminds us. He points out the problematic nature of any such attempt independent of specific education and culture. The debate over what constitutes intelligence is involved, and of long duration. At the heart of the matter is the perception that some people seem to be more mentally astute, learn more readily and thoroughly, and be able to solve certain problems more effectively than others. Even so, the matter is multifaceted. The smarter/dumber dichotomy, alluring though it may be, is much too simplistic to describe what is meant by intelligence, at least as psychologists and researchers in the field use it.

A number of unresolved issues complicate matters. Is intelligence a unified construct, or are there different types of intelligence? What roles do environment and heredity play in determining an individual's intelligence? Is intelligence specific to the culture in which one lives? Can intelligence be taught? How can intelligence best be measured? Perhaps in the years to come, answers to these questions will become more definitive as research on brain function moves forward.

Serious thinkers have had diverse answers for each of these questions over the years. Charles Spearman (1927) maintained that there is something called *general intelligence,* which is a basic capacity affecting all mental tasks. Proponents of this view note that those who do well on one type of mental task tend to do well on most others. Evidence of this is the fact that math and reading scores correlate highly, suggesting that there could be a general factor present to explain this. Spearman was able to document statistically that it is possible to derive a single quotient from the results of various tests of mental ability. He called this quotient g for general intelligence.

L. L. Thurstone (1938), however, maintained that there are several—more than 200—distinct mental abilities, including numerical ability, spatial ability, and verbal ability. He reached this conclusion although tests of these presumably separate entities showed high intercorrelations. Thurstone's point was that a distribution of scores from different tests of mental ability could also be analyzed to show that they gathered around a number of distinct centers with each center measuring a particular cognitive ability (Singham, 1995). Thurstone's view is probably closer than Spearman's to that which most professionals subscribe today.

Hernstein and Murray's (1995) controversial book, *The Bell Curve: Intelligence and Class Structure in American Life,* caused considerable debate when, in the minds of many people, they attributed intelligence mainly to heredity. Their interpretation of preexisting data seemed to shift the center of gravity toward nature in the long-standing nature/nurture debate. Hernstein and Murray appeared to conclude that there is a unitary construct called intelligence that can be measured by IQ tests, and that Spearman's thesis was essentially correct. Critics have attacked everything from the implied social and political agenda they attribute to Hernstein and Murray to their "overly simplistic" analysis of the data. Those interested in pursuing the issues touched on here would do well to read Mano Singham's (1995) thoughtful analysis of the problems associated with this type of research on intelligence.

Although the layperson may continue to think of and talk about intelligence as if it were a single entity, certain professionals have been moving in another direction. Howard Gardner (1983, 1993) has proposed what has become a popular model that he calls *multiple intelligences (MI)*, and as we shall see, school districts from around the country have jumped at the chance to put his ideas into action. Gardner's (2003, 2004) work is especially attractive to those who have become discouraged with the traditional idea that intelligence and resulting accomplishment is based nearly exclusively on genetically endowed abstract reasoning abilities. They see people who show great aptitude or talent for this or that and wonder why, as Gardner has, the concept should not be expanded. I'll return to Gardner's work later in this chapter.

As if the issue were not already hazy, Daniel Goleman (1995) has proposed an entity that he calls *emotional intelligence*. Citing research on the brain and emotion, Goleman asserts that an individual's success can be better predicted by emotional health than by standardized IQ tests: "In a very real sense we have two minds, one that thinks and one that feels." Whether or not attention to this concept of intelligence will prove useful for educators and beneficial for children remains basically untested from an empirical standpoint. It corresponds to the current emphasis placed on disposition as a key part of achievement.

From the potentially wide range of issues and topics reasonably connected to the idea of teaching for intelligence, I have selected three of the most significant innovations. Each of the three is drawn from theoretical study and research in the general area of intelligence. Although there is some overlap, they do represent distinctly different approaches both to the study of intelligence and to the educational implications that might be drawn from such study. Their common thread is the long gestation period of theorizing and problem solving out of which they each have emerged.

Let us look first at the theory building of Reuven Feuerstein and his resulting educational program *Instrumental Enrichment*. Feuerstein's work emerges from the classic definitions of intelligence as the construct has been measured by IQ tests. The notable idea is that intelligence, according to Feuerstein, can be enhanced through appropriate teaching strategies.

Next, we examine Howard Gardner's theory of *Multiple Intelligences* and its rapidly expanding use in the schools. Gardner is concerned with the *content* of intelligence; that is, the different abilities behind intelligent behavior. Gardner points to recent advances in cognitive studies that he is convinced show best how to conceptualize intelligence. In brief, he describes intelligence in terms of a person's biopsychological potential.

Finally, we turn our attention to the theory building of Robert Sternberg and the resulting programs based on his *Triarchic Theory of Intelligence.* Sternberg's work represents a focus on cognitive *processes* used by people in thinking operations His research is based primarily in a field of psychology known as information processing.

Reuven Feuerstein's
Instrumental Enrichment

The ideas of Israeli clinical psychologist Reuven Feuerstein have been called "the most significant innovations in educational psychology of the twentieth century" (Burgess, 2000, p. 3). Feuerstein's work is rooted in his theory that intelligence is dynamic and not static, meaning that it can be altered with appropriate interventions. To that end, one of Feuerstein's more notable contributions to the field was his development of the *Learning Potential Assessment Device* (Feuerstein, 1979), an instrument that measures not merely the product of someone's thinking but the process itself. The student is presented with different problem-solving tasks, and, when needed, the test examiner *teaches* the student how to solve such problems to assess the extent to which the student has learned from the teaching. Thus, what emerges from the test-taking situation is a more dynamic assessment, which predicts the student's potential.

According to Feuerstein, cognitive development is dependent on direct intervention over time that teaches the mental processes necessary for learning how to learn. These interventions are sometimes called *mediated learning experiences.* In this sense Feuerstein's work builds on, or at least connects with, Lev Vygotsky's (1978) idea of the Zone of Proximal Development (ZPD): the range in which a learner can solve problems independently and the learner's ability to benefit from expert guidance.

Feuerstein's theorizing has led to the development of an elaborate curriculum called *Instrumental Enrichment,* which provides the kinds of needed mediated learning experiences (Feuerstein & Jensen, 1980, May; Feuerstein, Rand, Hoffman, & Miller, 1980). Frances Link (1991) describes the program as

> a direct and focused attack on those mental processes, which, through absence, fragility, or inefficiency, are to blame for poor intellectual or academic performance....In terms of behavior, Instrumental Enrichment's ultimate aim is to transform retarded performers, to alter their characteristically passive and dependent cognitive style to that of active, self-motivated, independent thinkers. (p. 9)

ties into brain / synapses / etc.

The program consists of a three-year series of content-free lessons, called *instruments,* which are grouped in 14 areas of cognitive abilities (see Fig. 8.1). It is intended for upper elementary-, middle-, and second-ary-level students. Students do *instruments* with paper and pencil for about 2–3 hours a week. The teacher serves as the mediating agent and the instruments are supposed to parallel the subject matter being taught. In this sense, the program integrates with the existing course of study while enriching it with intelligence-enhancing exercises. The program is suffi-ciently sophisticated to make it crucial that teachers have a considerable amount of teacher training in its use.

Figure 8.1 Feuerstein's 14 Instruments

Organization of Dots
Orientation in Space I
Comparison
Analytic Perception
Categorization
Instructions
Temporal Relations
Numerical Progressions
Family Relations
Illustrations
Transitive Relations
Syllogisms
Representational Stencil Design
Orientation in Space II

Does It Work? The Research

Advocates of the program say it does. Frances Link (1991) states "[e]mpirical data exist to document improvement in cognitive functions; improvement in self-concept [see Chapter 7 on self-esteem], improvement in reading, writing, and mathematics subjects after two years of imple-mentation" (p. 11). The claims embedded in this statement are wide rang-ing and perhaps not all are capable of being substantiated to the extent that one might hope.

A point of fundamental distinction between Feuerstein's program and many of the thinking skills programs described in Chapter 9 is that there is a Level II research base for *Instrumental Enrichment.* Within a few years of its development, a number of studies had been conducted on its effects. Savell, Twohig, and Rachford (1986) reviewed the initial body of research conducted in Israel, Venezuela, Canada, and the United States. They con-cluded that the evidence to that point showed positive effects for nonver-bal measures of intelligence in all four countries, "in middle and low social class groups, in groups considered normal, as well as groups considered culturally or educationally disadvantaged," as well as in the hearing impaired. The effects, however, on other outcomes such as self-esteem, impulsivity, classroom behavior, and achievement were either "absent, inconsistent, or difficult to interpret." The positive results, however, were tied to those studies in which teachers had at least 1 week of training and students were involved with *Instrumental Enrichment* for at least 80 hours over a 2-year period.

Sternberg and Bhana (1986) conducted a second review of the research. They expressed concern about "teaching to the test," particularly the IQ-type tests, on which Savell and others found positive gains. Nevertheless, Sternberg and Bhana were mildly supportive of the program: "[W]e believe that when the full program is administered by carefully trained, intelligent, motivated, and conscientious instructors, gains can be attained on standard kinds of IQ and aptitude measures" (p. 63). If they are right, the results seem promising. Whether this translates into higher achievement (as opposed to IQ and aptitude measure gains) is a related but distinctly different question.

Meanwhile, there have been a few studies in the literature of Level II and Level III research on *Instrumental Enrichment*. For example, studies by Hoon (1990), Offenberg (1992), Kaniel and Reichenberg (1992), and Mulcahy (1993) generally report positive results, suggesting that *Instrumental Enrichment* can improve children's thinking (and therefore intelligence) when implemented over a long period and with well-trained teachers. The quality of these studies could be questioned with regard to elements of design and control of variables, but as reviewers have noted, this is a difficult area in which to conduct research. The indications from the research to date are promising, but the fact that nothing of more recent vintage turns up could indicate either that we already have confirmation of the program's success or that interest has begun to wane.

Howard Gardner and the
Theory of Multiple Intelligences

Howard Gardner's book *Frames of Mind* was published in 1983 (reissued in 1993) and was intended primarily for a limited audience of psychologists and other workers in the field of intelligence. Gardner was critical of the then prevailing views of intelligence, especially the theory of intelligence as a single construct. His work as an investigator in Harvard Project Zero had convinced him, much as Thurstone had been convinced before him, that intelligence is composed of a number of distinct factors. Where Thurstone had thought that the number of different kinds of intelligence might be in the range of 200, Gardner more modestly settled on 7. He did speculate that there may be more, and he has added an eighth (nat-

uralist) with a promise of a ninth (spiritual). Gardner noted that brain research had shown that stroke victims, for example, who might show considerable language loss, still maintained other capabilities. This was proof
to him that certain functions are separate enough to make the case for different intelligences. Studying individuals who had great ability in one
area but might not excel at all in other areas also shaped Gardner's
thinking about separate intelligences.

Gardner questioned the value of the *general intelligence* construct,
along with the more traditional views of intelligence that defined it operationally by tests focused primarily on logic, verbal, and quantitative abilities. Instead he states that his interest is on those intellectual processes that
are not covered by the *general intelligence* concept. Gardner rejects the
commonly made distinction between intelligence and talent. Intelligence,
he claims, is basically what most people call talent in spheres beyond the
traditionally accepted abilities in linguistic and logical/mathematical
realms. Gardner has now identified eight intelligences and is looking for
more (Figure 8.2, p. 94). He writes:

> [A]s a species, human beings have evolved over the millennia
> to carry out at least these seven forms of thinking....Although
> all humans exhibit the range of intelligences, individuals dif-
> fer—presumably for both hereditary and environmental rea-
> sons—in their current profile of intelligences. Moreover, there
> is no necessary correlation between any two intelligences, and
> they may indeed entail quite distinct forms of perception,
> memory, and other psychological processes. (Gardner & Hatch,
> 1989, p. 5)

Gardner has cautioned that "MI theory is in no way an educational
prescription," and that "the theory does not incorporate a 'position' on
tracking, gifted education, interdisciplinary curricula, the layout of the
school day, the length of the school year, or many other 'hot button' educational issues" (1995, p. 206). Gardner has noted that many of the current
uses of the theory are misdirected, and states simply that the theory implies that we need to broaden our definition of intelligence to include
those other areas of mental abilities, cultivate them in children, approach
learning in a variety of ways, and personalize education.

Key

Figure 8.2 Howard Gardner's Multiple Intelligences

Linguistic intelligence involves sensitivity to the meaning of words, their order and syntax, the sounds, rhythms, and inflections of language, and the uses of languages.

Musical intelligence consists of sensitivities to rhythm, pitch, and timbre. It also has an emotional aspect. Gardner relates musicians' descriptions of their abilities that emphasize an individual's natural feel for music and not the reasoning or linguistic parts of musical ability.

Logical-mathematical intelligence emerges from interaction with objects. By a sequence of stages the person is more able to perform actions on objects, understand the relations among actions, make statements about actions, and eventually see the relations among those statements.

Spatial intelligence is the capacity to perceive the physical world accurately, perform transformations and modifications on these perceptions, and produce or recreate forms.

Bodily kinesthetic intelligence involves a person's ability to use the body in highly specific and skilled ways, both for expressive (the dancer) and goal-directed (the athlete) purposes.

Naturalist intelligence is the ability to draw on features of the natural world to solve problems (the chef, gardener, florist).

Intrapersonal intelligence is the ability to access one's own feelings and to label, discriminate, and symbolically represent one's range of emotions to understand behavior.

Interpersonal intelligence involves the ability to notice and make distinctions about others' moods, temperaments, motivations, and intentions.

One change that has occurred at least in part from Gardner's work is the broadening of means of assessing learning. He thinks this trend will continue and that it will bring about corresponding changes in the creation of environments more conducive to alternative and fair assessment practices. Gardner has further mused

> I hope that in the next twenty years, a number of efforts will be made to craft an education that takes multiple intelligences seriously....Perhaps, if careful studies are done, we will even know *why* some educational approaches work and why some do not. (1993, p. 250)

In the more than two decades following, educational policies have emphasized standardized and predictable outcomes, highlighting the tension between Gardner's theory and the traditional, common sense notion of how people think. Educational theorists such as Elliot Eisner (2004) point out that the contrast is one of philosophy, or the aim of education; studying the outcomes of student achievement related to teaching practices based on MI would be pointless if the aim is not academic achievement but personal growth.

Research on Multiple Intelligences: A Bridge Too Far?

At Level I Gardner claimed, "MI theory is based wholly on empirical evidence and can be revised on the basis of new empirical findings" (1995, p. 203). *Frames of Mind* (1983, 1993) included a survey of a wide range of literature and psychological research on intelligence that serves as the basis for MI theory. It is actually extensive, and work has been done to develop assessment instruments in an attempt to measure the intelligences (see Gardner & Hatch, 1989). Considerable work has been done through Harvard Project Zero to measure the intelligences and to implement some ideas in school settings; but to this point, from a technical measurement viewpoint, the results have been mixed at best.

As Gardner himself has said, educators have interpreted this theory in hundreds of ways. For example, at one school it was concluded that

> [w]e have found that multiple intelligences is more than a theory of intelligence; it is, for us, a philosophy about education with implications for how kids learn, how teachers should teach, and how schools should operate....For example, teachers can help a child whose strength is bodily-kinesthetic use that talent to learn multiplication facts or spelling words; capitalize on children's interpersonal intelligences by using the study of personalities as a pathway to the study of history; or use graphs and tables to record the similarities and differences among Native American tribes to help students with strong logical-mathematical intelligence. (Hoerr, 1994, p. 30)

Other far reaches include having kids singing (musical intelligence) the multiplication facts or dancing to the four basic food groups. This may well seem to make perfect sense, but there is little hard evidence that these uses of the theory actually lead students to learn more. Whether Gardner has liberated or hijacked (depending on your point of view) a concept that has been used with consistent meaning for more than 100 years is an open question. The term *multiple intelligences* has taken on a life of its own and has joined the lexicon of the profession, providing language to discuss more than one dimension of students' ways of knowing and learning. But as Cuban (2004) has critically pointed out, there is little more than anecdotal evidence of MI's success and even less report of expanding success into large scale replication studies.

The questions for researchers are whether school-based implementations of this theory lead to higher academic achievement (dependent variable) or increases in the eight intelligences (independent variable that would seemingly yield an improved dependent variable). Although the classroom practices implementing the theory are highly variable, there have been studies of student outcomes, typically using action research designs. One example included in a recent issue of *Teachers College Record* is Haley's (2004) study of second language learners. She reports MI induced success; but she focuses more on the need for flexible and diverse teacher perspective and response to students than the particular decisions she made to implement the theory in such ways that could be replicated. So, the jury is still out on academic achievement, but the possibilities for enhancing forms of intelligence, if one agrees that these various forms of intelligence are in fact that, remain attractive.

Robert Sternberg and the
Triarchic Theory of Intelligence

Although Gardner is representative of psychologists who have focused on the *content* of human intelligence, Robert Sternberg of Yale University has emerged as a leader among those interested in intelligence as a *process*. Sternberg is widely known as a leading *information processing (IP)* theorist. He has synthesized his research-based construct into a theory of intelligence that quantifies IP abilities. By Sternberg's definition, to think productively is to be able to process information effectively. His theory identifies a three-part (triarchic) description of mental abilities: contextual intelligence, experiential intelligence, and componential intelligence. He has also identified six factors basic to successful information processing (Figure 8.3).

Sternberg's pioneering efforts in information processing and a resultant theory of intelligence (1990) emphasize thinking processes common to everyone. New perceptions of what intelligence means have begun to emerge from his work. Sternberg has developed what he calls a "triarchic theory of intelligence," which breaks down cognitive behavior into thinking, adapting, and problem solving. Thinking, which he calls "componential intelligence," includes planning, performance, and knowledge acquisition.

Adapting, which Sternberg calls "contextual intelligence," is composed of selecting, reshaping, and maximizing ideas. And problem solving, which he calls, "experiential intelligence," involves insight, automaticity, creativity, and efficiency.

Figure 8.3 Robert Sternberg's Six Factors

◆ **Spatial ability,** or the ability to visualize a problem spatially; skills one would associate with geometry, geography, architecture, mechanical drawing, art, map making and interpreting.

◆ **Perceptual speed,** or the ability to grasp a new visual field quickly; something that brings to mind the playing of Nintendo video games or piloting a jet aircraft.

◆ **Inductive reasoning,** or the ability to reach conclusions and generalize from evidence or other information.

◆ **Verbal comprehension ability,** or the ability to comprehend text either quickly or at deeper levels.

◆ **Memory,** or the ability to store and retrieve information and ideas.

◆ **Number ability,** or the ability to manipulate numerical ideas and to learn algorithms.

It should be noted that Sternberg is doubtful that cognitive theories such as his own can necessarily improve teaching. A theory of intelligence is one thing; implementing such a theory in a classroom is another altogether. He also addresses the idea of whether thinking skills (see Chapter 9) can be applied generically or whether they are domain-specific, a matter of great importance to those who teach subjects in school settings. He suggests that people, rather than the skills themselves, are the issue. He suggests that some pupils (as well as teachers) are domain specific whereas others are domain general. Yet, he does maintain that we can "achieve meaningful increases in intellectual abilities" (1996, p. 51).

In seeming contradiction to his statement of skepticism about school-based applications, Sternberg, focusing specifically on those aspects of intelligence related to creativity, has identified a number of strategies "that teachers and administrators may use to make students, staff—and themselves—more creative" (1995–1996, p. 81). Among those *strategies* are encouraging the questioning of assumptions, modeling creativity, allowing mistakes, encouraging risk taking, and letting students define problems.

Sternberg's (2004a) more recent focus has been on developing *expert students* who think wisely. He contrasts the traits of experts with those of the less skilled, as exhibited by five fallacies: unrealistic optimism, egocentrism, omniscience, omnipotence, and invulnerability. However, our focus is on the classroom innovations that have resulted from his theory, and he continues to conduct fairly rigorous tests of his hypothesis that teaching *triarchically* results in improved intellectual outcomes.

Research on the Triarchic Model

The Level I research base carried out by Sternberg and his colleagues in the development of the triarchic theory is substantial. He built his work on the already extensive development of theories of information processing. The logical next step appears to be the development of instruments or measuring devices of some kind designed specifically to test intelligence as a process, as he suggests it is. His work has been put into practice on a limited scale through the Yale Practical Intelligence for School Curriculum, and an evaluation study that shows these skills can be taught (Sternberg, Okagaki, & Jackson, 1990).

In the decade that followed, Sternberg and colleagues (see Grigorenko, 2002) directed several studies on hundreds of middle school and high school students; all of these studies are supportive of his theory that the triarchic approach is more successful than the traditional emphasis on memorization or the merely analytical. Although this could pose a conflict of interest concern because he is validating his own theory, the studies are designed for appropriately rigorous replication, so there is hope for further research to confirm or dispute his findings.

The relative newness of Sternberg's theory means that it has not been put into practice to the extent that the other two models have been. Time will tell whether the theory remains credible, and, in the likely event that it will, to what extent it can be used successfully in school settings.

Conclusion

The pioneering works of Feuerstein, Gardner, and Sternberg suggest that intelligence, like bowling, can be taught and enhanced. This idea runs counter to traditional assumptions that intelligence is something you are endowed with only. There is much evidence to suggest that intelligence can be raised, including the well-known illustration of recent generational gains in intelligence test scores by Japanese school children. That they and other Asian countries have witnessed a considerable rise in the average height of the population in the space of a generation is also well documented. The thinking that better diet, health care, and exercise have brought this about in a relatively short time span encourages those who advocate intervention strategies of the intellect.

The work cited in this chapter is both more foundational and theoretical than the examples found in the closely related Chapter 9. In a sense, this chapter serves as potential Level I research for the teaching of thinking skills, our next topic, in school settings. Whether developers can or will take full and thoughtful advantage of the profound ideas of Feuerstein, Gardner, and Sternberg is yet another matter.

9

Thinking Skills Programs

We have a lot of evidence that teaching content alone, and hoping it will cause students to learn to think, doesn't work. The teaching of content alone is not enough.

Arthur Costa

There is a danger that the teaching of "thinking skills"—if it survives to become part of mainstream educational practice —may one day become to thinking what diagramming sentences and memorizing rules of grammar too often have become to writing.

John Baer

Most teachers do not know what intellectual standards are nor why they are essential to quality thinking.

Linda Elder and Richard Paul

There is a need for "new thinking." The thinking of the last millennium was based heavily on analysis and judgment: "what is" thinking. There is a need to proceed to "what can be" thinking.

Edward de Bono

Almost all national, state, district, and school lists of goals include something from the grab bag called *thinking skills*. Thousands of people have attended the international conferences on critical thinking held annually at Sonoma State University in California and sponsored by the Foundation for Critical Thinking. In addition, the Association for Supervision and Curriculum Development (ASCD) has published a guide describing 27 commercial programs designed for teaching thinking–problem solving–critical thinking skills (Costa, 1991). A number of these programs claim widespread usage and success. The developers of the Higher Order Thinking Skills (HOTS) program, for example, claim that it has been used by 2,000 schools in 49 states (Pogrow, 1995).

Thinking skills is a general term that tends to incorporate problem solving, critical thinking, higher-order thinking, divergent thinking, and creative thinking; and, as noted in the previous chapter, thinking skills are also tied into various views on intelligence. The Thinking Skills Research Centre at the University of Newcastle upon Tyne in England has issued an executive summary that informs us that "'thinking skills' and related terms are used to indicate a desire to teach processes of thinking and learning that can be applied in a wide range of real-life contexts." Such skills include "information processing, reasoning, enquiry, creative thinking and evaluation" (Wegerif, 2004, p. 1). The summary goes on to note that because complex thinking requires effort and produces valued outcomes, which "makes higher order thinking hard to define. Nonetheless, it is possible to recognize higher order thinking and teach it" (Wegerif, 2004, p. 1).

Even for a profession that often seems to have little respect for the meaning of words, the terminology regarding thinking skills is rather loose. The various goals lists one finds in the literature tend to be skills-focused, typically employing such terms as critical-thinking skills, higher-order thinking skills, problem-solving skills, strategic-reasoning skills, productive-thinking skills, and so on, all used more or less interchangeably. The common ground seems to encompass the kinds of school experiences that purport to transcend memory work, textbook usage, drill and practice, and patterned, repetitive assignments.

The implication of all this is that these skills are located at a higher place on some taxonomic register and, therefore, ought not to be confused with lower-level thinking skills such as remembering or explaining—skills for which, if one can believe the rhetoric, there will be decreasing demand in the twenty-first century. Before we look at programs and their effectiveness, here are two pieces of advice: (a) Be wary of programs that promise to deliver decontextualized, content-free skills of any kind; and (b) be wary of programs that claim to know how to get students ready for an unknown and infinitely complex future.

Thoughts About Thinking

One would be hard-pressed to find someone who thinks that thinking skills are unimportant, more so these days as it becomes increasingly obvious to everyone that the knowledge explosion makes it ever more difficult to master content. There are, however, several problems that seem to be endemic to the entire area labeled *thinking skills.*

For starters, there is little agreement about what thinking skills actually are. Virtually every program has a list of skills to be developed, but in many cases the concepts are abstract with a range of definitions applied to any given thinking skill. For example, classification is often identified as an important thinking skill because it is so associated with scientific thought and expression. But what is meant by the term *classification*? Putting things in groups? Organizing whole taxonomies? Recognizing that different attributes lead one to assign something to a particular category? This is vexing because *classification* is a rather concrete skill compared to, say, *evaluation.*

Another problem is that of measuring thinking skills. It is a difficult challenge compared to measuring certain physical skills, such as one's ability to run 100 meters in so many seconds. I know of no outstanding thinking skills test, particularly one with a performance base, to which I could refer you. Selected portions of standard IQ tests are about as good as anything we have. And the several tests specifically designed to measure thinking skills that are available have no agreed-on validity if for no other reason than they define the various constructs differentially. However, it has become ever more the case that test makers are including opportunities for test takers to explain the thought processes that led them to a response. This is a start.

A third issue is whether thinking skills can be taught successfully to students independent of content. This remains a matter of some debate. Most experts have concluded that they probably cannot. So, the issue of transfer is problematic. Can someone who has been taught how to analyze (a typical skill) use analysis as a generic skill applicable to chemistry, literature, geography, personal problems, or any given problematic situation? It doesn't seem likely, although there may be something to it. And how does one teach others to analyze in a generic sense? Analysis, after all, can be based on evidence, experience, intuition, or other factors. Here is the essence of the argument: The better one's knowledge of something, the better one's position to meaningfully analyze it. Having knowledge, even in considerable store, does not guarantee one's ability to analyze; an absence of knowledge, however, of a given field precludes any ability to perform meaningful analysis in that field.

Apparently, not everyone agrees. Edward de Bono (1991, 2004) suggests that thinking can be directly taught as a skill or set of skills. His thinking skills program, called CoRT, an acronym for Cognitive Research Trust, emphasizes content-free thinking strategies. An example is the *Plus, Minus, Interesting (PMI)* strategy. Students are given a hypothetical situation and are asked to list as many "pluses," "minuses," or "interestings" as they can about the problem. One of the situations is,

"What if all cars were painted yellow?" According to de Bono, activities like these enable students to use effective thinking strategies that have transfer value to unknown future situations. De Bono's optimistic assertion, however, has little empirical support.

Another issue is that of a huge assumption that may not, in fact, be warranted. That assumption is that teachers themselves possess these various thinking skills. If they do not, how could they possibly teach them? In his book *A Place Called School*, curriculum researcher John Goodlad wrote,

> The emphasis on facts and recall of facts in quizzes demonstrates not just the difficulty of teaching and testing for more fundamental understanding but the probability, supported by our data, that most teachers simply do not know how to teach for higher levels of thinking....(Goodlad, 1984, p. 237)

The extent to which teachers possess these abilities, or could themselves be taught to model or teach them, is largely unknown. Goodlad's comments were written more than two decades ago, but they could well be the stuff of a fruitful research agenda.

Lastly, we know little about how people think. We know much more about the products of people's thoughts than we know about how they arrive at those products. Vast philosophical and scientific arguments are waged over the brain-versus-mind issue, just to name one example. There is some considerable debate about whether thinking is a conscious or an unconscious process (Baer, 1988). So, if we are not sure how people think, how can we proceed with the business of teaching them how to think in such a way that is compatible with given individuals' styles or approaches to situations that demand thinking? Perhaps apropos of that, the current model of practice that one can readily deduce from extensive classroom observation is that thinking skills are something students already possess in varying degrees; and like citizenship, it is something you bring to and experience in your work, not something that is directly taught by teachers.

All of this notwithstanding, there seems to be no shortage of would-be innovators willing to jump into the breach. Programs abound, and the thinking skills movement is marching full force across the country. A useful perspective for considering these matters was offered some years ago by Brandt (1984, 1988), who used the modifying terms, *for, about,* and *of.* He described teaching for thinking as the engagement of content and learning activities and the development of language and conceptual abilities through teacher questioning, student-to-student interaction, group discussions, and so on. Brandt identified teaching about thinking as encouraging students to be aware of their thinking, reflecting on it, and learning to control it, what is often referred to as *metacognition.*

Students are regularly asked to monitor their own thinking and make deliberate use of various thinking frames in such programs as Talents Unlimited, CoRT, and Tactics. In this light, Brandt suggested that teaching of thinking represents the attempt to teach particular mental skills such as summarizing, paraphrasing, and decision making. This last concern is no doubt the weakest area, and the one we know least about.

The thinking skills movement is manifest in two forms: (1) the adoption of specific thinking skills curricula or programs (see Figure 9.1 for a partial list) and (2) the development and implementation of a matrix of thinking skills to be infused by teachers throughout the curriculum by a school district or perhaps by a given school. The former often involves the implementation of one or more of the more popular commercial programs. The latter represents an *infusion* model where teachers agree to introduce and revisit certain desired thinking skills across a variety of subject areas. In either case, the efforts are intended to focus on the teaching of thought processes in which students are perceived to be lacking or in need of greater proficiency.

Figure 9.1 Sample Thinking Skills Programs for Schools

Cognitive Research Trust (CoRT)

Higher Order Thinking Skills (HOTS)

Instrumental Enrichment

Odyssey

Philosophy for Children

Project Impact

Strategic Reasoning

Structure of the Intellect (SOI)

Tactics for Thinking

Talents Unlimited

Thinking to Write

Invariably, one finds reference to such skills as analysis, synthesis, evaluation, decision making, creativity, critical thinking, information processing, problem solving, organization, communication, and reasoning. Whether these are in fact skills in the same sense as those needed by an expert carpenter or golfer is not always clear. The more tangible an operation (for example, skillfully using bow and arrow or needle and thread), the more readily we can agree that we have identified a skill, or set of skills, and something that can be taught as well. But even in such concrete situations, a truly skilled person is someone who can coordinate, articulate, and make seamless a number of subskills that come together into a whole, which, to quote the oft-cited Gestalt expression, is greater than the sum of its parts. Figure 9.2 provides an example of a typical set of thinking skills and accompanying strategies.

Most thinking skills programs are sufficiently complex to require a considerable amount of material as well as faculty inservice training if they are to succeed. Through training sessions teachers are acquainted with detailed descriptions of the skills to be taught, sample lesson plans, activities, evaluation techniques, and more. Usually, emphasis is placed on strategies whereby teachers can incorporate thinking skills into different subject areas and apply them to various age levels. Some of the programs are designed to stand alone as curriculums in and of themselves. These are often used in so-called gifted-and-talented classes.

Program Implementation

To give you a clearer picture of what these programs are like, two such are presented here, one commercial and one state-developed example. They are reasonably representative of the range of programs available.

Talents Unlimited

Talents Unlimited was developed in the early 1970s and has been adopted in states across the country as well as in a number of other nations. With trainers nationwide, Talents Unlimited claims to be one of the most widely used thinking skills programs in the country. It has been disseminated through the U.S. government's National Diffusion Network. The program "emphasize[s] and celebrate[s] critical and creative thinking, multiple intelligences, and the spirit of learning" (TEC Talents Unlimited, 2004).

Figure 9.2 A Taxonomy of Thinking Skills

I. **Thinking Strategies**
Problem Solving
1. Recognize a problem
2. Represent the problem
3. Devise/choose solution plan
4. Execute the plan
5. Evaluate the solution

Decision Making
1. Define the goal
2. Identify alternatives
3. Analyze alternatives
4. Rank alternatives
5. Judge highest-ranked alternatives
6. Choose "best" alternative

Conceptualizing
1. Identify examples
2. Identify common attributes
3. Classify attributes
4. Interrelate categories of attributes
5. Identify additional examples/nonexamples
6. Modify concept attributes/structure

II. **Critical Thinking Skills**
1. Distinguishing between verifiable facts and value claims
2. Distinguishing relevant from irrelevant information, claims, or reasons
3. Determining the factual accuracy of a statement
4. Determining the credibility of a source
5. Identifying ambiguous claims or arguments
6. Identifying unstated assumptions
7. Detecting bias
8. Identifying logical fallacies
9. Recognizing logical inconsistencies in a line of reasoning
10. Determining the strength of an argument or a claim

III. **Information-Processing Skills**
1. Recall
2. Translation
3. Interpretation

4. Extrapolation
5. Application
6. Analysis (compare, contrast, classify, seriate, etc.)
7. Synthesis
8. Evaluation
9. Reasoning (inferencing): inductive, deductive, analogical

Source: Adapted from Beyer, B. K. (1988a). Developing a scope and sequence for thinking skills instruction. *Educational Leadership, 45*(7), 27.

Talents Unlimited is based on the following three assumptions, according to Schlichter et al. (1998, p. 36):

1. People have talents (strengths or preferences) for different thinking processes.
2. Training in the use of these thinking processes can enhance one's potential in various areas of talent and at the same time foster positive feelings about oneself.
3. Training in particular thinking processes can be integrated with knowledge or content in any subject area and can enhance academic achievement.

Instruction is focused on 19 thinking skills to be applied to academic content in five talent areas as seen in Figure 9.3.

A detailed staff development program is required before and concurrent with implementation. The staff development inservice emphasizes understanding of the thinking skills and strategies to help the teacher integrate the 19 key skills into the academic curriculum. In addition, the inservice acquaints teachers with lesson materials.

The Georgia Critical Thinking Skills Program

Writing as a Thinking and Learning Tool

The GCTSP, as the Georgia Critical Thinking Skills Program (1999–2004) is known, was designed to promote thinking and learning in the classroom. The program identifies specific instructional strategies that teachers can use to teach content while also nurturing critical, creative, and independent thinking.

The program is K–12 and is intended for all content areas of the curriculum. The program involves professional development, lesson and unit plans, assessment standards, examinations, and other teacher resources. Ten critical thinking areas have been identified by the program's developers. Figure 9.4 (p. 108) lists each of those areas.

Figure 9.3 Talents Unlimited's Six Talent Areas

Talent	Processes	Sample Activity
Productive Thinking	To generate many, varied and unusual ideas and then to add onto those ideas to improve them.	In a math unit on surveying and graphing: think of a variety of unusual topics for a survey to conduct and graph.
Communication	To convey needs, feelings, and ideas effectively to others. (Related skills: description, comparison, empathy, nonverbal communication, and the networking of ideas.)	In a 5th grade American Revolution unit: to describe the emotions of different groups of colonists, role-play both Loyalists and Rebels as they hear a reading of the Declaration of Independence.
Forecasting (cause-and-effect relationships)	To look into the future to predict things that might happen or looking into the past to consider what might have happened.	For a parent poll on their school's dress code: generate predictions about the possible causes for low returns on the survey.
Decision Making	To outline, weight, make final judgments, and defend a decision on the many alternatives to a problem.	To order materials through the Scholastic Books campaign: make final selections by considering such criteria as cost, interest, and reading level.
Planning	To design a means for implementing an idea by describing what is to be done, identifying the resources needed, outlining a sequence of steps to take, and pinpointing possible problems.	Students who are studying the unusual characteristics of slime mold are asked to design experiments to answer questions they have generated about the behavior of the mold.
Academic	To develop a base of knowledge and/or skill about a topic or issue through acquisition of information and concepts.	Students read from a variety of resources to gain information about the Impressionist period and then share the information in a discussion of a Monet painting.

Source: Adapted from Hobbs, D. E., and Schlichter, C. L. (1991). Talents Unlimited. In Costa, A.L. (Ed.) (1991). *Developing minds: Programs for teaching thinking.* Alexandria, VA: Association for Supervision and Curriculum Development, pp. 73–78.

Figure 9.4 GCTSP Critical Thinking Skills

♦ **Inductive Learning.** Inductive learning helps students connect new content with prior knowledge. Students examine, group, and label data to draw conclusions or make predictions. The discovery learning involved heightens student motivation to learn and ability to retain and apply what has been learned.

♦ **Metaphorical Expression.** This strategy uses direct and personal analogies and compressed conflicts to teach new concepts or to deepen existing concepts.

♦ **Decision Making.** Students make decisions by studying background information, examining data, establishing alternatives, and analyzing consequences. They then communicate their decisions, provide support, analyze others' decisions, and practice consensus building and debating skills. Students take into account long-term effects of decisions and from and test hypotheses.

♦ **Student-Centered Integrated Learning.** This technique integrates learning styles, interests, needs, and abilities of students with strategies and tools. Teachers assess their own learning styles and become familiar with those of their students to accommodate differences.

♦ **Concept Attainment.** Students learn concepts through study of examples and nonexamples. They form, test, and refine hypotheses about the material they are learning. They identify critical attributes of important concepts. Finally, they demonstrate concept attainment by generating their own examples and nonexamples.

♦ **Circle of Knowledge.** This strategy is used as a framework for effective discussions. It involves posing a question to the class which is then discussed in cooperative small groups before returning to whole class discussion.

♦ **Compare and Contrast.** Students' attention is focused on similarities and differences. Data are collected on items based on certain attributes. Graphic organizers are used to analyze the data. Students then draw conclusions, make predictions, and synthesize their information.

♦ **Inquire/Mystery.** These two strategies are based on inquiry teaching. Students are presented with new content in the form of discrepant event, question, riddle, or mystery. They then collect data and form hypotheses to explain the discrepant event. Clues are examined to reach systematic conclusions.

♦ **Assessing, Thinking, and Learning.** ATL is designed to link curriculum, instruction, and assessment by teaching teachers to design appropriate tasks congruent with instructional goals and objectives. Teachers are taught to use and design rubrics, observation checklists, and portfolios.

♦ **Strategic Interdisciplinary Teaching.** This involves three models for the design of interdisciplinary curriculum: alignment, enhancement, and integration. Content is integrated from different disciplines, thinking skills, strategies, assessments, the real world, and learning styles.

Adapted from Georgia Critical Thinking Skills Program, 1999–2004. Georgia Department of Education.

The Research Base for Thinking Skills Programs

Can We Get There From Here?

Certain problems seem to be inherent in the research on thinking skills. Any evaluation of the research base must be done with the following things in mind:

- *It lacks definition.* It is difficult to conduct research in an area for which there exists no generally agreed-on set of definitions of terms. Mathematics achievement, by way of contrast, can be operationally defined by a set of constructs, although even this can be debated. Mathematics is largely defined by the various textbooks in use, by the goal structure of the National Council of Teachers of Mathematics (NCTM), and by the various standardized tests that are available. One can make no such parallel claims about thinking skills. Remember the Supreme Court justice who said that although he couldn't define pornography, he knew it when he saw it? Suppose we could say we know good thinking when we see it. It would be at least a place to start, but even if we could say that, it's a pretty shaky foundation on which to build.

- *Measurement validity problems.* We are not particularly adept at measuring thinking skills. A few such tests exist, such as the Cornell Critical Thinking Test. Some IQ and abilities tests contain scales that may be somewhat appropriate to this area, but the skills are diverse (see Figs. 9.2 and 9.3) and difficult to measure and evaluate. We are left measurement instruments specific to a given curriculum or local program. These instruments, although often interesting, are plagued by problems of reliability, validity, and subjectivity. We may be years away from valid, reliable, agreed-on instruments of assessment.

- *Questionable causality.* Given the first two problems, it follows that the means to achieve curriculum alignment seem presently insurmountable. Thinking skills no doubt develop over a long period, and they routinely defy attempts to trace their realization to a specific unit or curriculum experience. In addition, it has been suggested by more than one observer that school environments in general may not be particularly supportive of the thinking skills that advocates tend to promote. As Arthur Costa has noted, "the change in student behavior is bound to be diverse and elusive" (Brandt, 1988b, p. 11).

- *Content-specific domains.* The idea that thinking skills are content specific and cannot be taught generically must be seriously entertained until it is discredited. We don't think that will happen. And if this is so, how does one construct content-free tests to measure thinking skills?

♦ *Qualitative data.* Mostly, we are left with observations, impressions, and anecdotal records to document increases in student thinking skills. Any teacher who has ever had to fill out that part of a report card knows what shaky grounds we are on when we give a + to Mary for her ability to "solve problems independently." And how many teachers would take either the credit or the blame for the pluses and minuses we marked in the category for the 30 kids in that class?

Basic Research on Thinking

At Level I, one finds a surprisingly small amount of information claimed by thinking skills advocates about basic or pure research in this area. However, it occurs to us that the basic research can be traced mainly to two areas: brain research and cognitive science. It is
reasonable to assume that the work of such researchers as Gardner, Feuerstein, and Sternberg, cited in the Chapter 8, forms much of the theoretical basis of some, but not all, thinking skills programs.

No doubt we are on the threshold of important knowledge of human brain function. The research referred to in Chapter 6 on brain-based learning is the best we can do for now to give you any insights into this area. Much is at stake here including heredity, nutrition, and experience.

The work in cognitive science includes such stage theories as those advanced by Piaget (1970) and Kohlberg (1987), research in information processing such as that done by Robert Sternberg (1990, 2004), and research in constructivist thought such as that conducted by Driver (1983), Bruner (1996), and Dewey (1938). The work of Lev Vygotsky (1986) in the area of the codevelopment of language and thought is extremely important. A book well worth reading to acquaint you with these areas is *Cognitive Development Today* by Peter Sutherland (1992).

Of course, one would be remiss if one were to neglect to mention the work of Benjamin Bloom, whose *Taxonomy of Educational Objectives for the Cognitive Domain* (1956) has influenced the development of more than one lesson plan or district guide over the years. Bloom suggested that a hierarchy of thought exists. At the lower cognitive register are found, in ascending order, knowledge, comprehension, and application; at the higher cognitive register are found, in ascending order, analysis, synthesis, and evaluation. These six levels of cognition have been accepted by millions as gospel and have been used as a template for teacher questions, lesson plan objectives, and anything else related to student thinking.

The taxonomy has recently been revised by a group led by Anderson and Krathwohl (2001) of the original team, responding in part to the above complaint (Figure 9.6). The theory is refined with each stage subtly renamed with the famous verbs for which teachers have known the taxonomy for developing behavioral objectives.

Figure 9.6 Revision of Bloom's Taxonomy

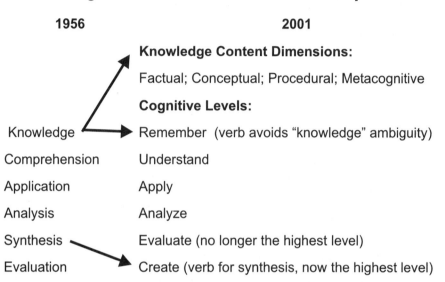

1956

2001

Knowledge Content Dimensions:

Factual; Conceptual; Procedural; Metacognitive

Cognitive Levels:

Knowledge → Remember (verb avoids "knowledge" ambiguity)

Comprehension → Understand

Application → Apply

Analysis → Analyze

Synthesis → Evaluate (no longer the highest level)

Evaluation → Create (verb for synthesis, now the highest level)

Source: Anderson, L., Krathwohl, D., Airasian, P., Cruikshank, K., Mayer, R., Pintrich, P., et al. (2000). *Taxonomy for learning, teaching and assessing: A revision of Bloom's Taxonomy of Educational Objectives.* New York: Pearson.

Actually, Bloom's Taxonomy is an imaginative theoretical construct with little empirical foundation. Is it really true, for example, that synthesis requires greater intellectual endeavor than comprehension? It is probably the case that to synthesize something, comprehension is required, just as it may be that to comprehend something, synthesis of some kind is required. And is a simple evaluation a higher intellectual function than a penetrating analysis? The proof simply isn't there.

Bloom's overly simplistic use of the terms that are the essence of his taxonomy is disquieting. To equate knowledge, for example, with lower registers of cognition when it ought to be abundantly clear that knowledge of something can be profound as well as trivial is to visit semantic confusion on us all. However, the complaint regarding the ambiguity of the knowledge term is duly addressed with the new emphasis on dimensions of knowledge.

Is There Any Evidence? Levels II and III Research

Given the ambiguities of research at Level I, it is predictable that the research at Level II is rather weak. A number of studies have investigated the development of higher-order thinking skills (a construct that has not really been established) as educational outcomes, but they are scattered throughout the literature on mastery learning, cooperative learning, outcome-based education, and peer coaching, among other topics, and are not research studies on the kinds of programs we describe in this chapter. For example, Hembree (1992) examined problem-solving attainment primarily in mathematics instruction and concluded that heuristics training provided the largest gains in problem-solving performance, but with a number of limitations. This tells us, however, little about thinking skills programs per se, either commercially or teacher-developed.

A number of claims are found in popular education journals such as *Educational Leadership* describe the benefits of these programs, but there does not seem to be even a modest number of published empirical studies to support most of the supposed benefits. For certain advocates of thinking skills programs (as with many other innovations mentioned in this book) this lack of research seems to be no obstacle. Stanley Pogrow (1995) appears to have discovered a new type of research, called "pattern sense making," that overrides traditional cause- and-effect studies. For schools using his Higher Order Thinking Skills (HOTS) program he states:

> It seemed natural to form a network to exchange information and ideas. The network makes possible a more realistic type of research than is possible in the highly controlled (contrived) settings of limited scope and limited duration in which most educational research takes places.

Such an arrangement allows for information flow and spontaneous feedback. This research, Pogrow writes,

> has generated fundamental new knowledge about the nature of the learning needs of educationally disadvantaged students. In addition, this approach to research has generated different conclusions from those of conventional research—conclusions that I believe are more valid and valuable for making national and school policy than those generated from either the prevalent quantitative or qualitative research techniques. (p. 20)

Although Pogrow furnishes us with an original theoretical paradigm, he develops a specific program and he conducts the research himself. Not only are the results efficacious, by his own admission, but his theoretical work has made possible conclusions that are "more valid and valuable" than those derived using other techniques. Perhaps.

The difficulties and ambiguities of thinking skills assessment have not gone unnoticed by those who have reviewed the research. Norris' (1985) review focused more on the general nature of critical thinking than on any cause-and-effect relationships. It is, however, a useful review for anyone contemplating curriculum changes in this area. He concluded that we really don't know much about critical thinking and sensibly offered only a few tentative conclusions, among them that critical thinking is not a generic tool and that it is sensitive to context.

Both the Norris review and that by Sternberg and Bhana (1986) highlighted the problems associated with the research on thinking skills, and those problems remain. Sternberg and Bhana's review sought to determine whether thinking skills programs are "snake-oil remedies or miracle cures." They evaluated five programs that had been cited in the annals of program evaluation and found most of the research to be weak in design and possibly biased. Even setting aside these serious problems, they found the results to be inconclusive and none of the evaluations useful for determining which portions of the programs worked and which did not. They concluded, "Some thinking skills training programs are probably not a whole lot better than snake oil, but the good ones, although not miracle cures, may improve thinking skills" (p. 67).

Cotton (1992) was more sanguine about the research base at Level II and Level III. She examined 33 "key documents, [of which] 22 are research studies or evaluations." The other 11 were reviews or syntheses of research. In these studies, thinking skills were defined in a wide variety of ways, including analysis, synthesis, evaluation, making predictions, making inferences, metacognitive activities, and a host of other things. She reached these conclusions:

+ Thinking skills instruction enhances academic achievement.
+ Research supports instruction in many specific skills and techniques, including study skills, creative and critical thinking skills, metacognition, and inquiry training.
+ Various instructional approaches enhance thinking skills.
+ Computer-assisted instruction helps to develop thinking skills.
+ Research supports the use of several specific thinking skills programs, including a number of those listed in Figure 9.1 (p. 102).
+ Training teachers to teach thinking skills leads to student achievement gains. (pp. 4–6)

In spite of Cotton's optimism, it seems difficult to mount much of a case for either the amount or quality of the research used to support such broad conclusions as these. Of course, you should examine for yourself the studies that Cotton reviewed. But short of doing so, critically reread any one of the foregoing six conclusions. The claims are somewhat reminiscent of the effective schools claims in that they can confuse cause and effect, are not weighted in helpful proportion, and raise the specter of unaccounted for variables and rival hypotheses. The claims can point in basically the right direction, but the evidence is not sufficient at this point to meet any clear standards. You may prefer to think of them as promising hypotheses in need of further testing.

Chang et al. (2002) tested the learning effects of a concept-mapping strategy with 126 fifth graders. They designed three concept-mapping approaches: map correction, scaffold fading, and map generation—to determine their effects on students' text comprehension and summarization abilities. The results were varied: the map-correction method enhanced text comprehension and summarization abilities, and the scaffold-fading method facilitated summarization ability. This well-constructed study offers some promise.

The professional literature, especially that chronicled in policy journals, not to mention the many teacher magazines, is replete with success stories, but few penetrating analyses. The advocates and enthusiasts are out there in profusion (e.g. Foil & Alber, 2002). Thinking skills has become one of the lucrative inservice and materials areas, and at its worst it preys on the vulnerability of professionals of goodwill who so much would like to improve the quality of students' thinking. Who can blame teachers for hoping these techniques will work, especially with the era of accountability combined with a trend toward inclusion that expands the academic diversity of their classrooms. In particular, students with learning disabilities struggle with extracting relationships from expository text, especially if it is implicit. Perhaps this is why some of the strongest studies lately have been focused on these students.

Baker, Gersten, and Scanlon (2002) reviewed recent studies on comprehension and expressive writing abilities, citing the promising use of concept maps and other "content enhancement techniques." DiCecco and Gleason (2002) noted that results have been inconclusive regarding the potency of graphic organizers (GO) as a comprehension tool. They write,

> When factual knowledge was assessed via multiple choice tests and quizzes, no differences were found between treatment and control conditions. As in other GO studies, both groups demonstrated attainment of facts and concepts. But when relational knowledge was assessed, the two groups responded differentially. On essays that required application, the GO group provided significantly more relational knowledge statements than students in the No GO group did. (p. 306)

Because they used a prolonged treatment and essays, their design incorporated other factors such as classroom environment and reflective thought.

Sturm and Rankin-Erickson (2002) studied middle school learning disabled students' writing across different treatments. Their results showed that student descriptive essays produced in the hand- and computer-mapping conditions demonstrated significant increases above baseline writing samples on number of words, number of T-units, and holistic writing scores. They also found that students' attitudes toward writing were significantly more positive in the computer-mapping condition when compared to no-mapping and hand-mapping conditions. It would make sense to think that their improved attitude toward writing means an improved attitude toward thinking and being aware of their own thoughts as they do so means that they are more reflective. This, however, is a stretch, and assumes much more than the quip, "the research shows."

Finally, Astleitner (2002) compared web-based and traditional text-based instruction as adjuncts to critical thinking, which he defined as evaluating arguments. He found no achievement difference in scientific analytical reasoning between university students by treatment. However, the web-based students who were also given supplemental guides such as graphic organizers showed greater satisfaction in the learning experience, suggesting another example of some other factors at play. So, such support may well offer some help when strategies are integrated with good content in an atmosphere that is genuinely conducive to the engagement of reflective thought.

Conclusion

It would be unreasonable to claim that thinking-skills programs fail to provide students with thinking skills. There just isn't much strong evidence that they do. The research in this area is muddled to say the least. It is not easy, for example, even to define or document the separate existence of thinking skills. Attempts to organize them into hierarchies may bear little resemblance to reality. Most of the evidence in favor of these programs is anecdotal. Still, when one examines the activities and teaching strategies found in most of the programs, they seem to have some potential.

At this time, any decision to purchase and implement particularly a commercial thinking skills program and to invest teachers' time in inservice training to make it go cannot be reasonably based on the research evidence. Ironically, the pure research base is good and improving almost daily, but the connections between pure and empirical research and the work of program builders are primitive. However, if in your professional judgment a particular thinking skills program looks good to you because of the interesting activities and strategies, that may be a logical basis on which to do some of your own higher-level thinking and give it a try.

10

Direct Instruction

DI interventions have been shown to produce superior performance with preschool, elementary, and secondary regular and special education students and adults. They have produced superior results with various minority populations, including nonEnglish speakers.

Gary L. Adams

It's a matter of balance...and Direct Instruction may in fact be limiting for some people in that it doesn't allow them to be as creative as they might....It prescribes, it's limiting, it's structured, it tells you exactly how it should be done.... Classrooms ought to be more than worksheets, ought to be more than multiplication facts....It's got to be reading plus and reading for a purpose.

Bertha Pendleton

What ever you do, don't stick this state with the DISTAR program.

Anonymous school district
curriculum director

The College of Education of the University of Oregon consistently leads the nation's institutions of higher education with respect to research dollars per faculty member (2004). The vast majority of those funds are awarded to researchers in the area of direct instruction. Perhaps the most well-known efforts at the University of Oregon are led by researchers Siegfried Engelmann and Douglas Carnine, who have developed a high-profile method of phonics-based reading curriculums, called Direct Instruction (DI). A recent meta-analysis in the *Review of Educational Research* (Borman, Hewes, Overman, & Brown, 2003) identified DI as one of only three models of comprehensive school reform that is supported by "strongest evidence of effectiveness."

✳ What if somebody could come up with a method of teaching
children how to read that was simple and worked every time.
That sounds like the impossible dream to parents and school
kids. But we found such a method. And you may be shocked to
find out that most schools refuse to try it.

This was how Hugh Downs of ABC-TV began a 1996 episode of *20/20,*
the long-running television news magazine. During Downs' interview
with Professor Engelmann, the originator and developer of DI,
Engelmann made the claim that in his many years of working with DI he
has never found a student who couldn't learn to read.

Given the problems with basic literacy that this country faces, could
this be the miracle cure we have all been looking for? It sounds too good to
be true. The never-ending quest for a silver bullet seems for once to have
been satisfied. Advocates say search no more—it is just a matter of applying the principles of DI in classrooms. And yet, it has detractors, critics,
and opponents. Why is this so? This chapter contains an examination of
the evidence in support of and against DI, and let you reach your own
conclusion. I will define it, search for theory building and empirical evidence, and see whether program evaluations tend to support its use or
not.

What is Direct Instruction?

There is some confusion over the terminology, so let us begin there.
First, it is useful to distinguish between direct instruction (d.i.), and Direct
Instruction (DI), although there is a relationship. Direct Instruction refers
to a range of about 60 instructional programs, developed by Engelmann
and his colleagues, that set standards of learning based on specific techniques and teacher-directed sequences, whereas d.i. refers to the work of
Barak Rosenshine (1979, 1986), and others, which is based on a highly organized and structured, teacher-directed, task-oriented approach to instruction. Obviously, there is common ground here, the commonality
being primarily that of a basic skills, linear, teacher-directed approach to
instruction. Philosophically, both are, roughly speaking, educational
manifestations of a point of view known as essentialism, an educational
philosophy that emphasizes basic skills, teacher direction, grades, tests,
and traditional discipline.

Linda Darling-Hammond and Jon Snyder (1992) quote Rosenshine's
description of where direct instruction occurs:

> Academically focused, teacher directed classrooms using se-
> quenced and structured materials. It [d.i.] refers to teaching ac-
> tivities where goals are clear to students, time allocated for in-
> struction is sufficient and continuous, coverage of content is

extensive, the performance of students is monitored, questions are at a low cognitive level...and feedback to students is immediate and academically oriented. In direct instruction, the teacher controls instructional goals, chooses materials appropriate for the student's ability, and paces the instructional episode. The goal is to move the students through a sequenced set of materials or tasks. Such materials are common across classrooms and have a relatively strong congruence with the tasks on achievement tests. (p. 65)

opposite y
v w
learning

Adams and Engelmann (1996) wrote:

[T]he most common confusion is that Direct Instruction is simply teacher-directed instruction, the opposite of the so-called "child-centered" approaches (such as the open classroom or discovery method) in which the teacher is supposed to act as a facilitator for students. Traditional teacher-directed instruction is not Direct Instruction; it is just direct teaching or teacher-directed instruction. (p. 1)

Although this statement oversimplifies Rosenshine's rather elaborate description, it does draw attention to the useful idea that direct instruction is more generic, a larger tent so to say, than DI. Direct Instruction is a specific instructional approach consisting of (a) "Direct Instruction techniques and sequences that set standards by documenting what students can achieve," or (b) "commercial Direct Instruction sequences and materials that are designed for use by people who have not been trained directly by Engelmann and his colleagues" (p. 2). As we shall see, commercial variants of DI appear under different labels applied to reading, math, science, and language.

It is thus safe to say that DI is a specific example of d.i. Direct Instruction fits into Rosenshine's description rather well. DI proponents are quick to point out that their programs are not representative of many of the aspects of generic direct instruction. Lecture, for example, is a type of direct instruction, and DI programs are virtually lecture free. Wide-ranging, teacher-directed class discussions are also examples of direct instruction not found in Direct Instruction. So, like any variant of a larger set, there is commonality as well as divergence between it and other members of the set. This attempt to describe likenesses and differences can seem laborious, but without it confusion reigns. The focus in this chapter is primarily on DI because its research claims are manageable within the constraints of a chapter, whereas to assess the research findings in d.i. would take us into such labyrinthine corridors as lecture, seatwork, textbooks, teacher-led class discussion, and a range of variables rather numerous to say the least.

Direct Instruction was first implemented in 1968 as part of the U.S. Office of Education's Project Follow Through and has continued in use in a variety of states, districts, and schools around the country since that time. The first series in reading and arithmetic was known as DISTAR (Direct Instruction System for Teaching Arithmetic and Reading, later changed to Direct Instruction System for Teaching and Remediation). These and other instructional programs have been published commercially and have a variety of names (see Figure 10.1). In addition an entire series of instructional programs is available on videodisc and aimed at adult learners.

Figure 10.1 Direct Instruction Commercial Programs

Reading	Language Arts	Mathematics
◆ Reading Mastery I, II ◆ Reading Mastery: Fast Cycle ◆ Reading Mastery III, IV, V, VI ◆ Corrective Reading: Decoding ◆ Corrective Reading: Comprehension	◆ Reasoning and Writing: Levels A–F ◆ DISTAR Language I, II ◆ Cursive Writing Program ◆ Expressive Writing 1, 2 ◆ Spelling Mastery ◆ Corrective Spelling Through Morphographs	◆ Connecting Math Concepts: Levels A–F ◆ Arithmetic I, II ◆ Corrective Mathematics ◆ Mathematics Modules

Source: Adams, G., and Engelmann, S. (1996). *Research on direct instruction: 20 years beyond DISTAR.* Seattle, WA: Educational Achievement Systems.

DISTAR was designed for use with K–3 children, particularly in compensatory school settings with lower achievers. It "emphasizes frequent teacher-student interactions guided by carefully sequenced daily lessons in reading, arithmetic, and language" (Engelmann et al., 1988). The developers describe the underlying assumptions of the Direct Instruction Model as

> (a) all children can be taught; (b) the learning of basic skills and their application in higher-order skills is essential to intelligent behavior and should be the main focus of a compensatory education program; (c) the disadvantaged must be taught at a faster rate than typically occurs if they are to catch up with their middle-class peers. (p. 303)

The Direct Instruction Model is guided by two major rules (Figure 10.2, p. 122) and includes carefully designed curriculums in reading, mathematics, social and physical science, language, handwriting, and fact learning. These curriculums are basic skills, to say the least: phonics and decoding skills, grammar rules, arithmetic operations, logical processes, research methods, and problem solving. The model also stresses increased teaching time, with at least two hours a day devoted to these specific skills. "Efficiently teaching" means "scripted presentation of lessons, small-group instruction, reinforcement, corrections, and procedures to teach every child by giving added attention to the lower performers (Engelmann et al., 1988, pp. 306–307). Basically, there is a lot of oral drill, recitation, and memory work. The scripted lessons include exactly what the teacher will say and do during the instructional time using procedures that have been field-tested and revised for effectiveness. This also permits a supervisor to identify deficiencies quickly and to provide appropriate remedies. Critics at the time and now have labeled such approaches to education as *teacher proof*, meaning that the procedures are so tightly scripted that even the worst of teachers could hardly go wrong. The idea, so critics claimed, was that "at last here is a method that even you can't screw up."

The DI model ideally requires extensive staff development and training. Teachers can and have used DI without formal training, but there is much they might miss by doing so. The equation is far more complex than merely putting a teacher in front of a group of students, even with the materials at hand, and allowing him or her to interpret along the way. Among its elaborate features, for example, is a procedure for keeping track of and coordinating all services given to an individual student, including nutrition, health, psychological, social, and guidance and counseling services. The major parts of the program are presented in Figure 10.3 (p. 123).

Since 1968 Direct Instruction programs have been used nationwide by a dedicated, but relatively small, numbers of teachers and professionals claim great success with it. The tenets have changed little since its inception 30 years ago, although it has probably become even more associated with teaching directed at low achievers and disadvantaged children than with high achievers. Its proponents say this is simply because the system works with low performers where other methods do not. They claim that it works equally well with average and high achievers, but obviously with fewer repetitions, shorter time needed for learning, and so forth.

Figure 10.2. The Two Major Rules of Direction Instruction

I.   Teach more in less time: X

- ♦ The model uses a teacher and an aide at levels 1 and 2 of the programs, usually in kindergarten and first grade. The aides are trained to teach and function fully as teachers and, thus, increase the amount of teacher-student interaction time.

- ♦ Programs are designed to focus on teaching the general use of information and skills where possible, so that through teaching a subject, the whole set is learned. For example, by teaching 40 sounds and skills for hooking them together students learn a generalized decoding skill that is relevant to one-half of the more common English words.

II.   Control the details of what happens:

- ♦ Daily lesson scripts are provided that tell the teacher exactly what to say and do. All teachers and aides use the DISTAR programs in reading, language, and arithmetic developed by Engelmann and his associates.

- ♦ Training is provided so that the staff knows how to execute the details of the program.

- ♦ Student progress and, indirectly, teacher implementation are monitored through the use of criterion-referenced "continuous progress tests" on the children every 2 weeks.

- ♦ Supervisors (1 for each 10 to 15 classrooms) are trained to spend 75% of their time actually in classrooms working with teachers and aides.

- ♦ Procedures for teachers, supervisors, administrators, and parents are detailed in implementation and parent coordinator manuals.

Source: Engelmann, S., Becker, W. C., Carnine, D., and Gersten, R. (1988). The direct instruction follow through model: Design and outcomes. *Education and Treatment of Children, 11*(4), 303–304.

Figure 10.3. Major Parts of the Direct Instruction Model

♦ Consistent focus on academic objectives.

♦ High allocations of time to small-group instruction in reading, language, and math.

♦ Tight, carefully sequenced DISTAR curriculum, which includes a task analysis of all skills and cognitive operations, and numerous opportunities for review and practice of recently learned skills.

♦ Ongoing inservice and preservice training that offers concrete, "hands on" solutions to problems arising in the classroom.

♦ A comprehensive system for monitoring both the rate at which students progress through the curriculum and their mastery of the material covered.

Source: Adapted from Meyer, L. A., Gersten, R. M., and Gutkin, J. (1983). Direction instruction: A project follow through success story in an inner-city school. *The Elementary School Journal, 84(2),* 243.

The Critics

There appears to be surprisingly little criticism of Direct Instruction in the literature. Nevertheless, that does not mean there is a lack of critics. Indeed, there are plenty. Curiously, however, DI has been largely unacknowledged except by its advocates. Perhaps the old saw, "ignore it and it will go away" obtains here. The following oblique mention of the DI approach, aimed primarily at phonics-based reading instruction, is offered by Zemelman and others (1998). They wrote: "Most children learned how to decode simple print. But we did not create a nation of mature, effective, voluntary, self-motivated, lifelong readers: on the contrary, most Americans stopped reading the moment they escaped from school" (p. 22).

There is, however, more than one way to "escape" from school. A study by Meyer and others (1983) of high school graduation rates for three cohort groups in the New York City schools showed that the dropout rates were statistically significantly lower among students taught by Direct Instruction than were those of a comparison group. And the percentages of those applying to and accepted by colleges were statistically significantly higher among the DI group than among the comparison group. Interestingly, Zemelman and others do not even mention either DI or d.i. in their coverage of reading research in their book, *Best Practice: New Standards for Teaching and Learning in America's Schools* (1998).

One does find in the writings of DI enthusiasts allusions to the objections of the critics. Critics, they say, argue that DI is old-fashioned, it is too much work for the teacher, it is more tiring, too regimented, promotes passive and rote learning, and stifles teacher creativity. To rebut these charges, to the extent that they are even made, there is no evidence offered; in fact, one seldom finds any written criticism from the critics. It seems to be basically ignored, much like Brussels sprouts, primarily based on personal distaste.

A common complaint by teachers about DI is that it is so regimented that it stifles their creativity. This is an interesting statement, to say the least. They reject it not because it doesn't work, but because it stifles teacher creativity. They feel limited. But it could at least be argued that teacher creativity is not the end product of schooling, student learning is. Imagine doctors rejecting a treatment, not because it didn't work, but because it cramped their style, stifled their creativity, or was too boring and tedious for them to use. Admittedly, this is a problem; teacher happiness and fulfillment is important. But perhaps one could put forth the scarcely novel idea that there is a time for everything—a time to be creative and a time to be didactic—especially if that didacticism is shown to work in the teaching of basic skills. As to the criticism of rote learning, there may be some degree of truth to it, even though DI proponents say that that is only part of what is learned. On the other hand, rote learning is necessary in the form of number facts, letter sounds, and so on, to provide the building blocks of higher learning.

The Research Base for Direct Instruction

Level I Research

The theoretical basis of both direct instruction and Direct Instruction is represented by a seemingly ad hoc mixture of behaviorism, cognitive science, and reductionism. When one peels away the layers and reaches the core, however, one encounters a clearly essentialist philosophy. Consider, for example, this ambiguity-reducing statement by Adams and Engelmann, authors of *Research on Direct Instruction: 20 Years Beyond DISTAR* (1996): "The first job of the teacher, therefore, is to teach basic skills and knowledge" (p. 27). Many, of course, would agree with this thought, but it does clearly put some distance between those who sympathize with it and those who advocate progressive education. Essentialism is largely a twentieth-century phenomenon, which rose to prominence based on its drumbeat attacks on progressivism. Educational essentialists of prominence include Arthur Bestor (1953), and more recently, E. D. Hirsch, Jr. (1987, 2001). Basically, essentialism promotes basic skills and knowledge, standards, testing, and mastery learning, while eschewing such approaches as nondirective learning, personalized curriculum, open-concept education, and developmentally appropriate practice.

That DI is behaviorist in orientation is clear. Emphasis is placed on objective and observable behaviors; reinforcement theory is promoted in the form of rapid feedback; the teacher (not the student) is expected to arrange the conditions of learning; and carefully planned, sequentially ordered teaching is carried out. Thus, one could reasonably find the theories of Pavlov, Watson, Skinner, and other giants of this movement as forming much of its backcloth. However, just as behaviorism has modified its stance against mental processes that cannot be observed, so does one find elements of cognitive science imbedded here. The type of cognitive science one encounters in DI is that branch related to information processing rather than to the developmental, environmental perspective advocated by Jean Piaget. *Reductionism* (Ellis & Fouts, 1996) suggests that learning can be broken down into constituent parts, and that simpler parts of whole complex ideas are more manageable for the learner when they are taught in some meaningful sequence that leads toward comprehension of the whole. This describes DI.

A final comment that seems in order in the search for Level I theory is that DI in fact represents something close to being purely evidence driven. In this respect, it emerges as an empirical model (Adams & Carnine, 2003). Over the past three decades, DI researchers have systematically sought for evidence of its efficacy, paying little attention to theory building or to matters of abstract philosophy Study after study has been conducted in such curricular areas as reading, language, and mathematics. They have asked the pragmatic question, "Does it work?" The sheer weight of the evidence published in respected journals is impressive. This is remarkably different from the many innovations that claim (often dubiously) a profound theoretical basis, but that offer little published evidence to substantiate academic or other effects. It is this very strength that may contain the elements of its weakness. Why, advocates and empirical researchers ask, is DI so little acknowledged and so reluctantly accepted? There may be a number of reasons, including a built-in bias toward progressive education on the part of teachers. But if that were all, how does one explain the phenomenal acceptance by teacher training institutions and school districts of such behaviorist-essentialist protocols as instructional objectives, Madeline Hunter's Instructional Theory Into Practice (ITIP), and mastery learning? Clearly, ours is a field more than willing to embrace eclecticism, with few qualms about a mixed progressive-essentialist agenda. Hunter was an extremely effective promoter of ITIP, an innovation that may have been more widespread and used in schools than any other of our time. She communicated a vision of ITIP that teachers, administrators, and professors in schools of education eagerly subscribed to although the empirical evidence one might wish for really never was there. Even good evidence is not easy to sell in the absence of a well-communicated vision. Regarding DI, this is unfortunate, because what we seem to have here, to paraphrase Cool Hand Luke's chain-gang boss, is a failure to communicate.

Levels II and III Research

An impressive research agenda has been carried out over the last four decades on DI instructional programs. Studies have been conducted on both small- and large-scale usage, for short periods of time and in the form of longer-term follow-up evaluations. Because of the nature of DI instructional programs, the research tends more often than not to be a combination of quasi-experimental and program evaluation designs, and for this reason we will discuss Level II and Level III research together.

Return with me for a moment to those thrilling days of yesteryear, to the 1960s and Lyndon Johnson's Great Society, when there seemed to be a lot more money for educational research than there is today. It was during this time that the U.S. Office of Education started Project Follow Through to the tune of $59 million, the priciest education research project ever funded. The project, which involved more than 170 communities, was designed to evaluate different approaches to educating economically disadvantaged students. "A wide array of instructional approaches were included in Follow Through, ranging from open classroom models, to cognitive models based on the theories of Piaget, to highly structured programs utilizing principles of contemporary learning theory" (Meyer et al., 1983). One of these instructional approaches was the Direct Instruction Model.

The Stanford Research Institute and Abt Associates were contracted to evaluate the effectiveness of the various models in the areas of basic skills, and cognitive and affective behaviors. To make a long story short, the Direct Instruction Model produced the most desirable results in all three areas. This included results superior in the cognitive areas to those instructional programs designed specifically to focus on cognitive outcomes, and results superior in the affective areas to those instructional programs designed specifically to focus on affective outcomes (Stebbins et al., 1977). The regimented protocols of DI are at odds with the progressive educational wisdom of the day; and as far as educational practice is concerned, these findings seemed to have been basically ignored.

Apparently convinced that there must have been a mistake, officials of the Ford Foundation funded an evaluation of the evaluation, which (not surprisingly) questioned certain conclusions drawn by the evaluators (House, Glass, & McLean, 1978). This critique resulted in several more in-depth analyses of the data generated by Project Follow Through, in which DI looked even better (see Adams & Engelmann, 1996, pp. 67–98, for a summary of these reports). If the research stopped at this point, we would say that the controversy surrounding the Follow Through studies could pose some reasonable threat to the research base. In the world of education, where such a premium is placed on the new, this is, after all, ancient history. There was, however, much more to come.

In the wake of Project Follow Through, research on the effectiveness of DI continued at both Levels II and III. Project Follow Through itself generated many follow-up studies of the long-term effects, the great majority of which supported the efficacy of DI. Having found results similar to those noted by Meyer and others (mentioned earlier in this chapter), Gersten and Keating (1987) noted that high school students who received Direct Instruction in primary grades had lower school dropout rates, higher test scores, and a higher percentage of college applications and acceptance. Finally, Gersten, Keating, and Becker (1988) conducted two longitudinal studies on the effects of Direct Instruction and found that the results consistently favored DI in educational outcomes such as graduation rates, dropout rates, and college acceptance, as well as in measures of achievement, especially reading.

Apart from Project Follow Through, scores of studies were conducted during the 1970s through this the first decade of the twenty-first century probing the effects of DI in the areas of language, mathematics, social and physical science, problem-solving and reasoning skills, reading, and spelling. A number of research reviews and meta-analyses have been conducted over the years, but we will mention just a few. Cotton and Savard (1982) reviewed 33 relevant documents that supported Direct Instruction as improving basic skills achievement and affective development, but they did not conclude that DI was appropriate for older students. White (1988) conducted a metaanalysis reviewing 25 studies with special education populations, which showed favorable results for DI, including the observation that not one research study favored the comparison group. They noted that the effects of DI were independent of such variables as handicapping condition, age group, or skill area. Adams and Engelmann (1996) conducted the most thorough review of the research. This impressive analysis of the literature, Project Follow Through publications, and metaanalysis of scores of Level II and Level III studies on the effects of DI are solid evidence of its efficacy, providing educators with a formidable research base.

Since its inception, DI has had a loyal group of adherents, and their names are prevalent in the DI literature, including the research studies. Among those are Becker, Carnine, Engelmann, Maggs, and Gersten. There is always cause for concern when the proponents of a program, and in this case a commercial program, are also the primary researchers. Conflicts of interest are always a strong possibility. In this case, however, this appears not to be an issue for several reasons. First, there are a number of researchers who have studied DI who are not connected to its commercial aspects, and their findings are basically the same. A recent study (Mills et al., 2002) ambitiously tracked 171 children who had been randomly assigned to the two early childhood models, one using direct instruction, the other using a cognitively oriented, child-directed approach. The results point to the efficacy of DI. Second, the research by prominent DI advocates is published in prestigious, peer-reviewed journals, an extremely important quality control point. Third, there has been no sustained or focused scholarly criticism that one can find challenging the quality of the research.

Conclusion

A curriculum director (whose comment serves as one of the opening quotes for this chapter), on learning of the soundness of the research base for Direct Instruction as an early years reading program, retorted, "I just don't like it, plain and simple." Well, okay. One can reasonably assume that when President George H. W. Bush said some years ago that he hated broccoli (costing him, no doubt, the broccoli growers' vote) that he already knew it contained essential vitamins and minerals. He just didn't like the stuff, plain and simple. Perhaps similar comments could be made about exercise, meditation, and adequate sleep, even though research has shown them to be beneficial. To stretch this thin metaphor even further, one can say with assurance that people even engage in practices that research has shown to be harmful, such as smoking and excessive drinking. It is a part of the human condition that gaps exist between evidence of something's worth and our willingness to embrace it. Contrariwise, we seem to be willing to embrace claims for which there is in fact little or no supportive evidence.

There is a recurring refrain in American education, one based on the idea of advocates of this or that creating a straw man of the opposition and then systematically pummeling the straw man. John Dewey noted this problem in his classic book, *Experience and Education* (1938). In his case, the argument was between the "old" education (traditional) and the "new" education (progressive). Dewey lamented the fact that each side oversimplifies and exaggerates the shortcomings of the other to advance its own argument. It doesn't work, he informs the reader. Why? Because you end up defining yourself as much by what you are not as by what you are.

Districts interested in a research-tested curriculum of basic skills for young learners and at-risk children should seriously consider DI It is, after all, one of a minority of educational innovations with evidence on its side. However, in a sound school program, there may well be room for both direct and indirect instruction. After all, both the school day and the school year are reasonably long.

11

Assessment

The only way to improve schools...is to ensure that faculties judge local work using authentic standards and measures... [I]t means doing away with the current extremes of private, eccentric teacher grading, on the one hand; and secure standardized tests composed of simplistic items on the other.

Grant Wiggins

Standardized tests are still the bread and butter of statewide assessment. But in all regions—north and south, liberal and conservative—alternative assessments have been added to the menu, if not as the main course, then at least as a side dish.

Lee Sherman Caudell

In the excitement about authentic assessment, it is important to be sensible. Just being different from traditional standardized tests will not guarantee that alternative tests are better.

Anita Woolfolk

The Movement

Alternative assessment strategies have emerged as a key element of the school restructuring movement. Like so many of the varied pieces of the vast and often contradictory school-restructuring puzzle, alternative assessment represents a frontal attack on the status quo. At the energizing source of the alternative assessment paradigm is a deep and abiding dissatisfaction with traditional assessment procedures, from high-stakes standardized tests to teacher-constructed measures of achievement. But it doesn't stop with mere dissatisfaction; the alternative assessment movement has produced a number of innovative ideas for taking student learning into account. Walter Parker (2005) captures the essence of the movement when he writes, "assessments should be geared to finding out students' abilities to apply knowledge and skills successfully in meaningful or 'authentic' tasks" (p. 242).

Like vi & yi, you need a mix.

As one might expect, an entire range of terms and phrases has emerged. The significant vocabulary includes *authentic assessment, performance assessment, practical testing,* and *direct testing.* Whatever the terminology, the move to alternative assessment practices has reached epic proportions. To place this movement into some kind of meaningful context, it is necessary to develop a contrasting image of more traditional assessment patterns and their effects on students.

Formative

Traditional Measures

Student progress is traditionally assessed and reported along a feedback continuum that incorporates everything from daily marks and test scores to semester grades and standardized test results. These marks take on a life of their own, creating a sense of reality in the minds of teachers, students, and parents. In fact, this reality may or may not have curriculum content validity: The tests and hence the grades that flow from them may or may not be well connected to the curriculum. There is a long history of discontent with both standardized and teacher-made tests.

From another viewpoint, standardized tests furnish communities, districts, states, and the nation with benchmarks of comparative scores over time and with one another. Thus we can compare any given district with its own past performance and with other districts; we can compare Vermont with Nevada, and so on. For all its perceived shortcomings, it is a relatively efficient system, one that has been around for at least 50 years. Still, the criticisms have become increasingly strident, and they cannot simply be ignored.

Thomas Toch takes standardized tests to task in his books, *In the Name of Excellence* (1991) and *High Schools on a Human Scale* (2003). He cites the many standardized tests that states have put in place as a means of holding teachers accountable. Thinking that such tests will lead to improved classroom performance because teachers will *know* that they have to prepare their students more adequately, state legislators have enacted legislation requiring tests in most states. Toch, however, sees this as nothing more than a return to "minimum competency testing," a movement that was tried and that failed in the 1970s. In a thoughtful passage, Toch wrote,

> Yet there is an immense paradox in the recent surge in standardized testing. Despite the key role standardized tests are playing in the reformers' accountability campaign, the bulk of the new tests are severely flawed as measures of the excellence movement's progress. One major reason is that the tests do not measure the sorts of advanced skills and knowledge that the reformers have argued all students should master....It is largely

How are assessments connected to curric?

How can we ? for understanding + or real world applications to get our points across if standardized tests aren't testing ? ?

Assessment   131

impossible to gauge from the results of such tests whether students are mastering the intellectual skills that have been the focus of the reform movement: the abilities to judge, analyze, infer, interpret, reason, and the like. Nor do the majority of the tests gauge students' more advanced knowledge of literature, history, science, and other disciplines. Indeed, the recent surge in standardized testing amounts to little more than an extension of the minimum basic-skills testing movement of the 1970s. (1991, p. 207)

This vexing problem carries with it yet another twist, as though it weren't enough to critique standardized tests (and teacher-made tests as well) for tending to measure only lower-register thinking and knowledge. In a 1973 article in the *American Psychologist,* David McClelland, a noted researcher who established much of the groundwork for the emotional intelligence movement, criticized standardized testing in a most basic sense. He proposed teaching to raise their test scores and testing abilities rather than aptitudes, designing tests so that scores would rise as students learned more, and abandoning multiple-choice formats—all of which is yet to happen. But his most basic suggestion for change was the idea that we need to stop ranking millions of people on their perceived knowledge and skills and start building tests that tap into motivations for learning, something that could actually be used to shape individual instruction (Lehman, 1994).

Teacher-made tests are yet another story. Consider this comment by Mehrens and Lehmann (1991):

Students sometimes complain that they are fed up with tests that are ambiguous, unclear, and irrelevant. Student comments such as "I didn't know what the teacher was looking for" and "I studied the major details of the course but was only examined on trivia and footnotes" are not uncommon. Nor are they necessarily unjustified. (p. 52)

It has been noted many times over that teacher-made tests are generally of low quality, particularly with respect to their validity and reliability as well as the observation that they tend to assess students primarily at low cognitive levels.

Authentic Assessment

Serious students of assessment are committed to a review of the entire educational system. This would involve a close look not only at how we have traditionally attempted to assess student learning but also of the effects on students of *how* their learning been assessed. The key to understanding the alternative assessment movement is found in a thoughtful consideration of the term *authentic assessment.* The term implies that, by contrast, it should replace assessment that is inauthentic, which means false. So the idea of authentic assessment is to create assessment strategies that measure more realistically and accurately those things that students are supposed to be learning.

Students proceed through their school years being evaluated daily, weekly, and quarterly, taking teacher-made tests, and doing assignments such as directed readings, reports, and projects. For this, they receive semester or yearly marks, frequently in the form of letter grades, sometimes supplemented by narrative teacher evaluations. In a seemingly unrelated process, once a year, sometimes less often, they take standardized tests in such basic skills areas as mathematics and reading, and in such content areas as social studies and science. These tests are, at best, variably connected to the curriculum that is actually taught at a given school. It is when the results are disappointing and they get in the newspapers that school people become so discouraged. In fact, a typical defensive reaction by teachers is that their students are learning many wonderful things that are not effectively captured by the tests. Of course, when the results are good we all seem to take them for granted.

In a more perfect educational world (the goal of school restructuring), it would be impossible to separate assessment procedures from curriculum content. In order to do authentic assessment, it stands to reason that we should be assessing what is being taught and hopefully what is being learned. First, authentic assessment should be as closely aligned as possible to the curriculum's day-to-day experiences. Here there really is little argument between traditionalists and those who would change the assessment paradigm. But good alignment is not enough. It's just a place to start.

Second, it is argued that teaching and learning should be authentic. This means that learning should focus on real-life situations. "Let students encounter and master situations that resemble real life." (Cronin, 1993, p. 79). The curricular implications of this view are clearly that school activities and projects should have a real-world cast to them. This argument has been around forever, and it essentially represents a philosophic divide between those who hold a purely academic-centered curriculum and those who hold a more society-centered curriculum. Consider, for example, Parker's (2005) principles of good assessment in Figure 11.1.

The Center on Organization and Restructuring of Schools at the University of Wisconsin at Madison has developed a framework for *authentic instruction,* and *authentic achievement* (Newmann & Wehlage, 1993). Newmann and Wehlage draw a distinction between "achievement that is significant and meaningful, and that which is trivial and useless." They use three criteria to define authentic achievement: "(1) students construct meaning and produce knowledge, (2) students use disciplined inquiry to

Figure 11.1 Principles of Good Assessment

Principle 1: Treat assessment as an integral part of curriculum and instruction.

Principle 2: Direct assessments toward essential learning.

Principle 3: Set high standards for teaching and learning.

Principle 4: Clarify targets early.

Principle 5: Assess student performance in authentic tasks.

Principle 6: Collect multiple indicators of learning.

Principle 7: Provide ample opportunities for students to learn.

Source: Parker, W. (2005). *Social Studies in Elementary Education.* Upper Saddle River, NJ: Pearson Prentice Hall.

construct meaning, and (3) students aim their work toward production of discourse, products, and performances that have value or meaning beyond success in school" (p. 8). One might safely presume that experiences that do not meet these criteria are "trivial and useless."

Not all advocates of alternative assessment procedures have such definitively articulated ideas about achievement, but the essence of their argument is the same: What we teach and what we assess are not what is important for students to learn. All too often, school learning is removed from the world that students will face when they leave school. Therefore, it behooves us to rethink our assessment techniques, and therefore our curriculum, to provide and assess learning that is authentic, not contrived. Such a statement presumes that school is not part of the real world.

The alternative assessment movement is obviously based on two related arguments: one deals with curriculum and the other with assessment. The first is the ancient, abiding debate over the curriculum and the relevance of school learning to the real world. The belief in such a dichotomy, of course, can serve as a self-fulfilling prophecy. The question becomes, "Does what students are taught in the schools apply to reality; that is, can they use their knowledge to solve problems, do their jobs, and lead their lives?" Second, "What do traditional evaluation strategies such as paper-and-pencil tests and standardized tests really measure, and whatever that is, is it important?"

The proponents of alternative assessment strategies have definite and predictable responses to these questions. School learning must be reality based, and the assessment of that learning must be more a natural, logical outgrowth of the learning experiences themselves. Many of those who hope to reform education agree and have joined the movement, seeing it as crucial.

There appear to be four reasons why alternative assessment is seen as a key to reform. First, alternative assessment strategies are seen as educationally superior to traditional methods. The strategies call for more formative and personalized assessment for the individual student, providing meaningful feedback to the individual, and thus creating the possibilities for more significant, useful learning. The focus shifts naturally to higher-level thinking skills and real-life applications that increase student interest and motivation.

A second line of reasoning is that alternative forms of assessment will provide a more adequate representation of what is actually being taught in the schools today. Current standardized tests lack validity as measures of the diverse curricular offerings. It's an interesting argument with a certain elemental appeal, but the idea behind good standardized tests is that they capture students' ability to apply concepts and skills, not their narrowly defined content information.

A third point is that authentic learning and alternative assessment strategies will facilitate the type of learning that is needed by employees to allow the United States to compete internationally. Here is an example. Students who use alternative assessment procedures are more involved in assessing their own learning and are therefore more aware of their learning. This metacognitive skill (reflecting on the processes of learning) is basic to problem solving, trouble shooting, and to working one's way through difficult, unpatterned situations. Thus, assessment becomes part of the learning experience and not something that is merely tacked on and without context. In the *real world,* you don't take periodic paper-and-pencil tests to measure how well you're doing. You do your job, which involves assessment of product quality, customer satisfaction, and worker productivity.

Fourth, alternative assessment strategies and resulting accountability will force intransigent teachers to change the way they teach children. Portfolios, student record keeping, journals, reflective discussions, and other related alternative assessment procedures are themselves metacognitive learning experiences and shape the school day. The amount of student-to-student interaction and time spent in reflective thinking increase; and before teachers and students know it, they have stepped off the conveyor belt that passes for learning and have entered a more seamless world where planning, activity, and assessment flow smoothly together. At least that's the argument. Ellis (2004), describing real-world assessment in an innovative curriculum, writes, "students conduct real-world investigations, and the idea is that any assessment should reasonably flow from that, especially in the form of some write-up, display, or performance" (p.83).

Alternative Assessment Strategies

A number of assessment strategies for teachers (Figure 11.2, p. 136) have emerged from all this. These strategies, or activities, are thought to be useful for measuring and enhancing critical thinking skills and the application of knowledge. Except portfolios, these strategies are not particularly new; good teachers are already using them extensively in their classrooms.

What is new, however, is the drive to replace the dominance of standardized tests in the eyes of the public and policymakers with these assessment techniques. At the extremes of the argument, enthusiasts wish to replace grades and tests completely with these strategies. Such a position is more about the use of the assessments for *grading* students than the use of alternative means to assess student *learning*. Assessment literacy involves increasingly sophisticated technical procedures used at all levels to determine whether learning has occurred. Richard Stiggins (2001) is one of many theorists to develop a classroom assessment framework, one that has achieved popular use in many teacher education programs.

Stiggins focuses on two dimensions of assessment: the targets of learning and the tools to measure what is learned. Teachers develop *blueprints* indicating they have thoughtfully identified the most appropriate way of testing students' learning according to the type of learning: facts, reasoning, skills, products, or disposition. The tools include selected response (the most traditional, with *one right answer*), essay (verbal or visual expressions of multiple ideas), performance, or direct communication.

One powerful contribution of the assessment literacy movement is the emphasis on rubrics for teaching and for assessment. Stiggins makes a good case that analyzing different criteria in a single product increases the efficiency of using it to measure many objectives, and helps students self-assess their progress. He is also known for developing the celebrated *6 Trait* writing analysis, a developmental model particularly well suited to process skills that do become more polished with practice. Those skills, rather than isolated facts, are of course the focus of reading, writing, and mathematics computation. A rubric is a self-assessment tool as well as a grading tool, because the descriptions of each stage of quality help the student analyze *what makes a good one.*

Stiggins neither promotes nor discourages any particular type of assessment but strongly makes the case that not all learning can best be measured the same way. One can readily see how this becomes a tool for *backward planning, reverse engineering,* or planning *with the end in mind.* Both the essay items and performance tasks identified in Figure 11.3 (p. 137) require rubrics because they involve more than one right answer and multiple criteria.

Figure 11.2 Assessment Alternatives

♦ **Computer adaptive testing:** Any assessment, other than multiple-choice questions or worksheets, that requires the student to respond to the assessment items or task with the aid of a computer.

♦ **Enhanced multiple-choice:** Any multiple-choice question that requires more than the selection of one correct response. Most often, the task requires the students to explain their responses.

♦ **Extended-response, open-ended:** Any item or task that requires the student to produce an extended written response to an item or task that does not have one right answer (e.g., an essay or laboratory report).

♦ **Group-performance:** Any assessment that requires students to perform the assessment task in a group setting.

♦ **Individual-performance:** Any assessment that requires the student to perform (in a way that can be observed) an assessment task alone.

♦ **Interview:** An assessment technique in which the student responds to verbal questions from the assessor.

♦ **Nontraditional test items:** Any assessment activity other than a multiple-choice item from which the student selects one response. These items or performances are rated using a predetermined set of performance criteria in the form of a scoring guide or a scoring rubric or in comparison to benchmark papers or performances.

♦ **Observation:** An assessment technique that requires the student to perform a task while being observed and rated using a predetermined set of scoring criteria.

♦ **Portfolio:** An accumulation of a student's work over time that demonstrates growth toward the mastery of specific performance criteria against which the tasks included in the portfolio can be judged.

♦ **Project, exhibition, or demonstration:** The accomplishment of a complex task over time that requires demonstrating mastery of a variety of desired outcomes, each with its own performance criteria, that can be assessed within the one project, exhibition, or demonstration.

♦ **Short-answer, open-ended:** Any item or task that requires the production of a short written response on the part of the respondent. Most often, there is a single right answer (for example, a fill-in-the-blank or short written response to a question).

Source: Adapted from Council of Chief State School Officers/North Central Regional Educational Laboratory. The status of state student assessment programs in the United States. Cited in Caudell, L. S. (1996). High stakes: Innovation meets backlash as states struggle with large-scale assessment. *NW Education, 2*(1), 36.

Figure 11.3 An Assessment Blueprint

TOOLS	Selected Response	Essay Items	Performance or Product	Personal Communication
TARGETS				
Knowledge				
Reasoning				
Skill				
Product				
Disposition				
SCORING	Key	Rubric	Rubric	Rubric

Source: Stiggins, R. (2001). *Student involved classroom assessment.*

Stiggins' primary contributions to the new paradigm include the idea of an assessment blueprint that matches targets to tools, the rubric tool to show development and complexity, and assessment as a domain worthy of serious staff development efforts.

Is It Working?

By the mid-1990s the alternative assessment movement had gained wide support throughout the country, and alternative assessment procedures were being implemented in nearly every state. Bond and Roeber's research (1995) found that "state assessment remains a significant tool for educational reform in 45 states." They noted, "Students are assessed most often with a combination of traditional and alternative assessments" and that the "use of assessments continues to grow" (p. 9). A decade or more later, the movement seems to have found a permanent niche.

As is so often the case in the annals of educational innovation, there were few skeptical articles early on. Blaine Worthen (1993), however, provided a careful analysis of the issues and sounded a cautionary note. We present his more salient points in Figure 11.4. In an earlier book Fouts and I wrote about these issues stating that "anyone who seriously sets out on the alternative assessment trail needs to consider these possible objections," and that Worthen's critique "is a useful primer in what might go wrong. The issues of conceptual clarity, standardization, public acceptance, feasibility, and technical quality, to name a few, are not trivial concerns" (Ellis & Fouts, 1996, p. 174).

Figure 11.4 Critical Issues
Facing Alternative Assessment

♦ **Conceptual clarity.** There is too little coherence of the concepts and language used about alternative, performance, authentic, and direct assessment.

♦ **Mechanisms for self-criticism.** Internal self-criticism is rather scarce among proponents of alternative assessment but is the only road to continuing improvement.

♦ **Support from well-informed educators.** Classroom teachers must be both willing and able to use the alternatives, so it requires much more assessment literacy.

♦ **Technical quality and truthfulness.** The crux of the matter is whether or not the alternative assessment movement will be able to show that its assessments accurately reflect whether a student's true abilities are relevant to adult life.

♦ **Standardization of assessment judgments.** How to standardize criteria and performance levels sufficiently to support necessary comparisons without causing them to lose the power and richness of assessment tailored to the student's needs and achievements remains a daunting issue.

♦ **Ability to assess complex thinking skills.** Do alternative modes of assessment necessarily require the use of more complex processes by students? Proponents cannot assume that students are using such skills just because they are performing a hands-on task.

♦ **Acceptability to stakeholders.** Alternative assessments are difficult to use to report learning outcomes for entire classes, school districts, or state systems to provide evidence for accountability.

♦ **Appropriateness for high-stakes assessment.** Does alternative assessment provide sufficient standardization—for all students, including ethnic minorities and others traditionally marginalized or underprepared for academic success—to defend high-stakes decisions based on such measures? Will the inevitable legal challenges aimed at critical decisions based on alternative assessments be more difficult to defend because of validity and reliability questions?

♦ **Feasibility.** Does alternative assessment produce sufficiently greater benefits to justify its increased costs, or is it simply not feasible for large-scale efforts?

Source: Adapted from Worthen, B. (1993). Critical issues that will determine the future of alternative assessment. *Phi Delta Kappan, 74,* 444–454.

Years later, it is worthwhile to examine the status of the movement in relation to these issues. Apropos of this, the following headlines have appeared in recent issues of *Education Week:* "The New Breed of Assessments Getting Scrutiny"; "Even as Popularity Soars, Portfolios Encounter Roadblocks"; "Kentucky Student Assessment Called 'Seriously Flawed'"; "New Assessments Have Little Effect on Content, Study Finds"; and "Assessment Reform at a Crossroads: A Retreat from Performance-Based Practice May Signal the Return to Failed Forms of Testing."

Indeed, some states that had adopted or attempted to implement statewide alternative assessment systems have begun to temporize. And efforts in other states are bogged down. Bond and Roeber (1995) wrote, "Although there have been some successes...the setbacks in California, Arizona, Indiana, and elsewhere indicate that widespread acceptance of performance assessment is certainly not automatic" (p. 25).

Worthen's analysis of the critical issues facing alternative assessment were right on target. Many of the issues he identified have yet to be resolved, and these problems have been pointed out by a number of writers (Neill, 1996; Caudell, 1996; Olson, 1995; Viadero, 1995; Bond & Roeber, 1995). Specific concerns remain:

◆ There are unresolved technical issues of reliability (basically consistency in scoring across scores and consistency in scoring from school to school or state to state) and validity (i.e., do they really reflect higher thinking skills, or life skills).

◆ As yet there is no way to standardize the assessments for *high stakes* purposes (e.g., accountability, program evaluation, and college admission).

◆ There is less-than-widespread public support among many parent and political groups.

◆ There is insufficient funding or commitment for the needed widespread teacher training demanded by alternative assessment procedures.

◆ There is no evidence that alternative assessment procedures are more equitable to certain groups than are traditional assessment procedures.

◆ The estimated costs of various alternative assessment procedures on a large scale run from 5 to 30 times the cost of standardized multiple-choice tests, with no evidence that there is a cost benefit to them.

All these issues are embedded in Worthen's earlier critique, and consequently, on a large-scale basis (state assessments, district assessments) the movement appears to have encountered a minor roadblock. Still, the alternative assessment movement has encouraged many teachers to examine their sense of the purpose of assessment, and that itself is an invaluable outcome.

Educational Research and Alternative Assessment

Researchers are just beginning to address the questions of whether or not the use of such assessment strategies actually changes teacher behavior, student learning, or the curriculum. Reports from Vermont and Kentucky suggest that the strategies can have a positive effect for changing classroom activities, whereas reports from Arizona and elsewhere suggest that that is not necessarily so. Research done by Martin-Kniep, Sussman, and Meltzer (1995), for example, has shown that the assessment piece can be a vehicle by which teachers examine the role of the teacher and student in the learning process, but a well-designed staff development program is probably vital to make this happen.

There are two clear strands of research interest: the design of the performance tasks that would be considered an alternative way to gather information about learning (compared to traditional paper-and-pencil, one-right-answer tests) and the design of the instruments used to assess learning in a given alternative performance task. As seen in Stiggins' blueprint (see Figure 11.3, p. 137), a rubric is the tool of choice to assess multiple criteria in one complex task.

An example of such a task is a concept map. This should make it possible for a student to demonstrate integrated knowledge. Fair enough. The problem is in the design of the rubric, because the map is primarily intuitively constructed with logic but great variety. Perhaps a more holistic format would serve the purpose of the teacher better than the type that reduces the parts to more easily measured criteria. For example, a concept map could be assessed for its number of concepts, hierarchal levels, and cross-links.

Besterfield-Sacre et al. (2004) attempted to develop "a quantitative, robust, and efficient scoring tool" for concept maps. They compared the results derived from the use of two different rubrics to score the same concept maps. They noted that the traditional rubric was good for reducing masses of information to a few numbers, but they questioned whether the final numbers were truly representative of what each student knew. They did find that the holistic rubric scores revealed more information and identified weaknesses in the program as students moved through it.

Research by Cotton (1995) identified the following assessment-related findings from among a long list of effective classroom and effective school attributes:

- Teachers make use of alternative assessments as well as traditional tests.
- Administrators and other building leaders develop and use alternative assessments.
- District leaders and staff support schools' development and use of alternative assessments.

However, these are only 3 of 59 characteristics that Cotton noted in her description of effective schools. Obviously, these findings cannot be considered terribly persuasive evidence to suggest that alternative assessment procedures will lead to greater student achievement. They merely tell us that alternative assessment procedures seem to be present in schools deemed effective.

Gredler (1995) sounded a note of caution regarding the use of alternative assessments as measures of learning. She examined what research there is on alternative assessment procedures and concluded that

> at present, portfolio assessments are not recommended as the primary source of evidence about the attainment of program goals in evaluations that compare curricula or programs. The lack of validity and reliability information makes judging a curriculum or program on the scores assigned to student portfolios problematic at best. (p. 435)

She stated further, "The use of portfolios for other purposes that differ from fostering individualized student growth or demonstrating the intrinsic value of a program, leads, to no surprise, to problems and unresolved issues" (p. 435).

Finally, one driving force behind the impetus to improve and even *standardize* alternative assessment is the mandate to include students with special needs in statewide testing procedures. With the implementation of the Adequate Yearly Progress requirements stipulated in the No Child Left Behind Act (NCLB) of 2001, states are greatly concerned about students who are not able to perform at target levels. Of course, they are no doubt also keen to help these challenged students learn to read and write and solve mathematics problems. As Byrne (2004) noted, "When students with disabilities are included in systemwide testing, their performance matters more to everyone" (p. 63). It is a cynical idea that learning disabled students should be given greater notice simply because their test results will be included in the mix. For whatever reason students are accorded greater attention, however, this may well serve to close the gap between teaching and learning on the one hand and assessment on the other.

Conclusion

The alternative assessment movement is in many ways a breath of fresh air in an atmosphere gone stale. Traditional tests and measures have so many obvious shortcomings that I hardly need to review that ground in the closing moments of this chapter. Still, it would be a strategic blunder to conclude that traditional measures have no value. It would be unwise to abandon them in spite of the allure of authentic approaches. Both are needed. As hybrid forms of the two types emerge, there seems to be hope for rapprochement. I will make the controversial statement here that teachers and students simply do not do enough assessing in school settings. We need more of it. Assessment at its best is the stuff of reflection, metacognition, communication, and moral judgment. I thank the alternative assessment movement for the reminder. In fact, the movement may be as much about teaching and learning strategies as it is about assessment. And its lasting contribution may well be the bringing of teaching, learning, and assessment into a seamless whole.

12

Mastery Learning

We believe this solution is relevant at all levels of education including elementary—secondary, college, and even at the graduate and professional school level.

Benjamin Bloom

Bloom's 1968 piece ["Learning for Mastery"] is indeed one of the most generative works to appear in the educational psychology literature in decades.

Glenn Hymel & Walter Dyck

In 1963 John Carroll wrote an article in the *Teachers College Record* entitled, "A Model for School Learning" (Carroll, 1963). It was in that article that Carroll laid the groundwork for mastery learning when he stated that time spent and time needed to learn are keys to achievement. Carroll emphasized that given sufficient opportunity to learn (allocated equity instruction time), and time spent actually learning (engaged learning time), the vast majority of students can achieve some specified, expected level of performance.

Benjamin Bloom is credited with making the concept practicable when he developed an instructional system designed to eliminate connotations of failure by allowing students to successfully acquire basic skills before moving on, in sequential fashion, to increasingly difficult skills. Bloom outlined his premise in an important article (1968), "Learning for Mastery." It is a clear path to trace the beginnings of this movement back to the work of Carroll and Bloom. Since those early days, mastery learning has found a niche, and has been used in over 30 countries around the world (Hymel & Dyck, 1993).

Mastery learning is distinguished from other approaches by focusing attention on the organization of time and resource to ensure that students are able to master instructional objectives. The compelling argument made by advocates is that mastery learning, when properly implemented, results in increased student achievement.

The theoretical construct on which mastery learning is based is simple: All children can learn when they are provided with conditions that are appropriate for their learning. This means that no two persons will necessarily learn at the same rate. We already know that, but surprisingly, schools seldom take it into account. In subject areas where the sequential learning of skills and concepts is at stake, it is all too often the case that when students fall behind, they are doomed to mediocrity of performance at best and failure at worst. This is indeed a tragedy if Bloom and Carroll are right: The material itself is not too difficult for the student to learn, and given an appropriate amount of time, the student in fact *would* learn it.

Reductionism at Work

Although the antecedent conditions of mastery learning have been traced back over the centuries, its basis for curricular application can readily be seen in the work of Ralph Tyler of the University of Chicago. Tyler argued that curriculum should be organized around clearly defined educational objectives, the achievement of which can be ascertained through measures that also reflect those objectives (Tyler, 1949). This position, which became popularly known as the *Tyler rationale,* has a certain appealing symmetry. It is a behaviorist position premised on the idea of reductionism. Reductionism states that most tasks can be reduced to smaller parts, which can be clearly identified and sequenced. This premise is at odds with most progressive learning theories that tend to be *holistic* in nature. Progressives argue that by reducing ideas to parts certain intangibles are lost in the process. So, we have the great philosophical divide over whether the whole is equal to or greater than the sum of its parts.

Tyler's thinking represented a refinement of those of his own mentor, Franklin Bobbitt, who in turn had been greatly influenced by the work of the inventor and engineer, Frederick Winslow Taylor. Taylor is considered to be the father of scientific management, particularly as it has been applied for nearly a century to industrial settings. He wrote a number of published articles in the late nineteenth and early twentieth centuries on such topics as piece-rate systems, notes on (conveyor) belting, and shop management. The idea in each was that any form of factory work done by unskilled laborers could be broken down into constituent parts, sequenced, mastered, and made more efficient. The goal, of course, was increased production of goods. Taylor's ideas became so popular and in demand that, in time, he published them in the small, but highly influential book *Principles of Scientific Management* (1911). It was only a matter of time before his ideas on factory work were appropriated by Franklin Bobbitt and Ralph Tyler, among others, and later by Bloom himself, as having potential for school learning.

At any rate, Tyler's celebrated rationale based on clearly purposed, specified, and measured experiences is essential to such classroom applications as behavioral objectives, lesson plans, teacher monitoring and adjusting, criterion-based testing, and therefore, mastery learning. The process is linear, beginning with purpose and ending with assessment, but it is also spiraled in that a successful assessment leads upward to the next level, and so on. An important part is the clear target, or outcome expected.

However, one does not need to start with purpose to maintain linearity. One can just as easily begin the process by stating the desired outcomes, which of course, is also a sense of purpose. Outcomes Based Education (OBE) is (or *was*—the term has largely disappeared from the scene) "a comprehensive approach to teaching and learning and to instructional management with roots in the Mastery Learning and Competency-Based Education movements of the early 1970s" (Murphy, 1984). Figure 12.1 illustrates the design-down principle in which one begins with clarity of focus on desired outcomes, which then become the controlling factor in curriculum and instruction decision making.

Figure 12.1 Outcome-Based Design Sequence: A Mastery Learning Exemplar

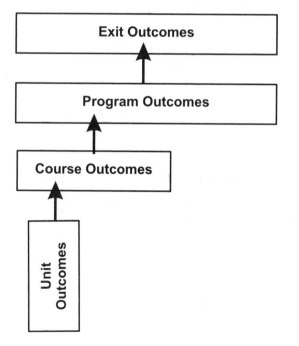

If the outcomes are taken seriously, the thinking goes, then expanded opportunities and support for learning to truly happen must be put into place. As you might imagine, this opens the door for mastery learning, generally an element of OBE. Figure 12.2 outlines the guiding principles.

Figure 12.2 Guiding Principles for OBE *Vlike b*

◆ **Clarity of focus on outcomes** Curriculum, instruction, and evaluation should all be closely aligned with the desired educational outcomes. Students should always know what learning is expected of them and where they are in relation to the expected outcomes at all times.

◆ **Design down from ultimate outcomes** Curriculum and instructional decisions should be determined by the desired educational outcomes, rather than the other way around.

◆ **Expanded opportunity and instructional support** Content coverage is replaced by instructional coaching to ensure that the content is mastered, using formative evaluation, *second chance* instruction, and continual teacher encouragement and support.

◆ **High expectations for learning success** The teachers' underlying philosophy is that all students can learn and expect high-quality work from students. Consequently, students may be expected to redo substandard work, take incomplete, and retake tests when necessary.

Source: Spady, W. G. (1988). Organizing for results: The basis of authentic restructuring and reform. *Educational Leadership, 46*(2), 7.

Built into the equation as an element of belief or philosophy of OBE is the success principle. The success principle implies that all students can learn and produce work of good quality, although it can take some students longer or more repeated efforts to do so than others.

Often mastery learning and OBE are thought of as synonymous. However, they are not the same thing. OBE was an overall planning and restructuring process at the macro level of school or district policy; it frequently involves mastery learning as a vital element. Mastery learning, as Benjamin Bloom defined it, is a *micro* level process. One implements it at the classroom level, and it is generally considered a part of the teaching and learning process. Thomas Guskey (1994) has made an interesting analysis of this relationship. He maintains that the guiding principles of OBE were set forth in Ralph Tyler's (1949) *Basic Principles of Curriculum and Instruction,* mentioned earlier, in which he posed four questions to be addressed by anyone who sets out to plan, develop, or implement a program of curriculum and instruction. In these four basic questions, Tyler addresses purpose, experience, organization, and assessment. Put another way, the questions ask why, what, how, and whether. That's all straightforward enough, and it would appear to encompass the required conditions of teaching and learning. Tyler's approach to curriculum and instruction is rational, logical, systematic, and linear. This is the basis of mastery learning:

- What educational purposes should the school seek to attain?
- What educational experiences can be provided that are likely to attain these purposes?
- How can these educational experiences be effectively organized?
- How can we determine whether these purposes are being attained?

Mastery learning is deeply invested in behaviorism. All the protocols are there: reinforcement, contingency planning, monitoring, and feedback with correctives and adjustments. It is safe to say that mastery learning is teacher-directed in the sense that the teacher directs the flow of learning, typically using a combination of teacher explication and prepared materials such as worksheets. The point is that students do not simply choose what they will do or how or when they will do it. Someone other than the student directs the learning. So, an element of behaviorism, de facto programmed learning, is either explicitly or implicitly present. Students are expected to demonstrate in some overt or performance sense that they have learned (mastered) the material to some acceptable level (typically, 80 percent correct) to move on to the next piece.

The argument is often made that mastery learning is method-neutral. But if it were, this would allow for indirect methods, including discovery and inquiry as well as self-realization activities. To carry out such activities using mastery protocols would seem curious, to say the least. It could well be said, however, that mastery learning is *content*-neutral simply because one could identify anything deemed worth learning and break it down into constituent, sequenced parts to be studied and tested.

Before we consider the practical implementation of mastery learning, let's clarify the major premises on which mastery learning procedure is founded:

- All students can learn and succeed, not necessarily in the same way or at the same rate.
- Success breeds success (just recall the old saying than nothing succeeds like success).
- Schools control the conditions of success.

A weekly after E "Catch up Club" - come w questions clarifications.

148   Research on Educational Innovations, Fourth Edition

w lunch time.

These three essential principles were oft-touted in the literature of outcomes based education, but they serve as a template for mastery learning in general.

I mentioned earlier that the idea that all students can learn the curriculum traces back to the work of John Carroll (1963). Carroll's thesis, which in time was adopted by Benjamin Bloom, was that the issue is not whether a student can learn the curriculum, but the length of time it might take the student to learn it. Carroll suggested that we have confused time with ability, unwittingly rewarding those who are able to keep up with the daily flow of events and punishing slower or more deliberate (not necessarily less intelligent) students.

The second premise, success breeds success, is something that each of us knows experientially. Some research has shown (Walberg, 1984) that the motivation to learn academic subject matter is primarily the result of prior learning. In other words, the rich get richer and the poor get poorer. The more you know, the more you want to know.

The third premise, schools control the conditions of success, is depressing if one thinks of the realities of school life for many children who walk down the lonely roads of mediocrity and failure every day. On the other hand, it is an empowering idea if one thinks of the possibilities. Again, the idea is that by reconceptualizing our sense of purpose, we will think in terms of success for all rather than a competitive system where learning is treated as a scarce resource available only to a few. *Tutoring*

build curric around outcomes Reversing the Order of Things

The traditional school-practice paradigm is one of writing objectives for a curriculum that is already in place or has undergone some degree of modification. Mastery learning turns the paradigm on its head. Desired outcomes are specified, and the learning sequence is built around them.

In mastery learning the curriculum and the resulting educational experiences flow from the outcomes that have been determined to be crucial. OBE advocates called this the design-down principle. That is to say, one begins by thinking about the loftiest outcomes possible long before one specifies the tasks and tests of school life. How that is different from beginning with goal statements, as some people have done for years, is unclear. Advocates of outcome-based education would answer that although people claim to have started with goal statements for years, the fact that they seldom questioned the given axioms of school life (time, subject matter, custody, etc.) speaks for itself. In other words most goal statements are made without thinking outside the box.

Accordingly all, or nearly all, students can learn the third-grade mathematics curriculum, for example, but they will naturally learn it at different rates. This ought not surprise us, but apparently it does given that in most classrooms the majority of students are expected to learn at roughly the same rate. Centuries ago, Aesop taught us in the fable of *The Tortoise and the Hare* that speed and accomplishment are not synonymous.

Level II Research

At Level II, some people like to point to the research base for mastery learning as evidence for the effectiveness of OBE (as I did in the previous edition of this book), but, as Slavin (1995) has stated, this is probably not correct to do. In any event, mastery learning does not necessarily show the efficacy of OBE because, as Guskey points out, the two are not really the same things. As Slavin writes, "This being the case, advocates on both sides of the debate have attempted to make inferences about OBE from other areas of research." When considered apart from mastery learning, we are not aware of small-scale experimental studies that look at the efficacy of outcome-based education, although there is no shortage of anecdotal stories and claims made about its value. Earlier, King and Evans (1991) also concluded that published research was limited. In fact, Slavin (1995) stated, "To my knowledge, no studies directly compare students in OBE classes or schools to students in similar control schools" (p. 14). We couldn't find any either.

Implementation of Mastery Learning

There are two forms of mastery learning, but they share common elements. One form is *individualized-instruction* and the other is *group-based mastery learning*. Individualized instruction is commonly based on the premise of continuous progress (note the linear terminology) where students work entirely at their own rates. Individualized instruction done within the frame of mastery learning involves the establishment of formative evaluation procedures along the way, mastery criteria for unit tests, and corrective activities for those learners who fall short of a given criterion on the first or following attempts. An interesting example of this form is known as the Kellar Plan or Personalized System of Instruction (Simmons, 1974). It is used mainly at the postsecondary level with unit objectives established for a course of study. Tests accompany each unit. Students can take the tests in different but parallel forms as many times as they need to until they achieve mastery or a passing score.

Another example of individualized-instruction mastery learning is used in certain private Christian schools. It is called ACE, or Accelerated Christian Education, a complete K–12 curriculum. In this program students progress on their own through a series of workbooks for each subject in the curriculum. Each unit has a test that students can take as many times as needed until they reach the mastery criterion, which is 80 percent correct. The role of the teacher is to monitor progress and to lend assis-

Aint like the teacher—e reboot in programs.

tance where it is required. In this program, students can complete the 13 years of education in more or less time, depending on their ability, motivation, rate of learning, and so forth.

The second form of mastery learning, group-based learning, is most closely associated with the work of Benjamin Bloom. Bloom posed an intriguing learning concept that he called the Two Sigma Problem (Bloom, 1984). He and his associates at the University of Chicago discovered that average achievers could raise their scores on criterion measures by two standard deviations (two sigma) if they were to shift from group learning to tutorial learning. What we are talking about here is moving someone from the 50th percentile to about the 98th percentile, which is not a bad move. This felicitous outcome appeared to hold up across subject matter boundaries. However, the noted researcher Robert Slavin has pointed out that the experiments were brief laboratory studies that he felt would not hold up under more prolonged school conditions.

Critics quickly pointed out, of course you can raise students' achievement by giving them individual attention as opposed to what happens in a class of 30 or so. But the real question is what happens in a tutorial that brings about the dramatic difference in achievement? The answer to that question might shed some light on how classrooms could be reconfigured to take advantage of the elements of tutorial teaching and learning. One answer could be found in peer teaching. Another could be found in cooperative learning. But mostly group-based mastery learning has been carried out using something along the lines of Madeline Hunter's Instructional Theory Into Practice (ITIP) procedures, which involve reducing learning to manageable units and daily lesson objectives, teaching to those objectives, formative evaluation activities, reteaching when necessary, and summative assessment. Figure 12.3 illustrates the group-based mastery learning approach.

Related to these principles is the recent focus on achievement goal theory. Of interest is not the teaching strategy of using continuous assessment to monitor linear progress but seeking to understand the motivation for learning. According to Elliot and McGregor (2001) there are four orientations that students can have: A *mastery-approach* goal is focused on learning as much as possible. Students would be motivated to meet a challenge or improve a score. In comparison, a *mastery-avoidance* orientation is seen in students who want to avoid failure. Students interested in public demonstrations of achievement have a *performance-approach* goal whereas those who are afraid of others seeing them as less able than their fellow students (or less than perfect) would have a *performance-avoidance* goal. This is an important theory because it addresses the underlying motivation of the student. Many opinions about mastery learning imply motivational theory, such as the encouragement of more chances or the discouragement of more work. The technique of mastery learning—frequent

Figure 12.3 Components of Group-Based Mastery Learning

- **Planning** Content or skill to be learned is analyzed and divided into small units with related specific objectives and performance criteria. Preinstruction assessment identifies instructional starting point.

- **Instruction** Teachers use appropriate strategies based on careful sequencing of the learning. In many instances, direct instruction is used involving modeling and practice.

- **Formative Evaluation** Assessment is frequently used throughout the instructional process to determine if the learner is mastering the sequential prerequisite skills.

- **Reteaching** Based on the formative evaluation results, the student is retaught material as needed with new or alternative approaches or examples and with additional practice.

- **Final Evaluation** Assessment to determine the degree to which the new content or skills have been mastered.

assessment, reteaching, and reassessment—creates a classroom environment that at least attempts to take into account motivation from the standpoint that the most powerful motivation to learn an academic subject is prior success with that subject.

The complexity of the group mastery learning model means that any one of the parts can be varied, making research design difficult. There is no limit to the refinements of the model. For example, one part of the model is reteaching: Anything the teacher does in direct response to the student's initial efforts. Another term for this is *feedback,* which puts a step between learning and the step of final evaluation. Konold and Miller (2004) recommended matching the type of feedback to the probable reason for the answer, as seen in Figure 12.4 (p. 152).

Such useful insights may well lead to further innovation, research (one hopes) and refinement of mastery learning. We'll have to wait and see. For the time being, most studies point to beneficial outcomes. A few questions have, however, been raised about mastery learning's efficacy over time. Let us turn our attention now to the research literature.

Figure 12.4 Differentiated Feedback Guidelines

If the student answers...	Then the teacher should...
Accurately and firmly	Affirm the accuracy; quickly move on
Accurately but hesitantly	Acknowledge with explanation
Incorrectly and carelessly	Correct answer, quickly move on
Incorrectly but without sufficient knowledge base	Prompt, cue, explain

The Research Base for Mastery Learning

The Level I foundation of mastery learning is confusing. Everyone from Pestalozzi to Skinner is supposedly a developer of the deep structure. The problem, of course, is the confusion that results philosophically when educators think that what they are doing effectively crosses the lines from essentialist to progressive orientations.

The amount of Level II research on mastery learning is formidable, if not terribly recent. But as one colleague quipped, "It appears the case has been made." Among those programs examined in this text, only the cooperative-learning research base compares favorably with it in quality and volume. The research base extends back over three decades. It includes individual studies, major reviews, best evidence syntheses, and meta-analyses of mastery learning research.

The earliest synthesis of mastery learning research was conducted by Block and Burns (1976). They found consistently positive results for mastery learning. They also reported that mastery learning improved affective outcomes. Thus students were not merely learning more; they felt better about school and themselves as a result of their experience.

Kulik, Kulik, and Cohen (1979) conducted the next review. Their review covered 75 studies of Kellar's Personalized System of Instruction (PSI). They found consistently higher achievement, less variability of achievement, and higher student ratings in college classes where PSI was used.

The most celebrated mastery learning studies were those conducted by Bloom and his associates (1984) mentioned earlier in this chapter. Bloom's research consistently showed that group mastery learning produced an effect size of 1.0. This means that students who are tutored and who raise their achievement 2.0 effect sizes, or two standard deviations, will raise their achievement one standard deviation above the mean in a group-based mastery learning situation. To raise achievement by an effect size of 1.0 represents an incredible outcome so great that one researcher called group-based mastery learning the educational equivalent of penicillin.

The individual studies and reviews continued apace. Guskey and Gates (1986) found positive effect sizes for students at both elementary and secondary levels. The effect sizes were not as large as those found by Bloom but were still deemed educationally significant. And contrary to what one might hypothesize, the most efficacious outcomes were found in language arts and social studies rather than in reading and mathematics where one might expect to find them.

Guskey and Pigott (1988) used a much larger database than those found in past reviews seeking the effects of mastery learning. Again, the results showed that mastery learning yielded consistently positive results with respect to both cognitive and affective outcomes. The findings were consistently positive across subject areas and types of measures used, whether criterion referenced or norm referenced. Effect sizes were larger at elementary levels than at secondary or college levels.

Kulik and Kulik (1986–87) examined the research that focused on the effects of *mastery testing*—a single facet of mastery learning. Of the 49 studies they reviewed, 47 indicated positive effect sizes. They suggested that even though mastery testing is only one part of mastery learning, it could be the most important part in helping to raise student achievement. Stallings and Stipek (1986) and Walberg (1985) also give mastery learning generally positive reviews and suggest that the research supports its implementation into the school curriculum. *as always*

The only cautionary note is sounded by Slavin (1987):

> I required that the studies had to have taken place over at least four weeks. The studies that produced the big effects—the ones that Bloom talks about and that are cited in a lot of other mastery learning syntheses—were conducted in three days, one week, two weeks, three weeks. Requiring that the treatment had to be in place for at least four weeks brings down the mastery learning studies to a very small number, and I think that even four weeks is really too short. (Brandt, 1988a, p. 24)

Slavin goes on to point out that in the few mastery learning studies where a genuine control group was in place, the difference in achievement between experimental and control groups was virtually nonexistent. Essentially, he appears to be saying that the studies in mastery learning lackfactors affecting external and internal validity. This would seriously compromise the practical effects of these studies.

Block, Guskey, Bloom, and Walberg have all questioned Slavin's conclusions. Guskey wrote that "[t]he results of these best-evidence syntheses...are often potentially biased, highly subjective, and likely to be misleading" (1988, p. 26). Guskey went on to say that Slavin used an "idiosyn-cratic approach" to reach his conclusions, and a considerable body of research shows that mastery learning works regardless of the length of the study. Block, Bloom, and Walberg agree.

Slavin developed an innovative model designed to make the most of mastery learning as well as interactive practices, named encouragingly *Success for All.* The mastery of each level of literacy is frequently assessed, resulting in a flexible grouping of students as they individually progress. Regarding the Level III research on *Success for All,* Slavin (2004) noted, "A problem in the longevity of innovations is that educators willing to imple-ment one innovation are likely to be receptive to other innovations, too, leading to a flitting from one program to another." With admirable can-dor he cited the need for rigorous research for more than empirical justifi-cation. He addressed the psychological strategy of his own innovation at a corporate level: continuous assessment under tutelage increases awareness of success and becomes its own self-perpetuating of successful innovation.

He also identified a more prosaic factor:

> Almost all SFA [*Success for All*] schools fund their facilitators, tutors, and other continuing costs out of Title I and other fund-ing sources that are both dedicated to improving the achieve-ment of children in high poverty schools and relatively reliable. (p. 67)

Accordingly he revealed, "The close match between the focus of SFA and that of Title I certainly has contributed to the maintenance of the pro-gram through the inevitable shifts in non-Title I funds that all schools ex-perience" (p. 67).

The Level III research, or that done at the program evaluation level—particularly that done on *Success for All*— is positive with regard to achievement outcomes. It, too, has its critics, but the fact that the federal government has given huge sums of money in support of SFA speaks to its reputation as a program that works.

Conclusion

The research literature in mastery learning is largely positive. Some of the best-known names in educational research circles have weighed in as supporters of this approach to teaching and learning. In spite of Slavin's well-founded concerns, the research championing mastery learning is about as strong as one can find in the annals of educational investigation. Study after study indicates the superiority of mastery learning over tradi-tional methods in raising test scores.

For those who favor an essentialist approach to education—that is, one that emphasizes direct instruction in basic skills—there appears to be much promise here. If one's goal is raising test scores, mastery learning would seem to be worth serious consideration. After all, raising test scores is hardly a trivial goal. On the other hand, those who favor a more experiential approach, such as that advocated in progressive literature, should probably look elsewhere.

The significance of the innovation, however, is in its use of assessment not just to measure learning but to be a recursive function of learning and motivation. Mastery learning in all its variety is a practical innovation that rests on the teacher's close monitoring and subsequent adjustment of instruction. At worst, children are left to monitor themselves; whereas at best, children are coached encouragingly through small increments of improvement.

13

Curriculum Integration ✱ key ✓ of my ideas

You must not divide the seamless coat of learning.

Alfred North Whitehead

Students resort to the extracurriculum because the curriculum is so stupid

Robert Hutchins

Herein lies one of the problems with the notion of integrated curriculum: Do theory and practice converge to produce more thorough or comprehensive learning experiences for students, or do teachers run the risk of leaving wide gaps in students' understanding of important concepts and subject matter?

Terrance Mason

All things are connected.✱

Chief Seattle

The nationwide restructuring movement, particularly the move to block scheduling, has led many schools to consider implementing of integrated curriculums. The main arguments for an integrated curriculum, or interdisciplinary studies as they are sometimes called, are threefold: (a) The knowledge explosion is real and there is simply too much information to be covered in the curriculum; (b) most school subjects are taught in isolation, and students never are able to make the connections; and (c) curriculum integration is designed around problems and concerns students have about themselves and their world.⌐ ✱

I mentioned that integrated curriculum and interdisciplinary studies are sometimes thought to be the same thing. Although this is true in a sense, there is a fine distinction. Integrated curriculum is thematic; students study broad themes such as *Problems of Living, Life in the Future,* or

Conflicts and their Resolution. Interdisciplinary studies, on the other hand, represent a combining of two or more subjects (disciplines) to build connections between or among disciplines. Social studies is in fact interdisciplinary in that it represents a blend of geography, history, civics, and other social sciences adapted to children's or adolescents' needs and capabilities. The wishes of purists aside, for a number of practical reasons, *integrated* and *interdisciplinary* often are interpreted as roughly the same thing. In either case, they are both products of the progressive philosophy of education.

One idea behind integration is that by combining school subjects around themes or projects, a certain economy is achieved because much of the repetitious material that occurs from subject to subject is eliminated. And flowing from the first idea is a second: When subjects are connected, students begin to see meaningful relationships because the subject matter serves as a vehicle for learning rather than as an end in itself. And to this can be added a third idea: A subject-matter-driven curriculum, particularly one based on separate subjects, fails to address students' concerns about themselves and the world around them. These are among the primary claims of the advocates of curriculum integration. A rationale for the integration of the curriculum is presented in Figure 13.1.

Figure 13.1 Arguments *for* Curriculum Integration

♦ **Psychological/developmental**—Research in developmental and cognitive psychology suggests that individuals learn best when encountering ideas connected to one another.

♦ **Sociocultural**—The current curriculum, especially in the secondary school, is basically obsolete and does not address the needs, interests, and capacities of today's students.

♦ **Motivational**—The integrated curriculum de-emphasizes rote learning and content coverage; and because it is often organized around student-selected themes and provides for choice, it enhances student interest and motivation.

♦ **Pedagogical**—The traditional curriculum is so vast and intractable that educators cannot hope to cover all the so-called essentials for productive living, and therefore they should focus their efforts on providing experiences leading toward internalization of positive attitudes toward learning.

Heightened teacher collaboration, greater student involvement, increased relevance, greater learner motivation and achievement, higher-level thinking, better content mastery, real-world applications, and fewer fragmented learning experiences are among the improvements that supposedly follow suit when a change to integrated curriculum is made. Most teachers and administrators dream of these outcomes, so the claims tend to be rather attractive.

Yet there are many obstacles to implementing this, in any of the variations, as Figure 13.2 shows.

Figure 13.2 Obstacles to Curriculum Integration

♦ **The trivialization problem**—It is sometimes appropriate for teachers to address ideas within a single content area, and some ideas are best understood without introducing confusing or inconsequential subject matter.

♦ **The skills problem**—A number of educators maintain that students can attempt interdisciplinary work only after they have mastered some elements of disciplinary knowledge; and if integration activities dominate the curriculum, there will be inadequate time to teach these skills.

♦ **The teacher knowledge problem**—If teachers lack knowledge and skills within multiple disciplines, their ability to integrate those disciplines is highly problematic.

♦ **The school structure problem**—Many teachers have never experienced subject integration, being products of discipline-based schooling throughout their lives, so vast retraining and reconceptualizing must take place.

♦ **The assessment problem**—The mode of assessment in most school systems is unable to effectively assess students' attainment of deep understanding, the stated goal of integrated learning.

Source: Adapted from Mason, T. C. (1996). Integrated curricula: Potential and problems. *Journal of Teacher Education, 47*(4), 263–270.

Integrating the curriculum is not a new idea. The learning done in most *natural* situations including apprenticeships, for example, tends to be seamless. But in school settings, the idea of integrated learning and teaching came to the fore as part of the progressive educational movement of the early twentieth century. In ways that modern educators cannot even realize, the progressive movement achieved much in this regard. Language arts and social studies, *subjects* taken for granted in today's elementary curriculum, are themselves interdisciplinary versions of several former separate subjects. And at the secondary level many districts have for several years integrated their mathematics programs, shucking off the old algebra–geometry–advanced algebra sequence. There are many other examples of progressive influence, from Future Farmers of America (FFA) to the growing tendency to do *real world* investigations, which by definition are problem focused, not focused on a single discipline.

The current trend, however, goes somewhat further than the prior attempts to coalesce, for example, history, geography, and civics into something called social studies. Today the movement is dedicated to crossing new frontiers between and among school subjects. It should be noted, however, that the philosophical premise remains the same as that advanced during the original progressive movement. Let's take a moment to examine that premise.

All Things Are Connected

Traditional school programs tend to be centered on subjects; the organizing focus in teaching and learning is on separate school subjects or academic disciplines. In most cases, those subjects are offered separately, even in elementary classrooms. At the secondary level, the distinction is even clearer, as signaled by the organization of the school faculty into departments based on academic disciplines. Each subject has a sequence to it that generally becomes more technical and abstract through the succeeding years. Each subject also has a scope within a given grade level. The scope of a subject has to do with how broad or wide ranging the treatment. The scope and the sequence tend to represent the boundaries of a given subject; but the point is that the focus is always on the subject and its domain of knowledge and skills. The best way to understand the traditional curriculum is to think of its dominant form, the textbook. This is so because most textbooks are written for a particular subject at a particular level such as fourth-grade mathematics. You could search far and wide for a textbook on, for example, combined mathematics and music for seventh grade, but it is doubtful that you would find it; and if you did, how many schools are ready to adopt it? Perhaps it seems absurd to suggest that a textbook might combine music and mathematics, but to the ancient Greeks, who clearly saw the connection, this would have been perfectly logical.

Curriculum integration, on the other hand, takes a much different approach to teaching and learning. It is far more than a mere blending of separate subjects. It represents a philosophy of student-centered, often socially relevant, learning. By placing the learner rather than the subject matter at the center of gravity, projects and activities take precedence over academic disciplines. This is so because this seems to be the way children and adolescents learn when given a choice. In other words, it is closer to the *natural* way that people learn. The academic disciplines, from such a perspective, are regarded as tools for learning rather than as ends in themselves. If they are tools, the argument goes, why not blend them wherever it makes sense to do so? After all, the apprentice carpenter does not take separate classes in hammers, saws, and nails. The carpenter is taught to build, and these are tools to be used in building.

for paper.

Teachers and students are generally involved together in the planning and development of the theme or issue chosen for study. Figure 13.3 provides a step-by-step approach to developing such a unit.

Figure 13.3 A Procedure for Developing Integrated Units of Study

Step 1—Selecting an organizing center. The *organizing center* is the focus of the curriculum development (i.e., theme, topic of study, or concept). Once parameters are explored, the topic must be broadened to provide a base for investigation from various points of view in preparation for the next developmental step.

Step 2—Brainstorming associations. A graphic device (i.e., planning wheel) is useful as teachers and students begin to explore the theme from the perspectives of various discipline fields. The organizing center for the theme is the hub of the wheel; each spoke is a discipline area. The open-ended technique of brainstorming is used to generate spontaneous ideas that will be recorded on the wheel.

Step 3—Establishing guiding questions to serve as a scope and sequence. This step takes the array of brainstormed associations from the wheel and organizes them. Now the course of study begins to take shape. A framework for the unit of study will develop naturally as scope and sequence-guiding questions are developed.

Step 4—Writing activities for implementation. Guiding inquiry questions have been formulated; now the means for exploring them must be developed. Activity design is crucial because it discloses what students will be doing. Bloom's taxonomy is a good guideline for activity design to ensure the cultivation of higher-level thought processes.

Source: Jacobs, H. H. (Ed.) (1989). *Interdisciplinary curriculum: Design and implementation.* Alexandria, VA: ASCD, pp. 63–56.

Integrated programs typically eschew textbook treatments. Thus the curriculum is changed in more ways than one. Most American schools use textbook-driven curriculums. Textbooks tend to configure and control both scope and sequence. But integrated curriculums focus on group activities and projects; textbooks, if they are used at all, are relegated to the status of resource material. The curriculum still has to come from somewhere, and if it is not to come from textbooks, what are its sources?

Integrated settings tend to use a site-based curriculum. This is disconcerting to commercial publishers because generic textbooks published for use everywhere are simply not applicable. Integrated curriculums are often tied to local issues, especially when those local issues have global

textbooks cost a lot of money.

connections such as studies of local water supplies, wetlands, and pollu-
tion. Equally often, units will be constructed around a compelling theme
such as local architecture, patterns in nature, or cultural heritage.

Frequently a study begins with a brainstorming session where the
teacher leads students through the construction of a *webbing,* which develops visual and open-ended connections. The webbing, or map, gives
focus and structure to the unit, project, or investigation while allowing
many avenues of individual or group work. This stage is crucial, apparently, because the sense of ownership or investiture in the curriculum is
thought by advocates to be a motivating force throughout the study.

A criticism of integrated or interdisciplinary curriculums is one that is
obvious to any essentialist. Because the units are teacher–student developed, they have a seemingly random flavor. The essentialist's need for an
orderly scope and sequence of knowledge and skills is often not met, to
say the least. To integrated studies advocates, who tend to be progressives, this is the beauty of such a curriculum. It is fair to say, however, that
integrated curriculums often tend to favor social studies, language arts,
and the arts, although not necessarily in any systematic way, while slight-
ing mathematics, and this is a serious problem. It is not insoluble, but it is
difficult to overcome.

There is also a phenomenon known as *the tyranny of integration.* Sometimes teachers become so committed to integrated studies that they find
themselves trying to integrate everything they teach. This can quickly
lead to a different kind of artificiality. The fact of the matter is that not everything probably can or should be integrated. Matters of discretion become paramount when such factors are weighed. Integration is a *means* to
an end and not an end in itself, a simple idea that is too easily forgotten.

The Research Base for
Curriculum Integration

Remember John Dewey?

The primary theoretical basis of curriculum integration is found in
progressive educational philosophy. The progressive movement, which
included such luminaries as John Dewey, William Kilpatrick, George
Counts, and Harold Rugg, reached its zenith earlier this century. It is a
child-centered approach to learning that places great emphasis on creativity, activities, *naturalistic* learning, real-world outcomes, and above all,
experience.

Progressive education came to be known for what it opposed as much
as for what it advocated. This was a matter of great concern to Dewey and
others. Progressives were opposed to the factory-like efficiency model on
which schools depended (and still do). They decried the artificial instruc-

Fan of constructivism, & not behaviorism.

tion and learning driven by textbooks and written exams. They said that school learning was so unlike the real world that it has little or no meaning to the average child. This led to the invention of the *extracurriculum*. The idea of the extracurriculum is that it is genuine; it is team- or project-oriented. Robert Hutchins, certainly no progressive, said it best: "Students resort to the extracurriculum because the curriculum is so stupid."

In his classic work, *Interest and Effort in Education*, Dewey wrote eloquently, establishing the thesis of progressivism and therefore of integrated studies:

> Our whole policy of compulsory education rises or falls with our ability to make school life an interesting and absorbing experience to the child. In one sense, there is no such thing as compulsory education. We can have compulsory physical attendance at school; but education comes only through willing attention to and participation in school activities. It follows that the teacher must select these activities with reference to the child's interests, powers, and capacities. In no other way can she guarantee that the child will be present. (Dewey, 1913, p. ix)

key & paper

Such theorizing about the nature of education is foundational to integrated curricular efforts. The other, more recent theoretical basis for integrated curriculum is found in constructivist theory. It was noted in an earlier chapter that constructivism is a theory of learning that states that each person must construct his or her own reality. The constructivity principle states that "construction should always precede analysis" (Post et al., 1997, p. 10). Put another way, this means that experience is the key to meaningful learning; it is not someone else's encounter abstracted and condensed into textbook form, but one's own direct experience. The current interest in the contributions to thought and language made by the Russian psychologist Lev Vygotsky (1962; see also Moll, 1993) especially bolstered the argument for the social interaction so readily prevalent in the group projects associated with integrated and interdisciplinary teaching and learning. So, in this sense, the traditional curriculum of learning alone and doing mainly seat work is not merely turned around, it is stood on its head. Although the work done in constructivist thought is recent, it is essentially in harmony with the earlier thinking of the progressives.

Advocates of integrating the curriculum also cite Level I research in the area of brain function (see Chapter 5). They point to research indicating that the brain seeks patterns and that this is a basic process. They believe that the brain actually resists learning that is fragmented, personally meaningless, and presented in isolation. On the contrary, they note that knowledge is learned more quickly and remembered longer when constructed in a meaningful context where connections between and among ideas are made (Beane, 1997).

But not everyone agrees. The author Thomas Sowell was particularly critical of interdisciplinary teaching and learning, calling it "another popular buzzword." He noted that much of what passes for interdisciplinary is in fact "nondisciplinary, in that it simply ignores boundaries between disciplines." He stated further that

> academic disciplines exist precisely because the human mind is inadequate to grasp things whole and spontaneously, or to judge "the whole person." Thus mathematics must be separated out for special study, even though it is an ingredient in a vast spectrum of other activities. (Sowell, 1995, p. 205)

Sowell's point of view is shared by those who think that depth of subject matter, crucial coverage, the sequencing of important skills, and other related concerns are inevitably shortchanged in interdisciplinary efforts. Furthermore, this point of view holds that there are indeed many opportunities to relate any single discipline to other spheres of knowledge. Good teachers have always done this while preserving the integrity of their discipline.

Before we leave Level I, let's acknowledge another theory behind curriculum integration: systems theory. Influenced by Kurt Lewin's field theory and Morton Deutsch's model of interdependence, systems theory can be seen in such wide-ranging practices as cooperative learning and multiculturalism. True integration is not just an overlapping of compatible concepts and patterns and skills from different academic domains; it is also the disposition to be tolerant and sensitive to other perspectives.

To be fair, many textbooks now mention the connection to other academic disciplines in teachers' resource materials. Although textbooks themselves are seen by purists as a perversion and a sellout, certain textbooks do suggest projects with a range of knowledge and skill, including elaborate rubrics that measure different criteria. The question for research is not whether it improves achievement. Instead, researchers will question whether the lack of projects and integration will explain any failure to achieve adequately on standardized tests. Why? Teachers report they have no time to do the fun stuff now that *adequate yearly progress* (No Child Left Behind Act [NCLB], 2001) on standardized tests is governing their curriculum. Evidence in support of integrated curriculum may come from documenting the results of not using it.

Bold Claims—Little Evidence

Research at Levels II and III is somewhat dependent on investigations of highly related topics such as block scheduling, team teaching, and self-contained programs, where by inference, one might conclude that these approaches at least lend themselves to integration. This can be described by the observation that curriculum integration is itself a large

🖈 ⌐ all 3 how you implement it. As long as active engagement.

Curriculum Integration   165

holding company of educational variables that, put together, defies classic research methods. There would simply be too many variables to control if one set out to do traditional controlled studies of the topic as a whole. Often curriculum integration is *integrated* into other reform efforts such as block scheduling, which make the task of isolating the curriculum as a treatment variable difficult, to say the least. Additionally, assessment of the outcomes most sought after by advocates of this type of curriculum arrangement is problematic because of the tendency of advocates to challenge the validity of traditional paper-and-pencil testing.

Integrated curriculum in the context of middle school learning and its more complete context is thoughtfully addressed by Beane and Brodhagen in the *Handbook of Research on Teaching* (2001). They cite a number of advantages of interdisciplinary studies for middle school students and teachers. Their allusions to the benefits are carefully contextualized: They claim its efficaciousness in settings where a fully realized range of middle school philosophy has been put into practice. Thus they avoid the overly simplistic notion that any given innovation can or should succeed unless systemic change is brought about.

A qualitative study by Hargreaves and Moore (2000) addressed the relationship between curriculum integration and "classroom relevance" in the practices of 29 grade 7 and 9 teachers in Ontario, Canada, schools. Hargreaves and Moore interviewed the teachers, compiling more than 1,000 pages of write-up. In addition they held several group meetings with the teachers and conducted in-depth classroom observations of up to 10 days each in four of the teachers' classrooms. The purpose of the study was essentially to document the planning, actions, and reflections of a group of teachers committed to integration. The descriptions they provide of the teachers' reflections about their work with students are indeed useful to anyone contemplating the implementation of an integrated curriculum. Hargreaves and Moore concluded that

> successful and stimulating integration, we have learned, is most likely when teachers put students and what is relevant and meaningful for students first, and when they have the knowledge and imagination to draw widely on their own and others' subject expertise to make that relevance into an experience that is also rigorous for students. (p. 111)

Hargreaves and Moore also reached another conclusion, curious in light of the fact that they provide no related achievement data to accompany their claim that the teachers' work involved

> the use of higher-order thinking skills, the exercise of problem-solving capacities, the application of knowledge to real problems, the valuing of creativity and invention, the embedding of

learning in real time and real life, and the importance of learning collaboratively as well as individually. (p. 111)

One might reasonably expect that in the light of such claims, some empirical means of validation might be presented.

Lake (1994) examined the available research and concluded that there
are "no detrimental effects on learning when students are involved in an
integrated curriculum" (p. 7). How one can conclude that there are no detrimental effects is unclear, but perhaps Lake means that there have been
no *documented* or discernible detrimental effects. She was able to locate a
few studies dating back as far as 1965 to show that some students actually
learned more in the integrated curriculum, and she noted some educational advantages such as teacher cooperation. She was cautious about
reaching conclusions about the benefits of integrated studies, however,
because of the limited amount of research.

Morrow, Pressley, and Smith (1995) reported the interesting results of
a well-crafted study of the effects of integrating literacy and science programs. Their results indicate "clear support for integrating literacy and
science instruction at the third-grade level with respect to the development of language arts competencies," which "did not come at a cost to science content learning" (p. 25). If advocates of integrating the curriculum
wish to substantiate their enthusiastic claims with empirical data, additional studies will have to be conducted. At this stage, the number of empirical studies remains so small that any kind of meaningful meta-analysis that might point to some generalized findings is precluded.

Czerniak, Weber, Sandmann, and Ahern's (1999) review of the literature offers one of the best recent surveys of research findings in curriculum integration. They note that virtually every one of the major professional organizations supports the idea of curriculum integration. This
same assertion is made as well by Zemelman, Daniels, and Hyde (1998).
Czerniak and colleagues, however, observed that "few empirical studies
exist to support the notion that an integrated curriculum is any better than
a well-designed traditional curriculum" (p. 421).

A problem that Czerniak and colleagues cited as not incidental is the
lack of any agreed-on operational definition of curriculum integration.
Like whole language, the term means many things to many people. Terms
often used interchangeably include interdisciplinary, fused, thematic,
connected, nested, transdisciplinary, multidisciplinary, and sequenced.
As they pointed out, this only compounds the confusion when it comes to
talking about effectiveness. Lederman and Niess (1997) made the same
two charges, namely the lack of empirical evidence and confusion over
the meaning of terms.

Czerniak and colleagues, searching for supportive evidence cited the
following: Beane (1996) reported that, on traditional measures of school

achievement, students who experience an integrated curriculum do as well as if not better than students who experience a separate-subjects curriculum. Stevenson and Carr (1993) reported increased student interest and achievement in integrated instruction as did Greene (1991).

So in fairness, although it can be said that little empirical evidence exists, there is in fact some. Czerniak and colleagues noted the irony of discipline-based standards set forth by the various professional organizations while those same organizations at the same time advocate integrated curricular approaches.

Vars (1996) concluded that "more than 100 studies" have shown that students in interdisciplinary programs "do as well as, and often better than students in so-called conventional programs" (p. 148). His review of the research in interdisciplinary curriculum and instruction is actually more a summary and synthesis of findings than a critical, analytic examination of the quality of the research. In this light, one ought to be reluctant to conclude that the research base is convincingly supportive of integrated or interdisciplinary efforts. A reasonable assessment is that the number of confounding variables and rival hypotheses is sufficient to warrant caution. Still, Vars' contribution is considerable, and interested readers are advised to examine the many published studies he cites. Vars wisely observed, "In short, research on the effects of interdisciplinary curriculum and instruction affirms the benefits of these approaches, but warns against raising unrealistic expectations in the minds of teachers, students, or parents" (p. 159).

The difficulties inherent in conducting good Level II research have not kept enthusiasts from making wide-ranging claims of the efficacious outcomes of interdisciplinary curriculums. The following six claims are presented in the name of so-called research done in this area. Although the claims are intriguing and possibly accurate, they seem to go well beyond any sound empirical base at this time.

The first claim is that *interdisciplinary curriculum improves higher-level thinking skills.* Here the term *metacurriculum* is invoked. The term *metacurriculum* refers to the larger, more transcendent ideas that emerge when people focus on problems to be solved rather than on the reductionist, bits-and-pieces activities that occupy so much of school life. The suggestion is that students will become more skilled in flexible thinking as they are placed in learning situations that address connections rather than the kinds of computation, workbook, and seat-work skills of the traditional separate-subjects curriculum. The evidence that exists to substantiate this claim seems to be missing.

This leads to the second claim that *learning is less fragmented.* Students are provided with a more coherent set of learning experiences and, therefore, with a more unified sense of process and content. For example, if a theme such as *patterns in the environment* is selected for study, then knowl-

edge and skills from the various disciplines must *cohere* or integrate because they are merely means to a more relevant end, rather than being
ends in themselves. This thought has considerable appeal. Who wants to
argue against coherence? It is based on a logical discontinuity, however,
that could lead to the conclusion that a teacher who uses an interdisciplinary curriculum is more likely to present a more connected, coherent world
view of learning than does a teacher assigned to teach a single subject. In
fact, connections are what any good, well-informed teacher attempts to
make, and it is just possible that both subject-specific and general teacher
knowledge may have as much to do with the making of connections than
anything else.

Claim number three is that *interdisciplinary curriculum provides real-
world applications, hence heightening the opportunity for transfer of learning*. It
is often the case that interdisciplinary units have real-world connections
built into them, but that could be said as well of units taught within the
frame of a separate subject. However, the probability is greater that real-
world applications will take place in interdisciplinary curriculum settings
than in traditional school circumstances. There may be something to the
claim that interdisciplinary efforts with their real-world emphasis lead to
learning transfer, but in light of the scant evidence it is more a matter of
speculation than conclusion. After all, it is possible that a real-world emphasis may get in the way of the delayed gratification, difficult and sometimes tedious, long-term work necessary to fit people for careers in, for example, physics or the arts. Most skilled pianists, for example, had to spend
many hours studying music theory and practicing piano, delaying
relevance for years in many cases.

The fourth claim is that *improved mastery of content results from interdisciplinary learning*. The case is made in the literature for better understanding, greater retention, and even academic gains as demonstrated by test
scores. Perhaps so, but the evidence is not sufficiently in place. More often
the argument is that there is no evidence leading to conclusions that interdisciplinary curriculum and instruction causes harm to student achievement when compared to other approaches.

Claim number five is that *interdisciplinary learning experiences positively
shape a learner's overall approach to knowledge*. The concept is that students
will develop a heightened sense of initiative and autonomy in their thinking conduct. Similarly, students improve their moral perspective by
learning to adopt multiple points of view on issues. This is an interesting
hypothesis that should be tested empirically.

Sixth, the literature claims that *motivation to learn is improved in interdisciplinary settings*. Students become engaged in *thoughtful confrontation*
with subject matter. More students are reached because of the greater
need for different perspectives and learning styles in solving broad-based
problems. Teachers become more motivated because teacher-to-teacher

contact is enhanced as team efforts are required in planning, teaching, and evaluating. It is difficult to make the counterclaim that such an assertion is false; however, the claim itself lacks evidence.

To conclude that these claims are largely unsupported does not mean that they should be dismissed out of hand. To be more precise, they should be treated as important hypotheses for some focused Level II research. If the claims are changed to hypotheses, we have before us an excellent research agenda that should keep investigators busy for several years, much like good Level II research has been successfully conducted for the cooperative learning agenda.

There appears to be a minimal amount of activity at Level III, with some notable exceptions. *Humanitas,* an interdisciplinary humanities program for secondary students, was evaluated in the Los Angeles Unified School District using what appears to be a careful design (Aschbacher, 1991). The program evaluation, carried out by the Center for the Study of Evaluation at UCLA, could easily serve as a model for this type of sorely needed research. Achievement comparisons of *Humanitas* students and other students from comparison groups showed that the program had positive effects on writing and history content knowledge during the first year. The improvement continued as students stayed in the program, which they did in greater percentages than did their counterparts in four comparison schools. Other sophisticated aspects of the evaluation included surveys of students, teachers, and administrators; observations in classrooms; analyses of teachers' assignments and examinations; reviews of student portfolios; and an examination of such *educational indicators* as school attendance, discipline problems, and *college-oriented* behaviors by students. Classroom observation, for example, showed that *Humanitas* students spent more time per day in thoughtful discussions with a greater number of students contributing than did comparison groups. And even though *Humanitas* students received assignments judged to be harder than those given to comparison group students, the *Humanitas* students liked school better than the other students. I recommend a careful reading of the evaluation study (Aschbacher & Herman, 1989) by personnel in any district interested in doing serious program evaluation. It is a sophisticated, penetrating analysis that serves not only as a guide for meaningful program assessment but for planning and implementing programs.

The Eight Year Study: 1932–1940

Delving deep into the last century, one encounters what is generally considered to be the most celebrated program evaluation study ever conducted. It was called *The Eight Year Study,* sponsored by the Progressive Education Association, which is now defunct but was a potent force in education. The Eight Year Study (Aikin, 1942) was intended to determine whether a curriculum designed to meet the "needs and interests" of students is as effective at preparing students for college as is a traditional, subject-centered program. The study involved 30 progressive or experimental high schools that were matched as closely as possible with traditional comparison schools. Much of the curricular experience in the progressive schools was interdisciplinary in nature. The results of the Eight Year Study showed that students from the progressive schools were as well prepared academically for college as their traditional counterparts and were more involved in such social and extracurricular activities as yearbook, student government, and clubs. In spite of the evidence, the many pressing issues of World War II obscured the results, and as Decker Walker wrote, "the reforms of this period survived only in isolated places and as the seeds of further reforms" (Walker, 1990, p. 72).

It may be stretching things a bit to claim the Eight Year Study as a program evaluation of integrated or interdisciplinary curriculums. However, many of the curricular offerings in the progressive schools were what are called *core curriculum,* which is a way of combining subjects like English and history, for example, into a single offering called *Social Living.* It be justfied that the Eight Year Study did much to bring about the demise of the junior high school. A great deal of middle school philosophy emerged from the progressive movement, and one of the middle school tenets is to coalesce subjects into integrated studies using block scheduling.

Other Research

Finally, there are some emergent research findings that offer tentative support to the use of an integrated curriculum. One source of such research is the updated effective schools findings. Effective schools research has been conducted for several decades, yielding a variety of lists of school characteristics that distinguish "more effective" schools from schools that are less so. These characteristics are thought by some to have a cause-and-effect relationship with respect to learning. However, please bear in mind that correlations derived by this type of research are not the same as cause-and-effect findings. Such attributions can really only be considered hypotheses, yet to be tested empirically. Still, these characteristics do point toward possibilities of why some schools may be better than others. Cotton (1995) identified the following among a long list of effective classroom and school attributes:

- ♦ Teachers provide instruction that integrates traditional school subjects, as appropriate.
- ♦ Teachers integrate workplace readiness skills into content-area instruction.
- ♦ Administrators and teachers integrate the curriculum, as appropriate.

A second body of research is emerging from the many restructuring efforts underway across the nation. Lee and Smith's study of 820 secondary schools led them to conclude that "the consistent pattern of findings allows us to make quite unequivocal statements about the organizational structure of high schools: students learn more in schools which are restructured" (Lee & Smith, 1994a, p. 23). About 25 percent of these restructured schools were using "interdisciplinary teaching teams" (Lee & Smith, 1994b).

There are obvious limitations inherent in any hard-and-fast attempt to apply this research to interdisciplinary teaching and learning. But the results reported in this chapter do give us a place to begin, a kind of port of entry to this intriguing landscape. What is needed now is a systematic way in which to enlarge both the quality and quantity of the findings derived from carefully crafted qualitative and quantitative research studies. Perhaps what it will take is the establishment of some sort of center for the study of integrated or interdisciplinary curriculum.

Integrated Curriculum has been discussed here in terms of connecting ideas across academic domains and perhaps combining content and skill objectives into projects. Advances in computer technologies have made possible another form of curriculum integration. Integrated Learning Systems (ILS) are computer-based programs that provide instruction and assessment to monitor and motivate students.

The Waterford Early Reading Program (WERP) is one such system. Paterson and colleagues (2003) studied eight schools using WERP for Kindergarten and first grade, comparing it to eight others without it. Their mixed-method design included observations, interviews, achievement data and a sophisticated statistical method to identify main effects. Their conclusion: "that the Waterford program failed to outperform non-Waterford classrooms in part because it did not stimulate or encourage the social constructions and interactions necessary for growth in early emergent reading and writing" (p. 205).

Conclusion

To approach the school curriculum from an integrated perspective rather than that of separate subjects is a compelling idea. We have all been told that separating academic disciplines for scholarly purposes probably makes sense, but even that premise can be questioned in light of the crossing of frontiers in, for example, biology and psychology or genetics and linguistics. But for children and adolescents who are still in the process of adapting, organizing, and otherwise constructing their own schema, such an artificial separation seems to make little sense. On the other hand, students can readily understand the purpose of a project or an activity based on an interesting theme or issue. Such reasoning would be stronger, however, if it were more fully supported by empirical evidence.

It is also the case that schools are often curious places where large numbers of people congregate but are expected to work separately and only rarely to collaborate. Obviously, integrated studies are a way of bringing people together. Teachers who have become involved in integrated efforts will often remark that they are really getting to know some of their colleagues for the first time even though they may have worked next door to them for years. Students, too, because of the project nature of integrated studies, are given greater opportunity to work with each other. Such experiences surely work to the greater benefit of teachers and students.

On the other hand, the claims made in the name of interdisciplinary curriculum are expansive and may only raise hopes beyond reasonable expectations. If you decide to approach the curriculum from an integrated perspective, you ought to do so for reasons of collegiality and real-world applications. But if you are expecting that such a move will result in higher test scores, well…the evidence is tentative at best.

Perhaps this is the time and place to say that higher test scores, an admirable goal, are not alone a sufficient reason for having schools. School is also about social intelligence, citizenship, participation, and decision making. These are the collateral learnings of the school experience. Please don't misunderstand the intent of this remark. It is not an argument for ignoring test scores. To do so would be folly. So, of course, the best answer is to raise test scores *and* meet participatory needs. This is the spirit in which you ought to consider curriculum integration. Professional judgment, whether in education or in some other field, is always a difficult, complex enterprise.

14

Cooperative Learning

An essential instructional skill that all teachers need is knowing how and when to structure students' learning goals competitively, individualistically, and cooperatively. Each goal structure has its place; an effective teacher will use all three appropriately.

David and Roger Johnson

The future of cooperative learning is difficult to predict. My hope is that even when cooperative learning is no longer the "hot new method," schools and teachers will continue to use it as a routine part of instruction. My fear is that cooperative learning will largely disappear as a result of the faddism so common in American Education.

Robert Slavin

Oh, they had cooperative learning when I was a kid; they just didn't call it that. They called it cheating.

former teacher Arlen King

Cooperative learning is one of the biggest, if not *the* biggest, educational innovations of our time. It has permeated all levels of teacher training from preservice to inservice. It has been estimated that as of 2005 more that 30,000 teachers and would-be teachers have been trained at the Minneapolis-based Cooperative Learning Center alone. And cooperative learning is not a peculiarly American educational phenomenon. It is touted from Israel to New Zealand, from Sweden to Japan.

The research claims that detail the elements of cooperative learning are more elaborate and documented than those of any other movement in education today. Study after study finds its way into the scholarly journals. Hundreds of articles, from research to practice, appear annually on this topic. The major professional subject matter associations have all published special editions showing how cooperative learning can be used in mathematics, social studies, language arts, science, and other subject areas.

The claims made on behalf of cooperative learning are legendary and sometimes controversial. Seemingly, advocates say, it can solve any educational problem. Researcher Robert Slavin (1989–1990), himself a recognized authority in the field of cooperative learning, warned us early on that

voice of reason when ← (o to comentary on
research
initiatives

> [a]nother danger inherent in the success of cooperative learning is that the methods will be oversold and under trained. It is being promoted as an alternative to tracking and within class grouping, as a means of mainstreaming academically handicapped students, as a means of improving race relations in desegregated schools, as a solution to the problems of students at risk, as a means of increasing prosocial behavior among children, as well as a method for simply increasing the achievement of all students. Cooperative learning can in fact accomplish this staggering array of objectives, but not as a result of a single three-hour inservice session. (p. 3)

Of course, Slavin is correct that a brief introduction to such a complex idea is hardly sufficient to accomplish anything more than a preliminary sense of what cooperative learning is. But note his agreement with the wide range of educational problems that cooperative learning can productively address! If it could do half these things, it would be the pedagogical equivalent of a cure for cancer.

What is this apparently wonderful thing called cooperative learning? How does it work? Can it really bring about basic academic and social changes for the better in classroom life? Let's take a closer look at it so that you can begin to decide for yourself.

how incorporate 4 curric?

Cooperative Learning Models

Cooperative learning takes on many different forms in classrooms, but all involve students working in groups or teams to achieve certain educational goals. Beyond the most basic premise of working together, students must also depend on one another, a concept called *positive interdependence*. From here cooperative learning takes on specific traits advocated differentially by different developers. In some cases, cooperative learning is conceived of as a generic strategy that one could use in practically any setting or in any course of study. In other cases, cooperative learning is conceived of as subject-matter–specific strategy. Figure 14.1 lists five of the major models of cooperative learning. They have much in common, but the differences among them provide useful distinctions. All five represent training programs for teachers who, having taken the training, should be equipped to implement the various attendant strategies in their classrooms.

Figure 14.1 Cooperative Learning Models

Model and Designer	Focus
Learning Together (David Johnson & Roger Johnson) ♦ Formal Base Groups ♦ Informal Base Groups ♦ Cooperative Base Groups	Generic group process theory and skills for the teacher for developing a cooperative classroom.
Structural Approach (Spencer Kagan) ♦ Roundrobin ♦ Corners ♦ Numbered Heads Together ♦ Roundtable ♦ Match Mine	Content-free ways of organizing social interaction in the classroom and for a variety of grade levels. Used for active processing and monitoring for understanding within any lesson. All grades.
Student Team Learning (Robert Slavin) ♦ Student Teams-Achievement Divisions (STAD) ♦ Teams-Games-Tournament (TGT) ♦ Team Assisted Individualization (TAI) ♦ Cooperative Integrated Reading and Composition (CIRC)	STAD & TGT— Structured events with assessment part. Most disciplines and grade levels. TAI—specifically for grades 3–6 mathematics. CIRC—specifically for grades 3–6 reading and writing.
Group Investigation (Shlomo Sharan & Yael Sharan) ♦ A general plan for organizing a classroom ♦ Uses a variety of cooperative strategies for several disciplines	
Jigsaw (Elliot Aronson) ♦ Interdependent learning teams regrouping to share separate investigations	Content, skills, or ideas that can be parceled out to individuals who put the pieces together cooperatively

Learning Together

David and Roger Johnson of the University of Minnesota are the authors of the *Learning Together* model. The model is based in a generic group process theory applicable to all disciplines and grade levels. Students are placed in formal or informal base groups that are charged with solving problems, discussing issues, carrying out projects, and other tasks. The Johnson and Johnson model is built on the five elements, which trace back to the theories of Morton Deutsch, mentioned previously in this text. Without any one of these five elements, the experience deteriorates into unstructured group work, for in theory each element contributes to the best learning interaction.

- ♦ **Positive Interdependence**—Students must believe and act on the belief that they are linked with other students to the point that they cannot succeed unless the other students also succeed.

- ♦ **Interaction**—Students must converse with each other face to face, helping one another with learning tasks, problems, and novel ideas.

- ♦ **Accountability**—Each student must be held accountable for his or her performance as contributor to self and the group.

- ♦ **Social Skills**—Students are taught and must use appropriate group interaction skills as part of the learning process.

- ♦ **Group Processing**—Student groups must regularly monitor what they are accomplishing and how the group and individuals might function more effectively.

Obviously, teachers must be trained in these elements, and they must be able to teach them to their students in turn. It is one thing to make a list of five elements of cooperative learning. It is quite another thing to operationalize them.

One of the more persistent criticisms of cooperative learning is that although groups may show progress, the individual, particularly the high-performing individual, learns little. Matters of individual accountability and achievement are addressed by Johnson and Johnson (2004) in their book, *Assessing Students in Groups*. Basically, they pointed out ways to assess individual performance in group settings, and they cite evidence of productive learning by all members of a group when the five elements are followed.

Student Team Learning

Robert Slavin of Johns Hopkins University has developed a cooperative learning model called Student Team Learning. His model is less generic than that of the Johnsons. In fact, it has at least four permutations, each of which is specifically designed to address different concerns. For example, his Cooperative Integrated Reading and Composition (CIRC) model is specifically designed for learning reading and writing in grades 3–6. His Team Assisted Individualization (TAI) model is designed for mathematics learning in grades 3–6. Slavin's approach to cooperative learning represents a sophisticated set of strategies which, as he has stated, cannot be acquired in a three-hour workshop session.

Other Models

Other notable models include Schlomo and Yael Sharan's (1992) *Group Investigation,* which is a general plan for organizing a classroom using a variety of cooperative tactics for different disciplines; Spencer Kagan's (1992) *Structural Approach to Cooperative Learning* includes such intriguing procedures as Roundtable, and Match Mine; and Elliot Aronson's (1996) *Jigsaw,* is composed of interdependent learning teams for academic content applicable to various age groups.

Used properly, cooperative learning is designed to supplement and complement direct instruction and the other teaching and learning activities typical of classroom life. Its main function is to replace much of the individual, often competitive, seatwork that so dominates American classrooms. John Goodlad's (1984) research showed that students on average start talk only 7 minutes per day. In cooperative learning environments, that figure changes dramatically.

It should be noted, as well, that the advocates of cooperative learning are not necessarily opposed to individualistic and competitive learning. Their opposition is to its near-complete dominance. Most cooperative learning advocates will say that there is a time and a place for each type of learning, but that there must be considerably more cooperative learning in classrooms than is presently the case.

Slavin's (1991) perspective is typical of the movement when he stated, "cooperative learning methods share the idea that students work together to learn and are responsible for one another's learning as well as their own" (p. 73). Slavin's well-stated phrase sums up the essence of cooperative learning. Read it carefully.

The Research Base for Cooperative Learning

Theory Building

The Level I research can be traced back to the theories of group dynamics and social interaction developed in the 1930s by pioneer researcher Kurt Lewin. Slavin noted, "A long tradition of research in social psychology has established that group discussion, particularly when group members must publicly commit themselves, is far more effective at changing individuals' attitudes and behaviors than even the most persuasive lecture" (Slavin, 1986, p. 276).

Lewin's ideas were further refined by the social psychologist Morton Deutsch, who derived a theory of group process based on shared goals and rewards. Deutsch (1949) postulated that when a group is rewarded based on the behavior of its members, the group members would encourage one another to do whatever helps the group to be rewarded.

The work of Lewin, Deutsch, and others led to new perceptions about the power of truly integrated groups to get things done, to sanction and support members, and to create a different social fabric. It is, of course, in one form or another, an old idea, and to their credit, cooperative learning advocates admit this rather freely. Socrates, for example, used cooperative dialogue between teacher and pupil to advance learning. The Gestalt movement in psychology, which arose in Europe late in the nineteenth century, furnishes much of the original paradigm. Its famous epigram, that "the whole of something is greater than the sum of its individual parts," is basic to cooperative efforts.

The pioneering work in perception and structural wholeness of such legendary psychologists as Max Wertheimer led to new insights regarding the strengths of collaboration in problem solving. What may have been felt or even known intuitively by some over the centuries (King Arthur's legendary Round Table comes to mind), now had a basis of well-grounded theoretical support. This set the stage for researchers to focus on the efficacy of cooperative group learning in school settings.

Empirical Studies

At Level II, the sheer amount of empirical evidence that has accumulated from research studies in cooperative learning is staggering. There are hundreds of published individual studies as well as many reviews, syntheses, and meta-analyses. There appears to be no review, synthesis, or meta-analysis that concludes that cooperative learning is deficient as a means to raise student achievement. In general, the conclusions are the same, and all tend to be mainly supportive.

Slavin's (1991) synthesis of the research on cooperative learning yields four main conclusions, each of which is consistent with the pure or basic research and theoretical model derived from Wertheimer, Lewin, Deutsch, and others. The conclusions are rather sweeping, but they have a sound empirical foundation:

- For enhancing student achievement, the most successful approaches have incorporated two key elements: group goals and individual accountability; that is, groups are rewarded based on the individual learning of all group members.

◆ When group goals and individual accountability are clear, achievement effects of cooperative learning are consistently positive; 37 of 44 experimental/control comparisons of at least four weeks' duration yielded significant positive effects, and none favored traditional methods.

◆ Positive achievement effects of cooperative learning have been found to be about the same degree at all grade levels from second on up; in all major subjects of the curriculum; and in urban, rural, and suburban schools. Effects are equally positive for high, average, and low achievers.

◆ Positive effects of cooperative learning have been documented consistently for such diverse outcomes as self-esteem, intergroup relations, acceptance of academically handicapped students, attitudes toward school, and ability to work with others.

A somewhat more recent meta-analysis was conducted by Z. Qin and David and Roger Johnson (1995) in which these researchers examined the effects of cooperative learning on problem solving. Having examined research studies done between 1929 and 1993, they concluded that cooperative learners outperformed their competitive counterparts in all four of the problem-solving areas examined: linguistic, nonlinguistic, well-defined, and ill-defined. These researchers concluded, "The practical implications of the finding that cooperation generally improves problem solving are obvious: On the job and in the classroom, cooperative groups will be better able to deal with complex problems than will competitors working alone" (p. 140).

Cooperative learning strategies are now considered basic to instructional competence. Actively involving students and monitoring their understanding, two skills expected of classroom teachers, are often accomplished with quick interactive and metacognitive exercises, such as *numbered heads together*. Cooperation itself is identified by many states' content standards as an objective, although it is not easily measured. It is easy to make a reasoned but subjective judgment; it is harder to develop an instrument that is reliable and proven to be valid at finding out what it means to find out.

One instrument for measuring cooperative learning can be found in Gillies' (2002) research for which she devised *schedules* (Figure 14.2) to gather data. She used these to measure student behavior states and verbal interactions during group sessions to study the residual effect of training. She observed fifth graders two years after their training, compared to those who had none. She used momentary time sampling at 10-second intervals over 10-minute periods to observe the four behavior states and six cognitive language strategies listed in Figure 14.2. Not only did she develop the three schedules, she included a rigorous interrater reliability exercise that yielded respectable ranges of 90–94 percent, 79–89 percent, and 75–83 percent respectively.

Figure 14.2 Gillies' Cooperative Behavior and Language

Behavior Schedule

Cooperative	Task-oriented; positively socially oriented; active attention to others in the group
Noncooperative	Competition; opposition; criticism; attain goals at the expense of others
Alone on-task	Independent; noninteraction with group
Alone off-task	All behavior not related to the task, i.e., spacing out

Verbal Interaction Schedule

Directives	Verbal and/or physical prompt to others
Unsolicited help	Explanations that were not invited
Unsolicited stop	Usually yes, no, or undetailed response
Interruptions	Calling out, or other distraction
Solicited help	Detailed and elaborate explanations
Solicited stop	Response following request for help
Other	Other speech not categorized as above

Language Strategy Schedule

Echoed	Mechanical repetition of others' speech
Unstructured	Loosely related stated out loud
Concrete	States relevant fact related to current discussion
Reasoned	Explanation with evidence
Generalized	Conclusion or principle based on current discussion
Evaluated	Considers multiple sources to make choice

Source: Adapted from Gillies, R. (2002). The residual effects of cooperative-learning experiences: A two-year follow-up. *The Journal of Educational Research, 96,* 15–22.

Although Gillies' (2002) findings were not surprising, the fifth graders who had been trained "exhibited less noncooperative behavior and less individual nontask behavior" (p. 18), we can benefit from her careful analysis of observed behavior. This elevates classroom management from a vague sense of compliance to a specific and teachable/learnable set of behaviors. Because the language strategies within the schedules are also part of the curriculum mandates, teachers can see the value of the cooperative learning model. The development of the three schedules and their reliability provides a convenient means to continue the research—perhaps at a school-wide level.

Program Evaluation

At Level III, Stevens and Slavin (1995a, b) conducted an impressive school evaluation study, the results of which revealed that cooperative learning could be effective in changing the school and classroom organization and instructional approach. Their research also shows that such large-scale implementation can be done effectively, and that learning can be enhanced for a variety of types of students when cooperative learning is used appropriately. They concluded their evaluation with this commentary:

> This study is the first and only evaluation of a cooperative elementary school. It is not merely another study of cooperative learning; it is the only study to evaluate cooperative learning as the focus of schoolwide change, the only study to evaluate cooperative learning in many subjects at once, and one of the few to show the effects of cooperative learning over a multiyear period. (p. 347)

This appears to be the only such published Level III research. This level of research is greatly needed by the profession, and unfortunately, it is seldom present in the annals of innovation. The hope is that this will be the first of many such studies on not only cooperative learning, but on all the innovations mentioned in this book.

Johnson and Johnson, who so ably launched the cooperative learning juggernaut, have come full circle, turning their attention to conflict resolution. A number of innovative guidance curriculums employ the cooperative learning model, and all efforts appear to support goals of improved learning, improved achievement, and an improved society. One such implementation studied by the Johnsons and colleagues (2002) was conflict resolution training integrated into a high school social studies curriculum. They pointed out that "Despite the abundance of school-based conflict training programs, most are not linked to conflict resolution theory and research and do not provide sound empirical evidence of effectiveness" and further stated that "conflict programs that are not linked to a theoretical framework cannot be systematically tested, refined, extended, or generalized across diverse school populations" (p. 305–306).

Apart from whether the students learned and applied the conflict resolution strategies, the study investigated achievement outcomes, which were positive, always an important finding because without such outcomes any innovation is unlikely to be sustained. Reading their study may encourage you to consider this integrative approach of incorporating conflict resolution training into academic courses.

Conclusion

Of all the educational innovations reviewed in this book, cooperative learning has the best and largest empirical base. It is not a perfect base, and as Slavin (1989–1990) pointed out, more research is needed at senior high school levels as well as at college and university levels. It is also instructive to note that a good beginning has been made in the conduct of much-needed program evaluation or Level III research. Slavin noted that the appropriateness of cooperative learning strategies for the advancement of higher-order conceptual learning is yet to be established firmly. However, the Qin, Johnson, and Johnson research mentioned earlier is a start in that direction.

This chapter concludes with the advice that for the administrator or teacher who wishes to bring about positive change in a more or less traditional school environment, cooperative learning would seem to be well worth exploring. To do it well takes considerable training and motivation. And to convince some parents and other community members that it is more than kids giving answers to each other will take some doing. These are comments one could make about any innovation, but in this case, the educator who chooses to implement it will have little trouble finding supportive evidence.

Some of pull names on popsicle sticks out of jars, & others, who also happen to ↓ ↑ students names on popsicle etc, lay ↑ out on ↑ tablet seemingly & together teams ↑ or thought.

15

Literacy:
Whole Language
and Its Discontents

Whole Language—two words that have become a label for an exciting grass-roots teacher movement that is changing curricula around the world....Never in the history of literacy education has there been such genuine excitement on the part of educators.

Dorothy Watson

A Whole Language approach that does not incorporate sufficient attention to decoding skills leaves in its wake countless numbers of youngsters who, in the words of one teacher, are surrounded by "beautiful pieces of literature that [they] can't read."

American Educator

Whole language has emerged as a complete pedagogy, rich, diverse, and complex.

Ken Goodman

Researchers Yange Xue and Samuel Meisels (2004) write that

> over the years there has been persistent disagreement among educators concerning the most appropriate approach to teaching children to read. The dispute centers around two polarized perspectives....Since the 1990s, the debate has shifted to one between phonics and whole language. (p. 191–192)

Whole language is a philosophy of how literacy best develops in learners. It represents a perspective on language and learning that is founded primarily on the use of literature programs, big books, predictable books, book discussion groups, authentic stories rather than basal readers, acceptance of developmental spelling, and emphasis on the writing process. It is based on the premise that human beings "acquire language through actually using it for a purpose, not through practicing its separate parts until some later date when the parts are assembled and the totality is finally used" (Altwerger, Edelsky, & Flores, 1987, p. 145).

Reyhner (2004) has cast whole language as constructivist, student-oriented, experiential, and interactive, emphasizing meaning in learning to read. By way of contrast, he cites its nemesis, phonics-based instruction as teacher-centered, skills oriented, and as a transmission (didactic) model of teaching reading. A clear lexical clue to the philosophical divide between whole-language *learning* (think progressive) and phonics-based *instructions* (think essentialist) should not go unnoticed.

The elements of whole-language learning are many, but a progressive, constructivist, and integrated language arts theme threads its way through each of them. Figure 15.1 illustrates a number of learner-centered procedures found in typical whole-language classrooms.

Figure 15.1 Elements of Whole-Language Learning

♦ Publishing original writing
♦ Composing and writing stories or report
♦ Performing skits and plays
♦ Writing stories in a journal
♦ Doing an activity or project related to a book or story
♦ Identifying the main idea and parts of a story
♦ Dictating stories to a teacher, aide, or volunteer
♦ Retelling stories
♦ Using context cues for comprehension
♦ Writing with encouragement to use invented spellings if needed
♦ Reading aloud
♦ Making predictions based on text
♦ Reading self-chosen books
♦ Remembering and following directions that include a series of actions
♦ Communicating complete ideas orally
♦ Learning new vocabulary
♦ Listening to teacher read stories where they see the print (for example, "big books")

Source: Xue, Y., and Meisels, S. (2004). Early literacy instruction and learning in kindergarten. *American Educational Research Journal, 41(1),* 204.

Whole language emerged as a force in the school curriculum for at least two reasons. One reason was a reaction to the skills-based language programs with their heavy emphasis on the technical (phonics, grammar, correct spelling, etc.) rather than the conceptual aspects of learning. The other reason is that new theories of learning have emerged in recent years, and whole-language advocates have been encouraged by these developments.

I mentioned previously that whole language is rooted in part in a learning theory called *constructivism*. Constructivism is based on the premise that the learner constructs all knowledge—personally, socially, or in combination—and therefore, learning is a more subjective affair than one might imagine. No two people can or should construct the same knowledge (although it might be similar); each of us has our own inimitable experiences, schema or knowledge structure, learning styles, and particular motivation to learn. Because this is so, the thinking goes, it is more appropriate to expose learners to broad ideas than to particular skills. The former permits individual accommodation, while the latter assumes that everyone (at least within a group) needs the same thing; and that same thing is a reductionist approach to learning as opposed to a holistic approach. Of course, this is an oversimplification: Whole language advocates have rarely said that the teaching of basic reading and grammar skills is always inappropriate; what we are talking about here are points of emphasis.

Some observers have noted the similarities between whole language and an approach that was popular a generation ago called *language experience*. Language experience was based on the premise that reading and writing should come primarily from the child's own experience rather than from predetermined, one-size-fits-all sources such as basal readers. For example, a teacher takes the class for a walk around the environs of the school, and afterward, using large pages of newsprint and felt pen, writes a story that the children tell based on the experience. The children would then practice reading and illustrating their own story. Often children in language experience classes would write and illustrate their own books, which they would share with others or give to their parents or others. The premise was twofold: reading and writing go together like hand and glove, and personal experience is the key to becoming a reader or a writer. The idea of *ownership* as a motivating force has been claimed by more than one group over the years. The idea can be traced back at least to Francis Bacon, who said the key to learning is found in experience, one's own and not someone else's.

Grabbing Hold of a "Slippery Quarry"

One of the major problems with the whole-language movement was its variety of definitions. It has been described as a "slippery quarry" and as "something hard to measure" (McKenna, Robinson, & Miller, 1990a). Even whole-language advocates openly admit that the concept is difficult to define and that it defies "a dictionary-type definition." Basically, whole language is a philosophy of teaching and learning that proposes that all language concepts are closely interconnected, to separate them is artificial, and they are best learned in a natural or *whole* manner. This description contrasts with the traditional reductionist, skill-focused approach to language where children begin with letters, sounds, blends, and phonemes, or what more than one proponent of whole language has called, *barking at text.* Instead, whole language flows from the child's personal, natural language patterns and with the reading and writing of stories and other forms of literature that draw on the child's experience.

The oft-cited analogy is the natural untaught process of learning to walk. Readers of this book who wish to pursue this issue of definition more deeply are encouraged to read "The Rhetoric of Whole Language," by Moorman, Blanton, and McLaughlin, and "Deconstructing the Rhetoric of Moorman, Blanton, and McLaughlin: A Response," by Goodman. Both articles appear in the October–December 1994 issue of *Reading Research Quarterly.*

Several key terms are closely associated with whole-language learning. One of those terms is *meaning-centered.* A meaning-centered approach seeks relevance and personal meaning and avoids isolated skills as the road to literacy. Another term found in the repertoire of whole-language advocates is *integration.* Because language is the root of much of our learning, whole-language classrooms provide integrated language experiences which touch variously on all parts of the curriculum—art, music, science, social studies, and so forth. And a third term is *natural learning.* We don't directly teach people to walk or even to talk. It happens along the way in a supportive environment. Therefore, the argument goes, so should learning to read and write be made as natural as possible.

An integral part of whole-language philosophy is the nurturing of the natural process by which a child comes to think about language as a result of his or her prior knowledge and life experiences. In this respect, the social and affective parts of learning are highly valued and attended to by whole-language teachers. Social experiences tend to be holistic and often highly charged effectively, for better or worse. They lend themselves to particularistic analysis only in retrospect. Figure 15.2 illustrates the set of common assumptions and beliefs held by many whole-language advocates. Perhaps in the most basic sense of learning, the difference between whole-language and traditional-language programs is that whole language emphasizes whole-to-part learning while traditional forms emphasize part-to-whole learning. In other words, they are diametrically opposing points of view. Figure 15.2 illustrates some of the differences between traditional and whole-language views of the curriculum.

Figure 15.2 Common Beliefs of Whole Language Advocates

According to whole-language theory, teachers should

- **Focus on meaning, not the part parts of language.** Children learn language from whole to part. Therefore, instruction in reading and writing should begin by presenting whole texts—engaging poems and stories—rather than zeroing in on the bits and pieces that make up language.

- **Teach skills in context, not in isolation.** Children learn the subskills of language most readily when these skills are taught in the context of reading and writing activities. Teachers should coach children in skills as the need for the skills arises, rather than marching children in lockstep through a sequenced skills curriculum.

- **Get children writing, early and often.** Reading and writing develop best in tandem. When children write, they master phonics relationships because they must constantly match letters with sounds to write what they want to say.

- **Accept invented spelling.** Whole language teachers do not expect perfect spelling from the beginning. Instead, they encourage children to make their best efforts. Invented spelling reveals the degree to which the young writers have cracked the phonetic code, and over time they will improve.

- **Allow pupils to make choices.** When children have some control over their learning, they are more motivated and retain what they learn longer.

Whole language is not

- Breaking language into its parts;
- Teaching skills in isolation or in a strict sequence;
- Relying on basal readers with controlled vocabulary;
- Using worksheets and drill; or
- Testing subskills.

Source: Adapted from the Association for Supervision and Curriculum Development. Whole language: Finding the surest way to literacy. *Curriculum Update* (Fall, 1995).

A review of the elements of curriculum and instruction found in Figure 15.3 revealed clearly that a basic difference is found between the two approaches with respect to learning goals, teacher role, student activities, materials used, methods of assessment, and the structure of the classroom. Needless to say, any teacher, administrator, or district contemplating such a basic change should be well aware of the implications, and should be able to defend such a change to parents and other interested parties.

Politics and Whole Language

There is another aspect of the whole-language movement, about which some whole-language enthusiasts are possibly unaware. At the deepest philosophical level, whole language represents something more than another way to teach kids how to read and write. Its source is found in a strong desire for education to play the role of change agent in the social and political fabric not only of schools, but society as a whole. This is hardly a new idea. George Counts (1932), who probably would have approved wholeheartedly of the politics of whole language, wrote *Dare the Schools Build a New Social Order?* on this theme. It is this social and political agenda that has fueled much of the debate about whole language.

A number of reading researchers and professionals have commented on this phenomenon, but one of the more penetrating analyses is provided by McKenna, Stahl, and Reinking (1994). They have identified the social-political aspect of the whole-language agenda as spelled out by certain leaders in the movement. They note that some whole-language advocates see "education as a vehicle for individual liberation and the classroom as a model for an egalitarian society" (p. 213). They interpret Kenneth Goodman, a prominent exponent of whole-language teaching, as someone who

> appears to see whole language, not as a method of teaching reading, but an aspect of an approach to creating a more just world. From this analysis, whole-language advocates do not see the goal of education as improving test scores. Their critique of test scores…is based on…a questioning of the imposition of a standard or norm on an individual child. (p. 214)

Indeed, a number of whole-language advocates are extraordinarily open about these beliefs. Edelsky, Altwerger, and Flores (1991) wrote that whole language "has a unique potential to be a liberatory pedagogy…." It is also, they continued, ideally suited for helping "subvert the school's role in maintaining a stratified society." Whole language "devalues the major language-based devices for stratifying people," and "huge chunks

Figure 15.3 Comparison of Traditional and Whole-Language Classrooms

Traditional

Whole Language

Learning Goals

Specific objectives in each subject area, usually identified by the school, district, or state. The objectives are hierarchical and tied to textbooks or teacher guides. The focus is on the product, with particular emphasis given to a student's deficits.

Teachers work with students to create a curriculum based on the interests and strengths of the individual student. Learning focuses on the process and learning in a functional context.

Teacher Role

A transmitter of information with major responsibility for determining what and how students should learn.

A facilitator of learning helping the student with the process of learning, sharing responsibility for learning with the student.

Materials

Basal readers, skill books and worksheets, social studies, math, language, science textbooks.

Student-selected reading materials, meaningful projects involving a variety of integrated materials from the various disciplines.

Class Structure and Activities

Students in traditional rows, with direct instruction predominant. Students may be grouped by achievement level. Minimal use of group learning activities. Teaching of skills in isolation from other parts of the curriculum with separate periods of the day for the various subjects.

Variable seating arrangements with considerable flexibility. Subjects integrated with language and reading, with considerable group and cooperative learning activities. Limited direct instruction, or only when the need arises within the context of the learning activities at a meaningful time.

Evaluation

Standardized tests, workbooks, worksheets, teacher-made tests that evaluate isolated skills mastery. The frame of reference for evaluation is an external standard or group norm.

Teacher observations of the learning process, writing samples, student self-evaluation, and portfolios. Students are evaluated against themselves to identify growth in various areas.

of time usually devoted to exercises are freed for projects in which students can analyze social issues like the systemic injustice and inequality that affects all our lives" (pp. 53–54).

The battle lines are sharply drawn. As McKenna and others noted in their analysis, "to compromise whole language would be to compromise that [political] goal." Critics point out that whole language is built on a theory that may be less about learning to read and write, except as tools of liberation, than about social change and "reorganizing power relationships in schools."

The Research Base for Whole Language

Whole language advocates claim that "the research base for whole-language philosophy is broad and multidisciplinary. It includes research in linguistics, psycholinguistics, sociology, anthropology, philosophy, child development, curriculum, composition, literary theory, semiotics, and other fields of study" (Newman & Church, 1989, p. 20). Movement leader Kenneth Goodman—who cites influences by such luminaries as Jean Piaget, Lev Vygotsky, Noam Chomsky, and the linguist Michael Halliday—proclaimed, "Whole language has emerged as a complete pedagogy, rich, diverse and complex" (1996, p. 135). These claims are daunting, and it might lead one to conclude that such a deeply structured Level I foundation augurs well for the results of this approach. The proof, however, is ultimately found in how or to what extent theoretical contributions are brought together to form a coherent teaching-learning construct or, in grander terms, a *complete pedagogy*.

Other examples of the claims are found in books such as *The Administrator's Guide to Whole Language* (Heald-Taylor, 1989), in which an entire chapter is devoted to whole-language research. Allusions are made to some 50 studies that cover a range of related topics including writing, oral language, reading, and developmental studies. Prominent among the researchers cited are Kenneth Goodman, Donald Graves, Delores Durkin, Marie Clay, and Frank Smith. This book was published at a time of largely uncritical enthusiasm and unbridled expansion of the whole-language movement.

Adams and Bruck (1995) reviewed the whole-language research base, concluding that to the extent to which whole-language proponents equate learning to read with learning to talk (i.e., that it is a *natural* process much like learning to walk), they are wrong. They concluded further that to the extent to which whole-language procedures minimize the role of skilled decoding in reading comprehension, they are wrong. And they conclude that the resulting pedagogical practices of whole-language teaching and learning are wrong. Adams and Bruck base their rather strong conclusions on a systematic examination in which they compare whole-language claims with empirical results.

Keith and Paula Stanovich (1995) added that "[empirical] research has consistently supported the view that reading is not acquired naturally in the same way as speech" (p. 93). Keith Stanovich maintained

> [t]hat direct instruction in alphabetic coding facilitates early reading instruction is one of the most well-established conclusions in all of behavioral science. Conversely, the idea that learning to read is just like learning to speak is accepted by no responsible linguist, psychologist, or cognitive scientist in the research community. (*American Educator*, 1995, p. 4)

Thus the conclusion that whole language has indeed a credible pure or basic (Level I) research foundation is debatable, to say the least. Furthermore, that the philosophical basis of whole language is one of a clearly thought-out theory of learning rests on its claim and is clearly challenged by Stanovich when he wrote:

> [T]hese [theoretical] ideas have unfortunately come into education half baked and twice distorted. Legitimate philosophy of science was picked up and reworked by scholars in a variety of humanities disciplines who were not philosophers by training and who used the work for their own—often political—agendas. (1993, p. 288)

The basic research and the theoretical model of whole language is its primary line of support. It rests, its critics say, on shaky foundations. The theoretical construct has been used to give both inspiration and direction to whole-language teaching and learning practices at the classroom level. It is to this level, that of implementation, that we now turn.

The practical questions are: What do students learn in whole-language classrooms? Do students attain higher levels of literacy? Is the learning qualitatively improved in whole-language classrooms? This is the domain of applied research (Level II). The best answer to those questions is that evidence is lacking. Let us see why this is so.

How Do We Do It?

Empirical researchers have observed that investigating the effects of whole-language instruction is difficult because of the lack of an agreed on definition of whole language. People simply mean different things when they use the term. To further compound the issue, a number of whole-language advocates claim that *traditional* methods of assessment are inappropriate when it comes to evaluating this approach to teaching and learning (McKenna, Robinson, & Miller, 1990a, p. 4). So if we have trouble defining it and we cannot apply traditional assessment measures to gauge its effectiveness, then where does this leave us?

McKenna, Robinson, and Miller (1990a) suggested a cooperative research agenda designed to treat these problems. They proposed that these eight steps be taken:

1. The concept must be defined to enable researchers to know whether a program represents whole language or not, or at least how to categorize a given program.

2. Both experimental and quasi-experimental research is needed.

3. Qualitative studies should also be employed.

4. The effects on student attitudes should be studied.

5. Longitudinal studies should be undertaken.

6. Learner characteristics as they interact with traditional and whole-language instruction should be identified.

7. Studies should identify the role of teacher variables in instruction.

8. Collaborative research partnerships between researchers and whole-language advocates should be developed.

Of course, this reasonable agenda is needed not merely for whole-language program assessment but for program assessment in general.

Some whole-language advocates, however, take strong exception to the idea of an imposed research agenda. In the article, "Whose Agenda Is This, Anyway?" Carole Edelsky (1990) wrote that traditional research forms have little relevance to whole language because "two competing views are more than different 'takes' on language arts instruction; they are conflicting educational paradigms. Each uses different discourse; maintains different values; and emanates from a different educational community" (p. 7). In a response to her response, McKenna and colleagues wrote, "in essence, people share a system of beliefs and they claim they have evidence to support their beliefs. But, when you look up what [whole-language advocates] cite as evidence, it is often just someone else's published beliefs" (McKenna, Robinson, & Miller, 1990b, p. 12). This has all the earmarks of a stalemate.

The debate about research methodology in the reading profession has obviously been rancorous, and suggestions have been made to resolve this dispute that "invoke a spirit of charity" (Stanovich & Stanovich, 1995). The strident nature of the debate is a reflection of how strongly these beliefs are held. As McKenna and others (1994) have noted, "[t]o compromise whole language would be to compromise that [political] goal." When people have such different worldviews, it would be naive at best and probably closer to folly to think that they might readily agree to a research agenda.

In fairness, it should be stated that many whole-language advocates are not necessarily opposed to any form of evaluation research. They do, however, question the appropriateness of the measures used, which are typically standardized tests. Such tests, whole-language proponents claim, isolate learning in bits and pieces and ask children to show their knowledge in unnatural settings.

What kinds of program evaluation do whole-language proponents advocate? First, they would propose that qualitative research, rather than quantitative, be emphasized. They suggest that writing samples that could be judged as process rather than product would be a place to start. Also, they are interested in determining students' attitudes toward learning to read and write. To get a sense of students' attitudes, it would be necessary to conduct personal interviews and to employ other, similar qualitative data-gathering procedures. Basically, some whole-language advocates feel that placing the assessment marbles in the quantitative-product bag is a mistake that leads to irrelevant conclusions about student learning. This leaves the potential consumer in a quandary because we can all appreciate the sensitivity toward attitude development and the employment of more *natural* measures of achievement. Then again, it is much easier to compare quantitative achievement results between this reading program and that one when districts are faced with the expensive decisions associated with program adoption and implementation.

Goodman (1996) has argued that

> [r]eductionist research in reading has inevitably focused on recognition of bits and pieces of language rather than on comprehension of real texts. But we can't assume that perception of letters and words in the process of making sense of real meaningful texts is the same as recognizing letters and words in isolation or in highly reduced contexts. And we can't assume that comprehension follows successive recognition of words. (p. 5)

This statement suggests rather strongly that, from Goodman's perspective, what we have are two completely different goal structures and agendas, one empirical-reductionist and the other global-expansionist. To compare them, it would seem, is not merely difficult but less than a good use of one's time. As Goodman wrote, "Whole language teachers have taken control of the body of knowledge about how reading and writing work and have built their own pedagogy on that knowledge—their teaching theory and practice" (p. 117). Such phrases as "have taken control" and "have built their own pedagogy" speak for themselves.

What We Do Know

In spite of all this, what does the research we do have say about the effectiveness of whole-language programs? A comprehensive review of the literature on whole-language effectiveness was conducted by Steven A. Stahl and Patricia D. Miller in 1989 and updated in 1994 by Stahl, Michael McKenna, and Joan Pagnucco. The reviews included both quantitative and naturalistic or qualitative studies but predate the change of data collection following the No Child Left Behind Act (NCLB). In 1989, Stahl and Miller wrote:

> Our review…concludes that we have no evidence showing that whole-language programs produce effects that are stronger than existing basal programs, and potentially may produce lower effects. The alternative, that whole language programs are too new to evaluate, also suggests a lack of evidence of their efficacy. In short, both views foster doubt as to the prudence of a widespread adoption of such an approach, pending evidence of its effectiveness. (p. 143)

This review of whole-language research outcomes was not without its critics. Many whole-language advocates rejected its definitions of whole language and the methodologies of the research itself (Schickendanz, 1990; McGee & Lomax, 1990). The 1994 Stahl and others review concluded again that whole language did not produce advantages in achievement, and that eclectic programs seemed to produce the most positive effects. They concluded that the evidence suggested that the strongest type of program

> might include a great deal of attention to decoding, especially in the early grades, but would give a greater emphasis to the reading of interesting and motivating texts.…[S]uch a program would incorporate much from whole language but include more teacher-directed instruction, especially in terms of decoding and comprehension strategies. (p. 182)

They also noted, however, that this is not likely to sit well with whole-language people because many of them are convinced that, "one cannot have a little whole language and a little of something else. Partial moves toward whole language are acceptable only as a way station to becoming a true whole language teacher" (p. 182).

Its staunchest critics have called whole language a *disaster,* and it is true that the empirical evidence in support of whole-language learning is tenuous to deficient at best. Increasing numbers of professionals and laypersons have concluded that there are major problems. Many children, particularly young children from homes where little reading takes place and who need to learn the basics, simply do not learn to read well when whole language is the principal philosophy guiding instruction. The notion put forth by whole-language advocates that learning to read is a naturalistic process much like learning to walk or talk (a notion that is disputed by many linguists and psychologists) breaks down in the absence of home-based role models either of learning to talk using proper grammar or learning to read when little evidence of reading is found in the home.

Reacting to the drumbeat of parent criticism and declining student achievement, the California Task Force modified its earlier embrace of whole language and is now advocating a more balanced approach with an increased phonics-based emphasis (California Department of Education, 1996). It should, however, be kept in mind that states and districts embraced whole language in the first place because of the perception that more traditional forms of literacy instruction were not meeting children's needs. Thus we have another example of the pendulum swing so recognizable to those who have been in the profession for considerable time, partly because of a superficial interpretation of data, that is, statewide tests before a trend was documented.

Figure 15.4 (p. 196) presents the highlights of California's revised emphasis on phonetic awareness, correct spelling, systematic, explicit phonics approaches, and other related reading instruction practices. Especially worth noting is the advocacy of early intervention programs for children at risk of reading failure. The *Report of the California Reading Task Force* contains much of the familiar rhetoric, including the insight that "there is a crisis" (California Department of Education, 1995, p. 1). Among other things, the California Task Force concluded that "many language arts programs have shifted too far away from direct skills instruction" (p. 1). Statutes instituted in 1995 require that the State Board of Education "adopt materials in grades one through eight that include systematic, explicit phonics, spelling, and basic computational skills" (1996, p. 1).

To be fair, the state was reeling from the first set of national report cards that compared it unfavorably to other states, and so with the assumption that the recent whole-language effort could be blamed for such a poor performance, it was vilified without much consideration that the results might have been even poorer without it. More recent standardized test results do not dispute this possibility for other reforms efforts have included the reduction in class size for younger grades and the elimination of dual language instruction for Spanish speakers.

Maryann Manning and Constance Kamii (2000) researched their article, "Whole Language vs. Isolated Phonics Instruction." The title alone falls short of a balanced agenda, but the study does appear to have been reasonably well designed. Two kindergarten classes were compared, one taught by a self-proclaimed phonics teacher and the other by a teacher

Figure 15.4 California's Balanced Approach to Reading

Program Components

♦ A strong literature, language, and comprehension program that includes a balance of oral and written language

♦ An organized, explicit skills program for the emergent reader that includes phonemic awareness (sounds in words), phonics, and decoding skills

♦ Diagnosis to inform teaching and assessment for accountability

♦ Early intervention program with individual tutoring for children at risk of reading failure

Instructional Components

♦ Phonemic awareness

♦ Letter names and shapes

♦ Systematic, explicit phonics

♦ Programmatic instruction in correct spelling

♦ Vocabulary development

♦ Comprehension and higher order thinking

♦ Appropriate instructional materials

Source: California State Department of Education (1996). *Teaching reading: A balanced, comprehensive approach to teaching reading in prekindergarten through grade three.* Sacramento: Author.

using whole-language methods. The research report yields an interesting portrait of the two teaching styles, based on results of a year-long series of carefully constructed interviews.

Manning and Kamii concluded that the difference in performance between the two groups could be described by the students' developing theories of language. The whole-language group showed less sophisticated achievement in the beginning of the year, but by January had equaled or exceeded the phonics group, and by the end of the year had maintained their progress while the phonics group showed more regression and confusion. If nothing else, this study serves as an object lesson illustrating the need for research designs that persist long enough to observe unintended and nonlinear effects.

So Where Does This Leave Us?

Whole language advocates continue to tout their approach primarily on the basis of theory, enthusiasm, and testimonials. Although these are significant factors that should not be cynically cast aside, they simply are not be enough to go on when it comes to spending big money on new programs and teacher retraining. The fact of the matter is that we simply lack the empirical evidence necessary to state that schools wishing to improve student reading ability and test scores in the areas of the language arts should adopt the whole-language approach. But here's the rub: Raising standardized test scores conflicts with the goals and objectives held by whole-language advocates. Their agenda, they state, is more complex than one in which learning outcomes can be captured by the reductionist mentality so pervasive in standard measures. So those who choose to adopt a whole-language approach to language arts must do so for reasons they find compelling, and those reasons will have to be sought in sources beyond the empirical record as it exists to date.

We want our children to learn to read, to use it as a knowledge-seeking tool, and to enjoy reading—three different but closely related outcomes. Some evidence exists to suggest that both teacher-directed, phonics-based instruction and some student-centered, literature-based learning are needed. What we need is a research agenda that will get us closer to the answers of sequence, balance, and the best use of children's learning time. There is a similar shortage of sound research on highly publicized (and expensive) phonics-based solutions, most famously the *Hooked on Phonics* product.

This chapter began with the debate between whole-language advocates of constructivist learner-centered methods and phonics advocates who insist on behaviorist principles of code breaking. As Xue and Meisels (2004) have concluded, we need both. They write: "Our findings suggest that, between the bottom-up (phonics) and top-down (whole language) models of reading, there is an intermediate position that incorporates both bottom up and top-down processes in constructing meaning from text (p. 222)." Xue and Meisels reasonably conclude that their own research provides empirical evidence that a combination of the two, rather than one or the other, represents the best approach.

Epilogue

Have not the verses of Homer continued twenty-five hundred
years or more without the loss of a syllable or letter; during
which time infinite palaces, temples, castles, cities have been
decayed and demolished?

Francis Bacon

The spirit of educational reform is endowed with perennial qualities. There seems to be a never-ending quest by educators for better programs, better delivery systems, or better ideas about how students learn. Each year new approaches are touted, and thousands of teachers and administrators find themselves in meetings, taking notes while listening to some guru who claims to have at last gotten to the heart of the matter. The claims themselves have an enduring nature, only the topics change.

University of Kentucky professor and writer Thomas Guskey (1996) likened the education profession's infatuation with educational innovations and fads with the infatuations of a young child. Guskey points out that young children are prone to infatuations that are "passionate, totally consuming, and held in staunch resistance to alternative points of view." Young children see only the positive qualities of the object of infatuation, and are blind to the faults no matter how obvious those faults may be to others. And, what imperfections the child does notice are "dismissed as inconsequential and unimportant." Only later with maturity do we realize the short-lived nature of these infatuations, and only with maturity do we develop a "richer understanding more likely to endure the tests of time."

Concerning education, Guskey went on to say that

> [a]lthough professional development in education cannot be considered young and innocent, it still appears to be caught up in infatuations, latching on to ideas, techniques, and innovations with innocence and naiveté. Devotion to these ideas is passionate and unfettered by criticism. Only positive attributes are perceived, while weakness and flaws pass unnoticed. And as is true in the case of most infatuations, the devotion tends to be short-lived. As a result, earnest but confused education leaders career from trend to trend. Their infatuations compel them to invest in the perspectives and programs that are currently in vogue, even though their use may not be justified by the current state of theory or sound evidence. (p. 34)

Few fields of endeavor are as vulnerable as ours is to miracle cures. After all, we want desperately to be efficient, to provide equality of opportunity for children, and to promote academic excellence. We want our schools to be places of good repute. Each of us wants own school to be talked about with expressions of admiration. We want our students to recall their days with us as times of hope and glory. And why not? Why expect less of ourselves?

Those teachers and administrators who have toiled in the vineyards of education over time come to know the rhythms of the school year. The hope and the high expectations of a golden September morning when the whole year lies before us and even the most mediocre student in the most mediocre class taught by the most mediocre teacher seems filled with the promise of success. We learn to know the ambiguities of a cold and dark January afternoon when the kids have left for the day and we're sitting at our desks wondering, *What's the point?* and *Why are we doing this?* And we've experienced that day in June when it's over once more; we made it, so did the kids and we're not sure how; they're saying goodbye to us; and where did the year go anyway? And that kid comes up to say goodbye, the one that everybody but us had written off, and hands us a note that simply says, "Thank you."

Maybe there is something more to teaching and learning than the quest for the latest program. Maybe it has more to do with a caring teacher and a group of kids who want to learn something than we are willing to admit in this age of innovation. Maybe the real answers were there all along, and they had more to do with decency, perseverance, character, and plain old high standards than we realized in our quest for the new. Still we look for help because it's a tough job and we want to do it right. How do we know when and whether to invest our time, our energy, the public's money, and the other resources that it takes to innovate?

The Graveyard of Lost Ships

To paraphrase singer Neil Diamond, there is no way to count or to measure the cost of the energy lost in the annals of educational innovation. Today's flagship is often tomorrow's abandoned shipwreck. There was the incredible new program that everyone talked about, and if you weren't up to speed, well....Now the same people who touted it can barely remember it. Where are they now? Where are all the miracle cures, the new curriculums and methods that at long last had arrived to rescue us from the depths of mediocrity. What about all the answers for low test scores, for low self-esteem, for apathy and indifference to learning.

Whatever happened to Values Clarification? Whatever happened to Outcomes Based Education, Career Education, TESA, GESA, and the other ESAs? And what of the New Math? The New Science? Competency-based Education? Behavioral Objectives? The Hunter Model? Glasser Circles? And the list goes on. It may be difficult to imagine it now, but there was a time when each of these items was the latest trend in educational circles. More than one of them sank beneath the waves leaving no wake in its path. Others were forerunners of later trends and thus contributed to a certain extent to the search for better schools.

Beyond Empiricism

Much of the space in this book has been devoted to a look at the research base supporting certain educational innovations. It is our contention that teachers and administrators should demand evidence before plunging ahead into some effort that is sure to go away in time if for no other reason than that it never had a solid empirical basis. But this is not to say that everything we do in the name of learning demands evidence based on carefully controlled studies. Some things that are done, or should be done, in the name of education are not of a nature to be empirically based.

An example of a promising idea that might reasonably be assigned to this category is *increased parent involvement* in their children's academic life. Researcher John Goodlad noted that where parents are involved, school tests scores are higher. His conclusion makes sense, but how could one conduct cause-and-effect experiments to determine the actual driving force in the mix of variables? We must in this case be content with correlation at Level II and try to document positive academic outcomes at Level III, program evaluation. But it does seem practical for building principals or classroom teachers to do everything they can to get parents meaningfully involved in their children's education. It not only is common sense; it supports a larger societal goal of family togetherness. Two closely related challenges schools should mount include an exponential increase in the amount of reading students are expected to do accompanied by a corresponding decrease in the amount of time they spend watching television. Obviously, both of these quests would require parental support.

These ideas lead to a closing statement that must be considered thoughtfully if we are truly serious about raising achievement levels. Schools are the direct responsibility of those entrusted to their care. We should expect good value from them. But school, it is easy to forget, is really only a subset of that something larger called education. Education is the responsibility of the society. The perspectives on the importance of learning, which our young people develop, come from all quarters of society. To the extent that the messages are uplifting, coherent, and supportive of one another, a society will do an honorable job of educating the young. Schools simply cannot do it alone apart from the larger society. A society's cultural, spiritual, and academic vision is communicated to the young through its art, architecture, music, religion, science, media, government, and social and family structures.

Research Questions to Ask

Anyone who contemplates educational innovation should ask three basic sets of questions. These questions have been at the heart of our own assessments of the programs reviewed throughout this book:

- ◆ What is the theoretical basis of the proposed program? How sound is that theoretical base?

- ◆ What is the nature of the research done to document the validity of the proposed program? What is the quantity and quality of the research done in classroom settings?

- ◆ Is there evidence of large-scale implementation program evaluation? What comparisons were made with *traditional* forms? How realistic was the evaluation? What was the duration? What was the setting?

My strong suggestion is that as you consider innovation, you pose these questions seriously. You definitely should ask them of the purveyors of innovations. And please don't settle for answers such as, "The movement is too new, too cutting edge. There simply has not been time for research." Too much is at stake.

A Closing Thought

We've looked together at a number of highly touted educational innovations in this book. In some instances, the evidence is supportive. In others this is not so much the case, especially where shaky theoretical foundations are concerned, few or dubious studies have been conducted, and program evaluation studies are lacking. The point is not to make a cynic of you or even suggest that you not *consider* an innovation until it has *proven* itself conclusively.

Caution, especially where large expenditures of funds and extensive teacher retraining are at stake, is the watchword. That is only prudent. A certain amount of risk taking, pilot programs, and efforts to transcend the ordinary qualities of school life are needed. Such efforts should be mounted as Level II investigations. That alone will separate your school or district from the bandwagon-hopping legions that *think* they are doing something innovative while actually practicing self-delusion. The other outcome of a commitment to Level II research is that your school or district really will become a pilot center, one that others begin to look to for leadership. When schools commit to this level of quality, we can all look forward to real progress, and perhaps the era of pendulum swings will come to a well-deserved end.

References

2021 Today. (2004). *Assessment with precision: Project 2061 building a collection of test items aligned with standards.* Washington, DC: American Association for the Advancement of Science.

Adams, G., & Carnine D. (2003). Direct instruction. In L. Swanson et al. (Eds.), *Handbook of learning disabilities.* New York: Guilford Publishing.

Adams, G., & Engelmann, S. (1996, 2001). *Research on direct instruction: 25 years beyond DISTAR.* Seattle, WA: Educational Achievement Systems.

Adams, M. J., & Bruck, M. (1995). Resolving the "Great Debate." *American Educator, 19*(2) 7–20.

Aikin, W. (1942). *The story of the eight year study.* New York: Harper and Brothers.

Altshuler, K. (1991). The interdisciplinary classroom. *The Physics Teacher, 29,* 428–429.

Altwerger, B., Edelsky, C., & Flores, B. (1987). Whole language: What's new? *The Reading Teacher, 41*(2), 144–154.

Anderson, K. (1991). Interdisciplinary inquiry. *School Arts, 91*(3), 4.

Anderson, L., Krathwohl, D., Airasian, P., Cruikshank, K., Mayer, R., Pintrich, P., et al. (2001). *A taxonomy for learning, teaching, and assessing: A revision of Bloom's taxonomy of educational objectives* (abridged ed.). New York: Longman.

Aronson, E. (1996). *The jigsaw classroom.* Boston: Allyn & Bacon.

Aronson, E., Blaney, N., Stephan, C., Sikes, J., & Snapp, M. (1978). *The Jigsaw classroom.* Beverly Hills, CA: Sage.

Arter, J. (1995). *Portfolios for assessment and instruction. ERIC Digest.* Greensboro, NC: ERIC Clearinghouse on Counseling and Student Services (ED 38890).

Aschbacher, P. R. (1991). Humanitas: A thematic curriculum. *Educational Leadership, 49*(2), 16–19.

Aschbacher, P. R., & Herman, J. L. (1989). *The Humanitas program evaluation final report, 1988–1989.* Los Angeles: UCLA Center for the Study of Evaluation.

Association for Supervision and Curriculum Development. (1995, Fall). Whole language: Finding the surest way to literacy. *Curriculum Update.*

Astleitner, H. (2002). Teaching critical thinking online. *Journal of Instructional Psychology, 29,* 53–76.

Baer, J. (1988). Let's not handicap able thinkers. *Educational Leadership, 45*(7), 66–72.

Bagley, W. (1938). An essentialist's platform for the advancement of American education. *Educational Administration and Supervision, 24,* 241–256.

Baker, S., Gersten, R., & Scanlon, D. (2002). Procedural facilitators and cognitive strategies: Tools for unraveling the mysteries of comprehension and the writing process, and for providing meaningful access to the general curriculum. *Learning Disabilities Research & Practice, 17,* 65–78.

Bandura, A. (1997). *Self-efficacy: The exercise of control.* New York: Freeman.

Battle, J. (1992). Culture-free self-esteem inventories (2nd ed.). Austin, TX: PRO-ED.

Baumeister, R. F. (1996, Summer). Should schools try to boost self-esteem. *American Educator,* 14–19.

Baumeister, R. F., Smart, L., & Boden, J. M. (1996). Relation of threatened egotism to violence and aggression: The dark side of high self-esteem. *Psychological Review, 103*(1), 5–33.

Beane, J., & Brodhagen, B. (2001). Teaching in middle schools. *Handbook of research on teaching.* American Educational Research Association.

Beck, C. (2001) Matching teaching strategies to learning style preferences. *The Teacher Educator, 37,* 1–15.

Bell, S., Ziegler, M., & McCallum, S. (2004). What adult educators know compared with what they say they know about providing research-based reading instruction. *Journal of Adolescent & Adult Literacy, 47,* 542–64.

Berliner, D. (2002). Educational research: The hardest science of all. *Educational Researcher, 31*(8), 18–20.

Besterfield-Sacre, M., Gerchak, J., Lyons, M., Shuman, L., & Wolfe, H. (2004). Scoring concept maps: An integrated rubric for assessing engineering education. *Journal of Engineering Education, 93,* 105–16.

Bestor, A. (1953). *Educational wastelands: The retreat from learning in our public schools.* Urbana: University of Illinois Press.

Beyer, B. K. (1987). *Practical strategies for the teaching of thinking.* Boston: Allyn & Bacon.

Beyer, B. K. (1988a). Developing a scope and sequence for thinking skills instruction. *Educational Leadership, 45*(7), 26–30.

Beyer, B. K. (1988b). *Developing a thinking skills program.* Boston: Allyn & Bacon.

Bland, C., & Koppel, I. (1988). Writing as thinking tool. *Educational Leadership, 45*(7), 58–60.

Beane, J. (1997). *Curriculum integration: Designing the core of democratic education.* New York: Teachers College Press.

Block, J., & Burns, R. (1976). Mastery learning. In L.S. Shulman (Ed.), *Review of research in education* (Vol. 4, pp. 3–49). Itasca, IL: Peacock.

Block, J., Efthim, H., & Burns, R. (1988). *Building effective mastery learning schools.* New York: Longman.

Bloom, B. (1968). Learning for mastery. *Evaluation Comment, 1*(2) [unpaginated].

Bloom, B. (1981). *All our children learning: A primer for parents, teachers and other educators.* New York: McGraw-Hill.

Bloom, B. (1984). The search for methods of group instruction as effective as one-to-one tutoring. *Educational Leadership, 41*(8), 4–17.

Bloom, B. (Ed.) (1956). *Taxonomy of educational objectives.* New York: Longman.

Bond, L., & Roeber, E. (1995). *The status of state student assessment programs in the United States. Annual Report.* Washington, DC: Office of Educational Research and Improvement.

Borman, G., Hewes, G., Overman, L., & Brown, S. (2003). Comprehensive school reform and achievement: A meta-analysis. *Review of Educational Research, 73*(2), 125–230.

Brandt, R. (1984). Teaching of thinking, for thinking about thinking. *Educational Leadership, 42,* 3.

Brandt, R. (1988a). On research and school organization: A conversation with Bob Slavin. *Educational Leadership, 46*(2), 22–29.

Brandt, R. (1988b). On teaching thinking: A conversation with Art Costa. *Educational Leadership, 45*(7), 10–13.

Brophy, J., & Alleman, J. (1991). A caveat: Curriculum integration isn't always a good idea. *Educational Researcher, 49*(2), 66.

Bruner, J. (1996). The culture of education. Cambridge, MA: Harvard University Press.

Bruner, J. (1960). *The process of education.* Cambridge, MA: Harvard University Press.

Bruner, J. (1966). *Toward a theory of instruction.* Cambridge, MA: Harvard University Press.

Brunn, M. (2002). Teaching ideas. *Reading Teacher, 55,* 522–526.

Burgess, R. (2000). Propelling the change, promoting continuity. In A. Kozulin & Y. Rand (Eds.), *Experience of mediated learning: An impact of Feuerstein's theory in education and psychology* (pp. 147–165). Oxford: Elsevier Science.

Burns, R., & Squires, D. (1987). Curriculum organization in outcome-based education. *The OBE Bulletin, 3.* San Francisco: Far West Laboratory for Educational Research and Development. (ERIC Document Reproduction Service No. ED294313).

Burr, W. (1992). Undesirable side effects of enhancing self-esteem. *Family Relations, 41*, 460–464.

Bushman, J. H. (1991). Reshaping the secondary curriculum. *The Clearing House, 65*(2), 83–85.

Byrne, B. M. (1984). The general/academic self-concept nomological network: A review of construct validation research. *Review of Educational Research, 54*, 427–456.

Byrnes, M. (2004). Alternate assessment FAQs (and answers). *Teaching Exceptional Children, 36*(6), 58–64.

Caine, R. N., & Caine, G. (1990). Understanding a brain-based approach to learning and teaching. *Educational Leadership, 48*(2), 66–70.

Caine, R. N., & Caine, G. (1994, 2004). *Making connections: Teaching and the human brain.* Menlo Park, CA: Addison-Wesley.

California Department of Education. (1995). *Every child a reader: The Report of the California Reading Task Force.* Sacramento: Author.

California Department of Education. (1996). *Teaching reading: A balanced, comprehensive approach to teaching reading in prekindergarten through grade three.* Sacramento: Author.

California Task Force to Promote Self-esteem and Personal and Social Responsibility. (1990). *Toward a state of esteem: The final report of the California Task Force to Promote Self-esteem and Personal and Social Responsibility.* Sacramento: California State Department of Education.

Cambourne, B. (1988). *The whole story.* Auckland, New Zealand: Ashton Scholastic.

Carnine, D. (1990). New research on the brain: Implications for instruction. *Phi Delta Kappan, 71*(5), 372–377.

Carroll, J. B. (1963). A model for school learning. *Teachers College Record, 64,* 723–733.

Caudell, L. S. (1996). High stakes: Innovation meets backlash as states struggle with large scale assessment. *NW Education 2*(1), 26–28, 35.

Chall, J. (1967). *Learning to read: The great debate.* New York: McGraw-Hill.

Chall, J. (1996). *Learning to read: The great debate* (revised ed.). Orlando: Harcourt Brace.

Chang, K., Sung, Y., & Chen, I. (2002). The effect of concept mapping to enhance text comprehension and summarization. *Journal of Experimental Education, 71*, 5–24.

Cochran-Smith, R. (2005). Aera Highlights. *Educational Researcher, 34*(2), 20–21.

Coopersmith, S. (1987). *Coopersmith self-esteem inventory*. Palo Alto, CA: Consulting Psychologists Press.

Costa, A. L. (Ed.) (1985). *Developing minds: A resource book for teaching thinking*. Alexandria, VA: Association for Supervision and Curriculum Development.

Costa, A. L. (Ed.) (1991). *Developing minds: Programs for teaching thinking*. Alexandria, VA: Association for Supervision and Curriculum Development.

Cotton, K. (1992). Teaching thinking skills. *School Improvement Research Series, Close-up #11*. Portland, OR: Northwest Regional Educational Laboratory.

Cotton, K. (1995). *Effective schooling practices: A research synthesis 1995 update*. Portland, OR: Northwest Regional Educational Laboratory.

Cotton, K., & Savard, W. G. *Direct instruction. Topic summary report. Research on school effectiveness project*. Portland, OR: Northwest Regional Educational Laboratory.

Counts, G. (1932). *Dare the schools build a new social order?* New York: John Day.

Crick, F. (1994). *The astonishing hypothesis: The scientific search for the soul*. New York: Scribner.

Cronin, J. F. (1993). Four misconceptions about authentic learning. *Educational Leadership, 50*(7), 78–80.

Cuban, L. (2004). Assessing the 20-year impact of Multiple Intelligences on schooling. *Teachers College Record, 106*, 140–146.

Czerniak, C., Weber, W., Sandmann, A., & Ahern, J. (1999). A literature review of science and mathematics integration. *School Science and Mathematics, 99*(8), 421–431.

Darling-Hammond, L. (1994). Setting standards for students: The case for authentic assessment. *Educational Forum, 59*(1), 14–21.

Darling-Hammond, L., & Snyder, J. (1992). Curriculum studies and the traditions of inquiry: The scientific tradition. In P. W. Jackson, *Handbook of research on curriculum* (pp. 41–78). Englewood Cliffs, NJ: Prentice-Hall.

de Bono, E. (1983). The direct teaching of thinking as a skill. *Phi Delta Kappan, 64*, 703–708.

de Bono, E. (1991). The Co, R. T., Thinking Program. In A. L. Costa (Ed.), *Developing minds: Programs for teaching thinking* (pp. 27–32). Alexandria, VA: Association for Supervision and Curriculum Development.

Deutsch, M. (1949). A theory of cooperation and competition. *Human Relations, 2*, 129–152.

Dewey, J. (1913). *Interest and effort in education*. Boston: Houghton Mifflin.

Dewey, J. (1938). *Experience and education*. New York: Macmillan.

DiCecco, V., & Gleason, M. (2002). Using graphic organizers to attain relational knowledge from expository text. *Journal of Learning Disabilities, 35,* 306–321.

Diez. M. (2000, May 3). Teachers, assessment, and the standards movement. *Education Week.* Retrieved 2004 from www.edweek.org.

Driver, R. (1983). *Pupil as scientist?* London: Open University Press: Milton Keynes.

Dubois, L., & Hirsch, B. (2000). Self-esteem in early adolescence: From stock character to marquee attraction. *Journal of Early Adolescence, 20,* 5–11.

Dubois, L., & Tevendale, H. (1999). Self-esteem in childhood and adolescence: Vaccine or epiphenomenona? *Applied and Preventive Psychology, 8,* 103–117.

Dusek, J. (2000). Commentary on the special issue: The maturing of self-esteem research with early adolescents. *Journal of Early Adolescence, 20,* 231–241.

Edelman, G. M. (1992). *Bright air, brilliant fire: On the matter of the mind.* New York: BasicBooks.

Edelsky, C. (1990) Whose agenda is this anyway? A response to McKenna, Robinson, and Miller. *Educational Researcher, 19*(8), 7–11.

Edelsky, C., Altwerger, B., & Flores, B. (1991). *Whole language: What's the difference?* Portsmouth, NH: Heinemann.

Eisner, E. (2004). Multiple Intelligences: Its tensions and possibilities. *Teachers College Record, 106,* 31–39.

Elder, L., & Paul, R. (1995). Critical thinking: Why teach students intellectual standards, I & II. *Journal of Developmental Education, 18*(3), 36–37; *19*(1), 34–35.

Elliot, A., & MacGregor, H. (2001). A 2x2 achievement goal framework. *Journal of Personality and Psychology, 80,* 501–519.

Ellis, A. K. (1991). Evaluation as problem solving. *Curriculum in Context, 19*(2), 30–31.

Ellis, A. K. (2004). *Exemplars of Curriculum Theory.* New York: Eye On Education.

Ellis, A. K., & Fouts, J. T. (1996). *Handbook of educational terms with applications.* Princeton, NJ: Eye On Education.

Engelmann, S., Becker, W. C., Carnine, D., & Gersten, R. (1988). The direct instruction follow through model: Design and outcomes. *Education and Treatment of Children, 11,* 303–317.

Erickson, F., & Gutierrez, K. (2002). Culture, rigor, and science in educational research. *Educational Researcher, 31*(8), 21–24.

Everett, M. (1992). Developmental interdisciplinary schools for the twenty-first century. *The Education Digest, 57*(7), 57–59.

Feinberg, W. (1999). The influential E.D. Hirsch. *Rethinking Schools Online, 13,* 3. Retrieved April 2005 from www.rethinkingschools.org

Ferreiro, E. (1978). What is written in a written sentence? A developmental answer. *Journal of Education, 160,* 25–39.

Feuer, M., Towne, L., & Shavelson, R. (2002). Scientific culture and educational research. *Educational researcher, 31*(8), 4–14.

Feuerstein, R. (1979). *The dynamic assessment of retarded performers: The learning potential assessment device, theory, instruments, and techniques.* Baltimore: University Park Press.

Feuerstein, R., & Hoffman, M. (1985). The importance of mediated learning for the child. *Human Intelligence International Newsletter, 6*(2), 1–2.

Feuerstein, R., & Jensen, M. (1980, May). Instrumental enrichment: Theoretical basis, goals, and instruments. *The Educational Forum, 44,* 401–423.

Feuerstein, R., Rand, Y., Hoffman, M., & Miller, R. (1980). *Instrumental enrichment: An intervention program for cognitive modifiability.* Baltimore: University Park Press.

Fisher, R. (1925). *Statistical methods for research workers.* London: Oliver and Boyd.

Flay, B., & Alfred, Carol (2003). Long-term effects of the positive action program. *American Journal of Health Behavior, 27.* S-6.

Flink, C., Boggiano, A., & Barrett, M. (1990). Controlling teaching strategies: Undermining children's self-determination and performance. *Journal of Personality and Social Psychology, 59*(5), 916–924.

Fogarty, R. (1991). *The mindful school: How to integrate curriculum.* Palatine, IL: Skylight.

Foil, C., & Alber, S. (2002). Fun and effective ways to build your students' vocabulary. *Intervention in School & Clinic, 37,* 131–40.

Gardner, H., & Hatch, T. (1989). Multiple intelligences go to school: Educational implications of the theory of multiple intelligences. *Educational Researcher, 18,* 4–9.

Gardner, H. (1983, republished 1993). *Frames of mind: The theory of multiple intelligences.* New York: BasicBooks.

Gardner, H. (1993). *Multiple intelligences: Theory in practice.* New York: BasicBooks.

Gardner, H. (1995). Reflections on multiple intelligences: Myths and messages. *Phi Delta Kappan, 77,* 206–209.

Gardner, H. (1999). *Intelligence refrained.* New York: BasicBooks.

Gardner, H. (2003). *Multiple Intelligences after twenty years.* Invited address American Educational Research Association Annual Meeting, 2003. Chicago.

Gardner, H. (2004). *Changing minds: The art of changing our own and other people's minds.* Cambridge: Harvard Business School Press.

Garger, S. (1990). Is there a link between learning style and neurophysiology? *Educational Leadership, 48*(2), 63–65.

Georgia Critical Thinking Skills Program (1999–2004). Athens, GA: State Department of Education.

Gersten, R., & Keating, T. (1987). Long-term benefits from direct instruction. *Educational Leadership, 44,* 28–31.

Gersten, R., Keating, T., & Becker, W. (1988). The continued impact of the direct instruction model: Longitudinal studies of Follow Through students. *Education and Treatment of Children, 11,* 318–327.

Gillies, R. (2002). The residual effects of cooperative-learning experiences: A two-year follow-up. *The Journal of Educational Research, 96.* 15–22.

Goleman, D. (1995). *Emotional intelligence.* New York: Bantam.

Goodlad, J. (1984). *A place called school.* New York: McGraw-Hill.

Goodman, K. S. (1989). Whole-language research: Foundations and development. *The Elementary School Journal, 90,* 207–221.

Goodman, K. S. (1994, October–December). Deconstructing the rhetoric of Moorman, Blanton, and McLaughlin: A response. *Reading Research Quarterly, 31,* 340–346.

Goodman, K. S. (1996). *Ken Goodman on reading: A commonsense look at the nature of language and the science of reading.* Portsmouth, NH: Heinemann.

Goodman, Y. M. (1989). Roots of the whole language movement. *The Elementary School Journal, 90,* 113–127.

Gredler, M. E. (1995). Implications of portfolio assessment for program evaluation. *Studies in Educational Evaluation, 21,* 431–437.

Greene, L. (1991). Science-centered curriculum in elementary school. *Educational Leadership, 49*(2), 48–51.

Grigorenko, E., Jarvin, I., & Sternberg, R. (2002). School-based tests of the triarchic theory of intelligence: Three settings, three samples, three syllabi. *Contemporary Educational Psychology, 27,* 167–208.

Grinder, R. (1982). The AERA annual meetings as reflected in the recent history of the association. *Educational Researcher, 11,* 20.

Guskey, T. R. (1987). Rethinking mastery learning reconsidered. *Review of Educational Research, 57*(2), 225–229.

Guskey, T. R. (1988). Response to Slavin: Who defines best? *Educational Leadership, 46*(2), 26.

Guskey, T. R. (1994). Defining the difference between outcome-based education and mastery learning. *School Administrator, 51*(8), 34–37.

Guskey, T. R., & Gates, S. L. (1986). Synthesis of research on the effects of mastery learning in elementary and secondary classrooms. *Educational Leadership, 43*(8), 73–81.

Guskey, T. R., & Pigott, T. D. (1988). Research on group-based mastery learning programs: A meta-analysis. *Journal of Educational Research, 81*(4), 197–216.

Ha, A. (2004, July 29). Coke or Pepsi? It's all in the head. *The Guardian.* Retreved May 2005 from www.hnl.bcm.tmc.edul.

Haley, M. (2004). Learner-centered instruction and the theory of multiple intelligences with second language learners. *Teachers College Record, 106,* 163–180.

Hand, J. (1989). Split-brain theory and recent results in brain research: Implications for the design of instruction. In R. K. Bass, & C. R. Dills (Eds.), *Instructional development: The state of the art, II.* Dubuque, IA: Kendall/Hunt.

Hansford, B. C., & Hattie, J. A. (1982). The relationship between self and achievement performance measures. *Review of Educational Research 52,* 123–142.

Hargreaves, A., & Moore, S. (2000). Curriculum integration and classroom relevance: A study of teachers' practice. *Journal of Curriculum & Supervision, 15*(2), 89–112.

Hargreaves, A., Earl, L., & Schmidt, M. (2002). Perspectives on alternative assessment reform. *American Educational Research Journal, 39,* 69–85.

Heald-Taylor, G. (1989). *The administrator's guide to whole language.* Katonah, NY: Richard C. Owens.

Hembree, R. (1992). Experiments and relational studies in problem-solving: A meta-analysis. *Journal for Research in Mathematics Education, 23*(3), 242–273.

Hernstein, R., & Murray, C. (1995). *The bell curve: Intelligence and class structure in American life.* New York: Free Press.

Hill, C. (2000). Developing educational standards. *Putnam Valley Central Schools Website.* Retrieved 2005 from http://putwest.boces.org/Standards.html

Hilliard, A. (1998). The standards movement—Quality control or decoy? *Rethinking Schools, 12,* (4). Retrieved 2004 from http://www.rethinkingschools.org

Hirsch, E. (1987). *Cultural literacy: What every American needs to know.* Boston: Houghton Mifflin.

Hirsch, E. (2001). You can always look it up—or can you? *Common Knowledge, 13*, 2–3.

Hobbs, D. E., & Schlichter, C. L. (1991). Talents Unlimited. In A. L. Costa (Ed.), *Developing minds: Programs for teaching thinking* (pp. 73–78). Alexandria, VA: Association for Supervision and Curriculum Development.

Hoerr, T. (1994). How the New City school applies the multiple intelligences. *Educational Leadership, 52*(3), 29–33.

Hoon, S. (1990). *Feuerstein's instrumental enrichment: An exploratory study for activating intellectual potential in slow learners.* (ERIC Document Reproduction Service No. ED329813.)

House, E. R., Glass, G. V., & McLean, L. D. (1978). No simple answer: Critique of the Follow Through evaluation. *Harvard Educational Review, 48,* 128–160.

Hunter, M. (1994). *Enhancing teaching.* New York: Macmillan.

Hymel, G. M., & Dyck, W. E. (1993). *The internationalization of Bloom's learning for mastery: A 25-year retrospective–prospective view.* Paper presented at the Annual Meeting of the American Educational Research Association. (ERIC Document Reproduction Service No. ED360333).

Interstate New Teacher Assessment and Support Consortium [INTASC] (1992). *Model standards for beginning teacher licensing and development: A resource for state dialogue.* Washington, DC: Council of Chief State School Officers.

Jacobs, H. H. (1991). Planning for curriculum integration. *Educational Leadership, 49*(2), 27–28.

Jacobs, H. H. (Ed.). (1989). *Interdisciplinary curriculum: Design and implementation.* Alexandria, VA: Association for Supervision and Curriculum Development.

Jagab, S. (1992). *Cooperative learning.* San Juan Capistrano, CA: Kagan Cooperative Learning.

Johnson, D., & Johnson, R. (eds.). (2004). Conflict resolution and peer mediation [Special issue]. *Theory into Practice, 42*(1).

Johnson, D., & Johnson, R. (1989a). *Cooperation and competition: Theory and research.* Edina, MN: Interaction.

Johnson, D., & Johnson, R. (1989b). *Leading the cooperative school.* Edina, MN: Interaction.

Johnson, D., & Johnson, R. (1994a). *Cooperative learning in the classroom.* Alexandria, VA: Association for Supervision and Curriculum Development.

Johnson, D., & Johnson, R. (1994b). *Learning together and alone. Cooperative, competitive, and individualistic learning.* Edina, MN: Interaction.

Johnson, D., & Johnson, R. (2002). *Circles of learning.* Edina, MN: Interaction.

Johnson, D., & Johnson, R. (2004). *Assessing students in groups: Promoting group responsibility and individual accountability.* Thousand Oaks, CA: Corwin.

Johnson, D., Johnson, R., & Holubec, E. (1988). *Cooperation in the classroom.* Edina, MN: Interaction.

Kagan, S. (1989). *Cooperative learning resources for teachers.* San Juan Capistrano, CA: Resources for Teachers.

Kagan, S. (1989/1990). The structural approach to cooperative learning. *Educational Leadership, 47*(4), 12–16.

Kahne, J. (1996). The politics of self-esteem. *American Educational Research Journal, 33*(1), 3–22.

Kaisa, A., Stattin, H., & Nurmi, J. (2000). Adolescents' achievement strategies, school adjustment, and externalizing and internalizing problem behaviors. *Journal of Youth and Adolescence, 29,* (3), 289–306.

Kaniel, S., & Reichenberg, R. (1992). Instrumental enrichment—Effects of generalization and durability with talented adolescents. *Gifted Education International, 8,* 128–135.

Kimura, D. (1992, September). Sex differences in the brain. *Scientific American, 267*(3), 118–125.

King, J., & Evans, K. (1991). Can we achieve outcome-based education? *Educational Leadership, 49* (2), 73–75.

Kohlberg, L. (1987). *Child psychology and childhood education: A cognitive-developmental point of view.* New York: Longman.

Kohn, A. (1994). The truth about self-esteem. *Phi Delta Kappan, 76*(4), 272–283.

Kohn, A. (2000). *The case against tougher standards.* Retrieved April 2005 from http://www.alfiekohn.org

Kohn, A. (2004). Challenging students—And how to have more of them. *Phi Delta Kappan, 86*(3) 184–194.

Kolb, D. A. (1985). *The learning style inventory.* Boston, MA: McBer.

Konold, K., & Miller, S. (2004). Using teacher feedback to enhance student learning. *Teaching Exceptional Children, 36,* 64–70.

Kozulin. A., & Rand, Y. (2000). *Experience of mediated learning: An impact on Feuerstein's theory in education and psychology.* Oxford: Elsevier Science.

Kulik, C. C., & Kulik, J. (1986–1987). Mastery testing and student learning: A meta-analysis. *Journal of Educational Technology Systems, 15,* 325–341.

Kulik, C. C., Kulik, J., & Cohen, A. (1979). A meta-analysis of outcome studies of Keller's Personalized System of Instruction. *American Psychologist, 34*(4), 307–318.

Lake, K. (1994). *School improvement research series VIII: Integrated curriculum.* Portland, OR: Northwest Regional Educational Laboratory.

Lee, V. E., & Smith, J. B. (1994a). *Effects of high school restructuring and size on gains in achievement and engagement for early secondary school students.* Madison, WI: Center on Organization and Restructuring of Schools.

Lee, V. E., & Smith, J. B. (1994b). High school restructuring and student achievement. *Issues in Restructuring Schools: Issue Report No. 7.* Madison, WI: Center on Organization and Restructuring of Schools.

Lehman, N. (1994). Is there a science of success? *The Atlantic Monthly, 273*(2), 83–98.

Lerner, B. (1996, Summer). Self-esteem and excellence: The choice and the paradox. *American Educator,* 9–13, 41–42 .

Levine, D. U. (1985). *Improving student achievement through mastery learning programs.* San Francisco: Jossey-Bass.

Levy, J. (1983). Research synthesis on the right and left hemisphere: We think with both sides of the brain. *Educational Leadership, 40*(2), 4, 66–71.

Lewin, K. (1947). *Field theory in social sciences.* New York: Harper & Row.

Link, F. (1991). Instrumental enrichment. In A. L. Costa (Ed.) (1991). *Developing minds: Programs for teaching thinking* (pp. 9–11). Alexandria, VA: Association for Supervision and Curriculum Development.

Linn, R. (2000). *Standards-based accountability: Ten suggestions.* CRESST Policy Brief. Retrieved May 2005 from www.cse.ucla.edu

Manning, G., Manning, M., & Long R. (1990). *Reading and writing in the middle grades: A whole-language view.* Washington, DC: National Education Association.

Manning, M., & Kamii, C. (2000). Whole language vs. isolated phonics instruction: A longitudinal study in kindergarten with reading and writing tasks. *Journal of Research in Childhood Education, 15,* 53–66.

Marchand-Martella, Slocum, T., & Martell, R. (2004). *Introduction to direct instruction.* Boston: Pearson Education.

Marcoulides, G., & Heck, R. (1994). The changing role of educational assessment in the 1990s. *Education and Urban Society, 26,* 332–339.

Martin-Kniep, G., Sussman, E., & Meltzer E. (1995). The North Shore Collaborative Inquiry Project: A reflective study of assessment and learning. *Journal of Staff Development 16*(4), 46–51.

Marzanno, R., & Kendall, J. (1997). The fall and rise of standards-based education. *A National Association of State Boards of Education Issues in Brief.* Retrieved February 2005 from www.mcrel.com/standards/articles

Marzanno, R., & Kendall, J. (1998a). *The status of state standards. A comprehensive guide to designing standards-based districts, schools, and classrooms.* Retrieved 2005 from www.mcrel.org/standards

Marzanno, R., & Kendall, J. (1998b). *What Americans believe students should know: A survey of U.S. adults.* Retrieved 2004 from www.mcrel.org

Marzanno., R., & Kendall, J. (1999). Awash in a sea of standards. *Standards at McREL.* Retrieved 2005 from www.mcrel.org/standards/articles/awash.asp

Marzanno,. R. Kendall, J., & Gaddy, B. (1999). Essential knowledge: The debate over what American students should know. *Standards at McREL.* Retrieved 2004 from www.mcrel.org.

Mason, T. C. (1996). Integrated curricula: Potential and problems. *Journal of Teacher Education, 47,* 263–270.

McCarthy, B. (1987). *The 4MAT system: Teaching to learning styles with right/left mode techniques.* Barrington, IL: Excel.

McClelland, D. (1973). Testing for competence rather than intelligence. *American Psychologist, 28,* 1–14.

McCutchen, D., Abbott, R. D., Green, L. B., & Beretvas, S. N. (2002). Beginning literacy: Links among teacher knowledge, teacher practice, and student learning. *Journal of Learning Disabilities, 35,* 69–86.

McGee, L. M., & Lomax, R. S. (1990). On combining apples and oranges: A response to Stahl and Miller. *Review of Educational Research, 60*(1), 133–140.

McGuire, J., & Heuss, B. (1994). *Bridges: A self-esteem activity book for students in grades 4–6.* Boston: Allyn & Bacon.

McKenna, M. C., Robinson, R. D., & Miller J. W. (1990a). Whole language: A research agenda for the nineties. *Educational Researcher, 19*(8), 3–6.

McKenna, M. C., Robinson, R. D., & Miller J. W. (1990b). Whole language and the need for open inquiry: A rejoinder to Edelsky. *Educational Researcher, 19*(8), 12–13.

McKenna, M. C., Stahl S.A., & Reinking, D. (1994). A critical commentary on research, politics and whole language. *Journal of Reading Behavior, 26*(2), 211–233.

McPike, E. (1996, Summer). Editor's introduction. In B. Lerner, Self-esteem and excellence: The choice and the paradox. *American Educator, 19,* 9–13, 41–42.

MDRC (2004). *School-based reforms in elementary and secondary education.* Retrieved February 2005 from www.mdrc.org

Mead, M. (1928). *Coming of age in Samoa: A psychological study of primitive youth for western civilization.* New York: William Morrow.

Mecca, A. M., Smelser, N. J., & Vasconcellos, J. (Eds.). (1989). *The social importance of self-esteem.* Berkeley: University of California Press.

Medina, J. (2003). Brainchild: Stress, learning and the human brain. *Response, 26*(4), 1–6.

Mehrens, W. A., & Lehmann, I. J. (1991). *Measurement and evaluation in education and psychology.* Orlando, FL: Holt, Rinehart & Winston.

Meyer, L. A., Gersten, R. M., & Gutkin, J. (1983). Direction instruction: A project Follow Through success story in an inner-city school. *The Elementary School Journal, 84,* 241–252.

Mills, P., Coler, K., Jenkins, J., & Dale, P. (2002). Early exposure to direct instruction and subsequent juvenile delinquency: A prospective examination. *Exceptional Children, 69,* 85–97.

Mitchell, W. H., & McCollum, M. G. (1983). The power of positive students. *Educational Leadership, 40*(5), 48–51.

Moll, L. C. (Ed.) (1993). *Vygotsky and education: Instructional implications and applications of sociohistorical psychology.* New York: Cambridge University Press.

Moore, J. (1986). Direct instruction: A model of instructional design. *Educational Psychology, 6,* 201–229.

Moorman, G., Blanton, W., & McLaughlin, T. (1994, *October–December*). The rhetoric of whole language. *Reading Research Quarterly, 27,* 309–329.

Morrow, L. M. (1992). The impact of a literature-based program on literacy achievement, use of literature and attitudes of children from minority backgrounds. *Reading Research Quarterly, 27*(3), 251–275.

Morrow, L. M., Pressley, M., & Smith, J. K. (1995). The effect of a literature-based program integrated into literacy and science instruction on achievement, use and attitudes toward literacy and science. *Reading Research Report No. 37.* Athens, GA: National Reading Research Center.

Mulcahy, R. (1993). *Cognitive education project. Summary project.* (ERIC Document Reproduction Service No. ED367682.)

Mullen, C. (2005). *Fire and ice: Igniting and channeling the passion in new qualitative researchers.* New York: Peter Lang.

Multon, K., et al.AQ: Please provide names of 6 authors before "et al."

 (1991). Relation of self-efficacy beliefs to academic outcomes: A meta-analytic investigation. *Journal of Counseling Psychology, 38,* 30–38.

Murphy, C. (Ed.) (1984). *Outcome-based instructional systems: Primer and practice. Education brief.* San Francisco: Far West Laboratory for Educational

Research and Development. (ERIC Document Reproduction Service No. ED249265).

National Association for Self-Esteem. (2004). AQ: Please provide additional source information if available. Retrieved 2005 from www.self-esteem-nase.org/research.shtml

National Council of Teachers of Mathematics. (1989). *Curriculum and evaluation standards for school mathematics.* Reston, VA: Author.

National Research Council. (2002). *Scientific research in education.* Washington, DC: National Academy Press.

Neill, M. (1996, February 28). Assessment reform at a crossroads. *Education Week,* 33.

Newman, J. M., & Church S.M. (1989). Myths of whole language. *The Reading Teacher, 44*(1), 20–26.

Newmann, F. M., & Wehlage, G. G. (1993). Five standards of authentic instruction. *Educational Leadership, 50*(7), 8–12.

Nickerson, R. S., Perkins, D. N., & Smith, E. E. (1985). *The teaching of thinking.* Hillsdale, NJ: Lawrence Erlbaum.

No Child Left Behind Act of 2001, 20 U.S.C. § 6301 *et seq.*

Norris, S. P. (1985). Synthesis of research on critical thinking. *Educational Leadership, 42*(8), 40–45.

O'Donnell, T. F., & O'Donnell, W. J. (1995). Multicultural myths. *American School Board Journal, 182*(7), 23–25.

Offenberg, R. (1992). *A study of the effects of instrumental enrichment on middle-grade, minority students* (Report No. 9225). (ERIC Document Reproduction Service No. ED361462.)

Olson, L. (1995, March 22). The new breed of assessments getting scrutiny. *Education Week,* 1.

Oxford English Dictionary. (1971). Oxford: Oxford University Press.

Pajares, F., & Viliante, G. (1997). Influence of self-efficacy on elementary students' writing. *Journal of Educational Research, 90,* 353–360.

Parker, W. (2005). *Social Studies in Elementary Education.* Upper Saddle River, NJ: Pearson Prentice Hall.

Paterson, W., Henry, J., O'Quin, K., Ceprano, M., & Blue, E. (2003) Investigating the effectiveness of an integrated learning system on early emergent readers. *Reading Research Quarterly, 38,* 172–207.

Paul, R. (1993). *Critical thinking: What every person needs to survive in a rapidly changing world* (3rd ed.). Santa Rosa, CA: Foundation for Critical Thinking.

Peterson, R. W. (1994). School readiness considered from a neuro-cognitive perspective. *Early Education and Development, 5*(2), 120–140.

Phelan, A., & Luu, D. (2004). Learning differences in teacher education. *Journal of Canadian Association of Curriculum Studies, 2*(1), 175–176.

Piaget, J. (1970). *Science of education and the psychology of the child.* New York: Viking Press.

Piers, E. V., & Harris, D. B. (1984). *Piers-Harris children's self-concept scale (The way I feel about myself).* Los Angeles: Western Psychological Services.

Pocock, A., Lambros, S., Karvonen, M., & Test, D., et al. (2002). Successful strategies for promoting self-advocacy among students with LD: The LEAD group. *Intervention in School and Clinic, 37,* 209–219.

Pogrow, S. (1995). Making reform work for the educationally disadvantaged. *Educational Leadership, 52*(5), 20–24.

Post, T. R., Ellis, A. K., Humphreys, A. H., & Buggey, L. J. (1997). *Interdisciplinary approaches to curriculum: Themes for teaching.* Upper Saddle River, NJ: Merrill/Prentice Hall.

Pressly, M. (1994). State-of-the-science primary-grades reading instruction or whole language? *Educational Psychologist, 29,* 211–216.

Qin, Z., Johnson, D. W., & Johnson, R. T. (1995). Cooperative versus competitive efforts and problem solving. *Review of Educational Research, 65,* 129–143.

Rayborn, R. (1992). Alternatives for assessing student achievement: Let me count the ways. In *Assessment: How do we know what they know?* (pp. 24–27). Union, WA: Washington State Association for Supervision and Curriculum Development.

Reiff, J. C. (1992). *What research says to the teacher: Learning styles.* Washington, DC: National Education Association Professional Library.

Resnick, L. B. (1987). *Education and learning to think.* Washington, DC: Academy Press.

Restak, R. M. (1984). *The brain.* Toronto: Bantam.

Reyhner, J. (2004). *The reading wars: Phonics versus whole language.* Flagstaff, AZ: University of Northern Arizona.

Roberts, J. (2002). Beyond learning by doing: The brain compatible approach. *The Journal of Experiential Education, 25,* 281–285.

Roeser, R., & Eccles, J. (1998). Adolescents' perceptions of middle school: Relation to longitudinal changes in academic and psychological adjustment. *Journal of Research on Adolescence, 8,* 123–158.

Rogers, C. (1969, 1994). *Freedom to learn.* Columbus, OH: Merrill.

Rosenshine, B. (1979). Content, time, and direct instruction. In P. Peterson, & H. Walberg (Eds.), *Research on teaching: Concepts, findings, and implications* (pp. 28–56). Berkeley, CA: McCutchan.

Rosenshine, B. (1986). Synthesis of research on explicit teaching. *Educational Leadership, 43*(7), 60–69.

Ryan, J., & Miyasaka, J. (1995). Current practices in testing and assessment: What is driving the changes. *NASSP Bulletin, 79*(573), 1–10.

Savell, J., Twohig, P., & Rachford, D. (1986). Empirical status of Feuerstein's "Instrumental Enrichment" (FIE) technique as a method of teaching thinking skills. *Review of Educational Research, 56, 381–409.*

Scheirer, M. A., & Kraut, R. E. (1979). Increasing educational achievement via self-concept. *Review of Educational Research, 49*(1), 131–150.

Schemo, D. (2002, January 9). Education bill urges new emphasis on phonics as method for teaching reading. *New York Times,* p. A16.

Schickendanz, J. A. (1990). The jury is still out on the effects of whole language and language experience approaches for beginning reading: A critique of Stahl and Miller's study. *Review of Educational Research, 60,* 127–131.

Schlichter, C. L. (1986) Talents Unlimited: An inservice education model for teaching thinking skills. *Gifted Child Quarterly, 30*(3), 119–123.

Schlichter, C. L., Hobbs, D., & Crump, W. D. (1988). Extending Talents Unlimited to secondary schools. *Educational Leadership, 45*(7), 36–40.

Schunk, D. (2000). *Learning theories: An educational perspective* (3rd ed.). Columbus, OH: Merrill/Prentice Hall.

Seifert, T. (2004). Understanding student motivation. *Educational Research, 46,* 137–50.

Sharan, S. (Ed.). (1990). *Cooperative learning: Theory and research.* New York: Praeger.

Sharan, S., & Sharan, Y. (1992). *Expanding cooperative learning through group investigation.* New York: Teachers College Press.

Shavelson, R., & Towne, L. (Eds.). (2002). *Scientific research in education.* Washington, DC: National Academy Press.

Simmons, F. (1974). *PSI, the Keller plan handbook: Essays on a personalized system of instruction.* Menlo Park, CA: W. A. Benjamin.

Singham, M. (1995). Race and intelligence: What are the issues? *Phi Delta Kappan, 77,* 271–278.

Skaalvic, E., & Hagtve, K. (1990). Academic achievement and self-concept. *Journal of Personality and Social Psychology, 58*(2), 292–307.

Slavin, R. (1986). *Educational psychology: Theory into practice.* Englewood Cliffs, NJ: Prentice Hall.

Slavin, R. (1987). Mastery learning reconsidered. *Review of Educational Research, 57*(2), 175–213.

Slavin, R. (1989/1990). Research on cooperative learning: Consensus and controversy. *Educational Leadership, 47*(4), 52–54.

Slavin, R. (1991). Synthesis of research on cooperative learning. *Educational Leadership, 48*(5), 71–82.

Slavin, R. (1995). Synthesis of research on cooperative learning. In J. A. Page (Ed.), *Beyond tracking: Finding success in inclusive schools.* Bloomington, IN: Phi Delta Kappa.

Slavin, R. (2004). Built to last: Long-term maintenance of Success for All. *Remedial and Special Education, 25,* 61–68.

Slavin, R., et al. (Eds.). (1985). *Learning to cooperate, cooperating to learn.* New York: Plenum.

Smelser, N. J. (1989). Self-esteem and social problems: An introduction. In A. M. Mecca, N. J. Smelser, & J. Vasconcellos, (Eds.), *The social importance of self-esteem* (pp. 1–25). Berkeley: University of California Press.

Sowell, T. (1993). *Inside American education: The decline, the deception, the dogmas.* New York: Free Press.

Sowell, T. (1995). *The vision of the anointed.* New York: BasicBooks.

Spady, W. G., & Marshall, K. J. (1991). Beyond traditional outcome-based education. *Educational Leadership, 49*(2), 67–72.

Spearman, C. (1927). *The abilities of man: Their nature and measurement.* New York: Macmillan.

Springer, S., & Deutsch, G. (1989). *Left brain right brain* (3rd ed.). New York: W. H. Freeman.

St. Pierre, E. (2002). "Science" rejects postmodernism. *Educational Researcher, 31*(8), 25–27.

Stahl, S., & Miller, P. (1989). Whole language and language experience approaches for beginning reading: A quantitative synthesis. *Review of Educational Research, 59*(1), 87–116.

Stahl, S., McKenna, M., & Pagnucco, J. (1994). The effects of whole language instruction: An update and reappraisal. *Educational Psychology, 29*(1), 175–185.

Stallings, J. (1987). *Longitudinal findings for early childhood programs: Focus on direct instruction.* (ERIC Document Reproduction Service No. ED297874).

Stallings, J., & Stipek, D. (1986). Research on early childhood and elementary school teaching programs. In M.C. Witrock (Ed.), *Handbook of Research on Teaching* (3rd ed., pp. 727–753). New York: Macmillan.

Stanovich, K. (1993). Romance and reality. *The Reading Teacher, 47,* 280–291.

Stanovich, K., & Stanovich, P. J. (1995a). How research might inform debate about early reading acquisition. *Journal of Research in Reading, 18*(2), 87–105.

Stanovich, K., & Stanovich, P. J. (1995b). Learning to read: Schooling's first mission. *American Educator, 19*(2), 3–6.

Stebbins, L., St. Pierre, R., Proper, E., Anderson, R., & Cerva, T. (1977). *Education as experimentation: A planned variation model. Vol. 4A–D. An evaluation of Follow Through.* Cambridge, MA: ABT Associates.

Sterbin, A., & Rakow, E. (1996). *Self-esteem, locus of control, and student achievement.* (ERIC Document Reproduction Service No. 406429.)

Sternberg, R. (1990). *Metaphors of mind: Conceptions of the nature of intelligence.* New York: Cambridge University Press.

Sternberg, R. (1995/1996). Investing in creativity: Many happy returns. *Educational Leadership, 53*(4), 80–84.

Sternberg, R. (1996). The school bell and the bell curve: Why they don't mix. *NASSP Bulletin, 80*(577), 46–56.

Sternberg, R. (2003). WICS as a model of giftedness. *High Ability Studies. 14*(2), 109–138.

Sternberg, R. (2004a). Four alternatives for education in the United States: It's our choice. *School Psychology Review, 33*(1), 67–78.

Sternberg, R. (2004b). What is an "expert student"? *Educational Researcher, 32*(8), 5–9.

Sternberg, R., & Bhana, K. (1986). Synthesis of research on the effectiveness of intellectual skills programs: Snake-oil remedy or miracle cures? *Educational Leadership, 44*(2), 60–67.

Sternberg, R., Okagaki, L., & Jackson, A. (1990). Practical intelligence for success in school. *Educational Leadership, 48*(1), 35–39.

Stevahn, L., Johnson, D. Johnson, R., & Schultz, R. (2002). Effects of conflict resolution training integrated into a high school social studies curriculum. *The Journal of Social Psychology, 142*, 305–332.

Stevens, R. J., & Slavin, R. (1995a). The cooperative elementary school: Effects on students' achievement, attitudes, and social relations. *American Educational Research Journal, 32*, 321–351.

Stevens, R. J., & Slavin, R. (1995b). Effects of a cooperative learning approach in reading and writing on academically handicapped and nonhandicapped students. *The Elementary School Journal, 95*, 241–261.

Stevenson, C., & Carr, J. (1993). *Integrative studies in the middle grades: Dancing through walls.* New York: Teachers College Press.

Stiggins, R. (2001). *Student-involved classroom assessment* (3rd ed.). New York: Pearson.

Sturm, J., & Rankin-Erickson, J. (2002). Effects of hand-drawn and computer-generated concept mapping on the expository writing of middle school students with learning disabilities. *Learning Disabilities Research & Practice, 17,* 124–140.

Sutherland, P. (1992). *Cognitive development today.* London: Paul Chapman.

Sylwester, R. (1981). Educational implications of recent brain research. *Educational Leadership, 39*(1), 6–10.

Sylwester, R. (1990). An educator's guide to books on the brain. *Educational Leadership, 48*(2), 79–80.

Sylwester, R. (1994). What the biology of the brain tells us about learning. *Educational Leadership, 51*(4), 46–51

Sylwester, R. (1995). *A celebration of neurons: An educators guide to the human brain.* Alexandria, VA: Association for Supervision and Curriculum Development.

TEC Talents Unlimited. (2004). Retrieved February 2005 from www.tec-coop.org

Thurstone, L. (1938). Primary mental abilities. *Psychometric Monographs, 1.*

Toch, T. (1991). *In the name of excellence: The struggle to reform the nation's schools and why it's failing and what should be done.* New York: Oxford University Press.

Toch, T. (2003). *High Schools on a Human Scale.* Boston: Beacon Press.

Tyler, R. (1949). *Basic principles of curriculum and instruction.* Chicago: The University of Chicago Press.

Vann, K. R., & Kunjufu, J. (1993). The importance of an Afrocentric, multicultural curriculum. *Phi Delta Kappan, 74*(6), 490–491.

Vars, G. (1991). Integrated curriculum in historical perspective. *Educational Leadership, 49*(2), 14–15.

Vars, G. (1996). The effects of interdisciplinary curriculum and instruction. In P. Hlebowish, & W. Wraga (Eds.), *Annual review of research for school leaders* (pp. 137–164). New York: Scholastic.

Viadero, D. (1995, April 5). Even as popularity soars, portfolios encounter roadblocks. *Education Week,* 8.

Vygotsky, L. S. (1962). *Thought and language.* Cambridge, MA: MIT Press.

Vygotsky, L. S. (1978). *Mind in society.* Cambridge: Harvard University Press.

Vygotsky, L. S. (1986). *Thought and language.* Cambridge, MA: MIT Press.

Walberg, H. J. (1984). Improving the productivity of America's schools. *Educational Leadership, 41*(8), 19–27.

Walberg, H. J. (1985). Examining the theory, practice, and outcomes of mastery learning. In D. U. Levine (Ed.), *Improving student achievement through mastery learning programs.* San Francisco: Jossey-Bass.

Walker, D. (1990). *Fundamentals of curriculum.* Orlando, FL: Harcourt Brace Jovanovich.

Walz, G. R., & Bleur, J. C. (1992). *Student self-esteem: A vital element of school success.* Alexandria, VA: American School Counselor Association.

Watson, D. (1990). Defining and describing whole language. *The Elementary School Journal, 90*(2), 129–141.

Wegerif, R. (2004). Towards an account of teaching general thinking skills that is compatible with the assumptions of sociocultural theory. *Theory and Research in Education, 2*(2), 143–159.

White, W. (1988). A meta-analysis of the effects of direct instruction in special education. *Education and Treatment of Children, 11,* 364–374.

Williams, S., Davis, M., Metcalf, D., & Covington, V. (2003). The evolution of a process portfolio as an assessment system in a teacher education program. *Current Issues in Education* [On-line],*6*(1). Retrieved July 20, 2004, from http:// cie.ed.asu.edu/ volume6/

Wittrock, M. C. (1981). Educational implications of recent brain research. *Educational Leadership, 37*(1), 12–15.

Wolfram, S. (2002). *A new kind of science.* Champaign, IL: Wolfram Media.

Worsham, A. M., & Stockton, A. J. (1986). A model for teaching thinking skills: The inclusion process (*Phi Delta Kappa Fastback, 236*). Bloomington, IN: Phi Delta Kappa.

Worthen, B. R. (1993). Critical issues that will determine the future of alternative assessment. *Phi Delta Kappan, 74,* 444–448.

Xue, Y., & Meisels, S. (2004). Early literacy instruction and learning in kindergarten: Evidence from the early childhood longitudinal study—kindergarten class of 1998–1999. *American Educational Research Journal, 41*(2), 191–229.

Yekovich, F. R. (1994). *ERIC/AE Digest. Current issues in research on intelligence.* Washington, DC: Office of Educational Research and Improvement.

Youngs, B. B. (1989). The Phoenix curriculum. *Educational Leadership, 46*(5), 24.

Zalewski, L. J., Sink, C., & Yachimowicz, D. J. (1992). Using cerebral dominance for education programs. *The Journal of General Psychology, 119,* 45–57.

Zemelman, S., Daniels, H., & Hyde, A. (1998). *Best practice: New standards for teaching and learning in America's schools* (2nd ed.). Portsmouth, NH: Heinneman.

INDEX